D0176040

ALSO BY DANNA KORN

*Kids with Celiac Disease: A Family Guide to Raising
Happy, Healthy, Gluten-Free Children*
(Woodbine House, Bethesda, MD, February 2001)

OTHER HAY HOUSE TITLES OF RELATED INTEREST

<u>Books</u>

*BodyChange™: The 21-Day Fitness Program for Changing Your Body . . .
and Changing Your Life,* by Montel Williams and Wini Linguvic

The Body Knows: How to Tune In to Your Body and Improve Your Health,
by Caroline Sutherland, Medical Intuitive

The Indigo Children: The New Kids Have Arrived,
by Lee Carroll and Jan Tober

Vegetarian Meals for People-on-the-Go: 101 Quick & Easy Recipes,
by Vimala Rodgers

*The Yo-Yo Diet Syndrome: How to Heal and Stabilize Your
Appetite and Weight,* by Doreen Virtue, Ph.D.

<u>Audio Programs</u>

*Body Talk: No-Nonsense, Common-Sense Solutions to Create Health and
Healing,* by Mona Lisa Schulz, M.D., Ph.D., and Christiane Northrup, M.D.

Eating Wisdom, by Andrew Weil, M.D., with Michael Toms

Healing Your Appetite, Healing Your Life, by Doreen Virtue, Ph.D.

Live Long and Feel Good, by Andrew Weil, M.D., with Michael Toms

Your Diet, Your Health, by Christiane Northrup, M.D.

All of the above are available at your local bookstore,
or may be ordered through Hay House, Inc.:

(800) 654-5126 or (760) 431-7695
(800) 650-5115 (fax) or (760) 431-6948 (fax)
www.hayhouse.com

The Art of Happy, Healthy, Gluten-Free Living

Danna Korn

Hay House, Inc.
Carlsbad, California • Sydney, Australia
Canada • Hong Kong • United Kingdom

Copyright © 2002 by Danna Korn

Published and distributed in the United States by:
    Hay House, Inc., P.O. Box 5100, Carlsbad, CA 92018-5100 • (800) 654-5126
(800) 650-5115 (fax) • www.hayhouse.com
    Hay House Australia Pty Ltd, P.O. Box 515, Brighton-Le-Sands, NSW 2216
phone: 1800 023 516 • *e-mail:* info@hayhouse.com.au

Editorial supervision: Jill Kramer • *Design:* Summer McStravick • *Index:* Debra Graf

    All rights reserved. No part of this book may be reproduced by any mechanical, pho-tographic, or electronic process, or in the form of a phonographic recording; nor may it be stored in a retrieval system, transmitted, or otherwise be copied for public or private use—other than for "fair use" as brief quotations embodied in articles and reviews with-out prior written permission of the publisher.

    The author of this book does not dispense medical advice or prescribe the use of any technique as a form of treatment for physical or medical problems without the advice of a physician, either directly or indirectly. The intent of the author is only to offer information of a general nature to help you in your quest for emotional and spiritual well-being. In the event you use any of the information in this book for yourself, which is your constitutional right, the author and the publisher assume no responsibility for your actions.

Library of Congress Cataloging-in-Publication Data

Korn, Danna.
    Wheat-free, worry-free : the art of happy, healthy gluten-free living
/ Danna Korn.
        p. cm.
Includes index.
    ISBN 1-56170-991-3
    1. Wheat-free diet—Popular works. 2. Gluten-free diet—Popular
works. I. Title.
    RM237.87 .K67 2002

                                                            2002002358

ISBN 1-56170-991-3

05 04 03 02 4 3 2 1
1st printing, August 2002

Printed in the United States of America

This book is dedicated to the many people in my life who have supported my efforts to help people learn to live and love the wheat-free/gluten-free lifestyle. Specifically, to my son, Tyler, who has inspired our family to be optimistic as we embark upon the realities of a gluten-free lifestyle; my daughter, Kelsie, whose zest for life and enthusiastic outlook are ever-energizing; my loving husband, Paul, who provides steadfast support, motivation, and encouragement; and to my family and friends who believe in my efforts. I feel so privileged to be able to offer even a little help to others, but I couldn't have written a single word if I didn't have such special people in my life.

Contents

Tables and Figures

※ ※ ※

Foreword

by Rich and Shelley Gannon

Oakland Raiders quarterback Rich Gannon was voted to his third consecutive Pro Bowl team following the 2001 season. His wife, Shelley, was an All-American gymnast at the University of Minnesota, and is now a full-time mother to their two daughters, Alexis and Danielle.

When we first found out that our daughter couldn't eat gluten, we thought that after a quick huddle, we'd have it all figured out. How hard could it be to cut out wheat, barley, rye, and oats? Not as easy as we first thought, we realized, and before we knew it, we were scrambling.

Our daughter, Danielle, began to get sick when she was two years old with what we now know are classic symptoms of a condition called *celiac disease*. It took more than a year, though, before she was finally diagnosed. Even though we eventually had a name for the condition, we had never heard of it and had no idea what was involved in living a gluten-free lifestyle.

People think that we live a "celebrity" lifestyle, and maybe to some extent, we do. But that doesn't make it any easier to understand what's gluten-free and what isn't, where to find gluten-free products, and how to handle the birthday parties and school celebrations that now have new meaning and provide new challenges. We know the lifestyle is tough for everyone, but moving between our home in Minnesota and our home in California (where we live during football season) doesn't make it any easier!

When Danielle was first diagnosed, one of the first people we were referred to and called upon was Danna Korn, who founded and runs R.O.C.K. (Raising Our Celiac Kids). We talked for hours, and she answered questions we didn't even know we had. Her first book wasn't published yet, but she was nearly finished writing it, and sent us the manuscript. *Kids with Celiac Disease: A Family Guide to Raising Happy, Healthy, Gluten-Free Children* was a godsend, even in its unfinished form.

Danna has lived the lifestyle, researched the medical aspects, and talked with thousands of people who have shared ideas, concerns, and inspirational moments. *Wheat-Free, Worry-Free: The Art of Happy, Healthy, Gluten-Free Living* is even bigger and better than her first book, but it is written in the same upbeat, witty, easy-to-read style.

As Danielle grows older, we know her needs—and ours—will change, and we will continue to face new issues. Danna's first book has helped us get to a point where life's a little easier now. Between her first book and this one, we know we're well supplied with practical suggestions for dealing with the unique challenges we'll face for the rest of Danielle's life.

Whether you're eliminating wheat or gluten from your diet because of allergies, intolerances to wheat and/or gluten, celiac disease, or personal preference, *Wheat-Free, Worry-Free* is *the* book you need. It has current medical information (combined with "life's lessons"), practical suggestions for dealing with a wheat-free or gluten-free diet, and a huge Resource Directory filled with contact information for hundreds of vendors and resources. It's easy to read, and will answer questions you haven't even thought of yet.

Acknowledgments

I'd like to thank everyone who took the time to offer input, suggestions, motivation, and encouragement, especially the renowned physicians and researchers who provided assistance in deciphering and translating complex medical research: Michelle Pietzak, M.D.; Alessio Fasano, M.D.; Peter Green, M.D.; and Cynthia Rudert, M.D.

Specifically, I'd like to offer my most sincere appreciation and admiration to the aforementioned Dr. Pietzak, pediatric gastroenterologist and renowned expert on the subject of celiac disease, who wrote one of the best sections of this book, spent more than her fair share of time editing the medical content, and dedicates an immense amount of time and energy to improving the health and lives of others.

Last, but definitely not least, I'd like to thank my editor and new friend, Gail Fink, who shared my vision and passion for this book. Gail has a meticulous eye, a gift for being able to appeal to every reader, and a flair for finesse and polish.

Introduction

Living and Loving the Wheat-Free/Gluten-Free Lifestyle

"Thy food shall be thy medicine."
— Hippocrates

Looking back on my life thus far, it seems to be divided into two clear-cut segments of time that I've come to think of as B.D. and A.D.: Before Diet and After Diet.

Until 1991, my family and I ate a fairly typical American diet. Sure, we tried to keep it balanced (extra cheese on the pizzas for an additional protein source), and we tried to keep the calories under control (okay, scratch the extra cheese), but we didn't spend a lot of time worrying about what we ate or the long-term effects food might have on our bodies. We pretty much took eating for granted, as I'm sure many people do. Hippocrates' words, "Thy food shall be thy medicine," were meaningless to us.

All of that changed in an instant. You'll find the whole story in Chapter 1, but the short version is that, after months of unexplained abdominal distention, diarrhea, and weight loss, our 18-month-old son Tyler was diagnosed with a condition called *celiac disease.* While we'd never even heard of this disease and didn't understand what it meant at first, reality quickly set in as we learned that Tyler could no longer eat wheat or gluten (a component of wheat, barley, and rye).

Millions of people are discovering that wheat makes them feel sick. Like Tyler, millions more are finding that it's not just wheat, but gluten, that makes them ill. In a society that covets foods such as bread, pasta, pizza, cookies, and crackers, it may seem nearly impossible to avoid wheat and gluten. Not only are obvious favorites such as cereals, cakes, and most baked goods off limits, but wheat is hidden in things you might never suspect—such as licorice, soy sauce, and some seasonings and additives. Gluten is even harder to avoid.

What about the emotional implications of eliminating these items from the diet? If you've ever tried to change your eating habits for any reason, you know how difficult it can be physically, socially, emotionally, psychologically, and even financially. The feelings of deprivation, loss of convenience, sadness, frustration, and confusion can be overwhelming. But when it means keeping yourself or someone you love healthy, happy, and worry-free, making the change can be well worth the effort. This book, loaded with helpful advice, important information on health and nutrition, and inspiring "attitude adjusters," is an essential resource for anyone giving up wheat or gluten.

Why You Should Read This Book

I'm guessing that if you've picked up this book, you fall into one of the following categories:

- You or someone you love, live with, or cook for has been diagnosed with a wheat- or gluten-related allergy, intolerance, sensitivity, or disease.

- You're exploring the idea of giving up wheat or gluten but haven't quite made up your mind.

- You're interested in the health and nutritional implications of wheat and gluten in the diet.

- You don't feel good, and wonder if eliminating wheat or gluten might help you feel better.

- You're investigating the gluten-free/casein-free diet for behavioral issues such as autism, Asperger's syndrome, attention-deficit disorder (ADD), or attention-deficit hyperactivity disorder (ADHD).

- You not only have a problem requiring you to eliminate wheat and/or gluten, but you also have diabetes and wonder how to incorporate the wheat-free/gluten-free diet into your diabetic diet.

- You've already eliminated wheat or gluten from your diet and want more information and some practical ideas.

A huge segment of the population has turned to the wheat-free/gluten-free diet for one or more of the reasons you just read. Wheat allergies affect millions of people, producing a wide range of symptoms from sinus problems to severe gastrointestinal distress. People with celiac disease (an autoimmune disease also called *sprue*), once thought of as rare but now known to be a common condition, must adhere to a strict, gluten-free diet for life. The wheat-free/gluten-free diet is also recommended for people with other autoimmune diseases, such as multiple sclerosis and lupus.

Researchers and proponents of the wheat-free/gluten-free diet also find it helpful in treating behavioral disorders. Some believe that the gluten-free diet helps with depression and even reduces or eliminates schizophrenic behaviors. Interestingly, many children with autism, Asperger's syndrome, ADD, and ADHD who try a gluten-free/casein-free diet often show remarkable improvement in their behavior. Even more important, the diet may prevent people from developing other, sometimes serious, associated conditions.

It doesn't have a fancy name, but the wheat-free/gluten-free diet is gaining in popularity as millions of people who have tried it discover that they feel better. Whatever your reasons for wanting to explore the wheat-free/gluten-free lifestyle, this book will provide you with the foundation you need to make informed choices and decisions, and will help you through the day-to-day practicalities as well as the emotional implications of living with dietary restrictions.

More than anything, this book is intended to be helpful, easy to read, and inspiring. Whether you're just interested in or considering the diet, or have been wheat-free/gluten-free for years, this book is filled with practical and emotional advice that will help you live—and love—the wheat-free/gluten-free lifestyle.

Why You Can Trust What You're About to Read

I've been where you are: I live the lifestyle, and I've dedicated my life to learning as much I can about the diet, the medical and scientific reasons why the diet works, and ways to develop and maintain an optimistic yet realistic approach to living the lifestyle. I'm committed to sharing my knowledge and experience with others.

You can trust what you read in this book because I have nothing to sell you except information and inspiration. No fancy foods. No strange miracle devices. None of the other incidentals that often accompany books on health and diet. I have no angles and no ulterior motives—just a desire to help you learn to live the wheat-free/gluten-free lifestyle.

This book isn't a fad diet book. The wheat-free/gluten-free diet doesn't promise to help you lose (or gain) 30 pounds in 30 days, nor does it come with the caveat that in order to enjoy the benefits of the diet, you have to buy expensive supplements or strange-looking contraptions. There are no sexy 23-year-old models claiming that the diet made their wrinkles disappear, and no paycheck-collecting celebrities espousing the benefits of the diet.

This book is based on more than a decade of practical experience living with a strict gluten-free diet. In the years that followed Tyler's diagnosis, I learned a great deal about our newly required lifestyle: how to navigate grocery stores and fast-food restaurants; how to communicate with doctors and other medical professionals; how to read labels and obtain detailed information from food manufacturers and distributors; and how to choose, buy, and prepare foods the whole family could enjoy. I've written this book in an effort to share my experience and make it easier for those who need or choose to follow a wheat-free or gluten-free lifestyle.

Beyond experience, this book is also based on scientific facts, medical research, and in-depth investigations into controversial and sometimes-confusing subject matter. As National Spokesperson for Celiac Disease Awareness, I have access to the latest research, publications, and product information on all related matters. I'm also witness to storms of heated controversy, political arm wrestling, unsubstantiated rumors, and inaccurate statements. In writing this book, I worked hard to assess the information—accurate, inaccurate, credible, and incredible—and sort it out for you with no particular spin on it.

I'm not a doctor, nor do I play one on TV. The medical information included in this book is based on published research, and while I've worked hard to distill fact from fiction, I'm at the mercy of reputable journals, peer reviews, and world-renowned researchers to validate scientific claims and medical literature. Some of the world's foremost experts on the subject of allergies, wheat/gluten intolerance, and celiac disease have reviewed this book for accuracy.

What *is* this book? It's a user-friendly guide to the art of happy, healthy, wheat-free/gluten-free living. It's also an attitude adjuster that I hope you'll find comforting and inspiring when you need a reminder of the bright side, a "friend" who's been-there-done-that, or a small kick in the tush to get you back on an optimistic track. Whether you're new to the diet or "an old pro," *Wheat-Free, Worry-Free* will help you understand the many reasons that a wheat-free/gluten-free diet may improve the way you feel—both physically and psychologically.

How to Use This Book

Wheat-Free, Worry-Free is divided into three parts. You can read one, two, or all three sections, based on the information you need and want. You don't have to read them all, nor do you have to read them in order, but of course I encourage you to read the entire book.

Don't worry if you're not the scientific type. The information has been written in a way that's easy to follow and understand. Just like the wheat-free/gluten-free diet, this book is intended to give you options and choices that feel right for you.

Part I: Is This Diet for You? Could you feel better if you cut wheat or gluten out of your diet? Are you at high risk of developing serious medical conditions if you continue to eat one or both of them? Could your behavior and emotions be under the influence of wheat or gluten?

Some people believe that wheat and gluten are the culprits behind just about every malady known to humanity. I've heard them blamed for everything from ear infections, nosebleeds, and vision problems to bad breath, backaches, and snoring. While those claims might sound ridiculous at first, it *is* the ambiguity of symptoms that makes conditions such as wheat allergies, gluten intolerance, and celiac disease so difficult to diagnose.

Part I explains who might benefit from the wheat-free/gluten-free diet, and why it makes so many people feel better—physically and psychologically. It describes dozens of conditions associated with eating wheat and gluten, most of which improve dramatically on a wheat-free/gluten-free diet. It also includes advice and tips about the medical tests you may need, and ways to communicate better with your doctor and other medical professionals to get the most appropriate and supportive medical care possible.

You may already know what condition you have, or you may not be interested in the details of why you'll feel better once you're wheat-free/gluten-free, and you may be tempted to skip to Part II. That's okay; the book is written in a manner so you can do that. But if nothing else, I encourage you to read Chapter 1 and the section about why doctors don't diagnose celiac disease more often. You may discover the answers to questions you didn't even realize you had.

Part II: Weaning from Wheat and Bootin' Gluten: How, What, and Where to Eat. This may be the part you've needed most—the everyday aspects of living life on a wheat-free/gluten-free diet. In Part II, you'll find comprehensive lists of safe and forbidden foods and ingredients, along with plenty of suggestions for shopping, menu planning, and cooking.

Many people on the wheat-free/gluten-free diet have additional dietary restrictions, including glucose and casein. This section includes information on specific concerns and challenges for people eliminating more than just wheat and gluten from their diets. There's even a chapter filled with delicious and easy-to-make recipes by cookbook author Connie Sarros, including wheat-free, gluten-free, casein-free, diabetic, and vegetarian items.

For many people on the wheat-free/gluten-free diet, the fear of eating out becomes imprisoning. You'll discover the importance of *not* living your life in a bubble, and you'll learn how to make special accommodations for yourself when you travel, eat at restaurants, and attend social functions. You'll find the answers to some big-picture questions, such as whether or not the entire family should be gluten-free, and how to handle holidays, special occasions, and taking holy communion at churches that serve gluten-containing hosts. By the time you finish Part II, you will be well equipped to live a happy, healthy, wheat-free/gluten-free lifestyle.

Part III: Wheat-Free Isn't Always Worry-Free: Dealing with the Emotions Behind the Diet. To adopt a wheat- or gluten-free diet is to adopt a new lifestyle, one that requires planning, flexibility, patience, and creativity. Adapting to this lifestyle can be accompanied by feelings of resentment and deprivation, special considerations, new responsibilities for the entire family, and an entirely new way of thinking about food. To think of it as a "diet" is akin to thinking that occasionally babysitting your nephew for an hour or two is just like parenting.

If you're feeling afraid, angry, deprived, or lonely, or you're grieving for the foods you'll never again eat, you're not alone. Everyone experiences a myriad of emotions, mostly—frankly—unpleasant ones. This part of the book focuses on those emotional ups and downs, and offers inspiration for dealing with them in an optimistic yet realistic manner.

Some of the advice in this section extends far beyond diet. You'll learn ways to improve your attitude and adopt a fresh, uplifting perspective on life in general and diet in particular. Possibly one of the most important chapters, "Family, Friends, and Strangers: Talking to Others about the Diet" explains why many of the people closest to you just won't "get" the concept of this diet, and offers advice on how to deal with the frustration and anger that can result. If you have or know kids on the wheat-free/gluten-free diet, be sure to read "Kid Conundrums and Answers to the Rest of Your Questions" for support and important reference resources. You'll also find bits and pieces of information that should resolve any lingering questions you may still have.

Tech Talk: Medical, Nutritional, and Scientific Details. If you want the details behind the diet, you'll find them in Tech Talk. This part of the book includes information about the nutritional deficiencies that can arise on the wheat-free/gluten-free diet and how to compensate for them. You'll find detailed nutritional requirements and recommendations for making your wheat-free/gluten-free diet a nutritionally sound and healthy one. If you're diabetic and trying to incorporate both diets into your lifestyle, the carbohydrate exchange information chart contained in this section will surely help. You'll also find a summary of the current research on sensitivities and intolerance, as well as specific medical references for celiac disease tests.

Resource Directory. One of the least creative but most valuable parts of this book is the Resource Directory, a comprehensive listing of products and services pertinent to the wheat-free/gluten-free lifestyle. It contains contact information for hundreds of food manufacturers, on-line shopping companies, and sources of information and support.

Throughout the book, you'll also find questions and comments from other people; you may recognize some of your own thoughts in what they've said. For more than a decade, I've counseled people from all over the world on the wheat-free/gluten-free diet. Day after day, I hear the same basic frustrations, fears, complaints, and concerns. These questions and comments, as well as the many creative ideas that people have shared with me over the years, inspired the content and format of this book. I hope they'll inspire you, too, and serve as a reminder that you're not alone in dealing with this new lifestyle. Others have done it, and you can, too!

Like any new lifestyle, adapting to the wheat-free/gluten-free diet is a process of metamorphosis, and it won't happen overnight. Some find it to be a difficult transition, while others sail right through it. This guide is intended to help you breeze into your new way of life—happy, healthy, wheat-free, and worry-free.

Part I

Is This Diet for You?

Could you feel better if you cut wheat or gluten out of your diet? Are you at high risk of developing serious medical conditions if you continue to eat one or both? Could your behavior and emotions be affected by wheat or gluten?

In this section, you'll find the answers to these and many other questions. You'll learn who might benefit from the wheat-free/gluten-free diet, and why it makes so many people feel better—physically and psychologically. You'll learn some basics about how digestion is supposed to work, and the critical impact of allergies, intolerance, sensitivities, and disease. You'll discover some skills for better communication with your medical professional, and you'll have the opportunity to explore a range of complementary approaches to wheat and gluten sensitivity.

Chapter 1

Going Wheat-Free/Gluten-Free: Usually a Matter of Chance, Not Choice

"Life is what happens to you while you're busy making other plans."
— John Lennon

O ur family has been living a gluten-free lifestyle since 1991, when our son, Tyler (well, okay, it was an original name when *we* thought of it), was diagnosed with celiac disease. Believed at that time to be a rare condition, celiac disease was anything but a household word, and most people were as knowledgeable about the condition as I am about quantum physics. We were truly on that figurative island in the middle of nowhere with no help in sight.

To paraphrase John Lennon, our life is what happened to us even though we had other plans—or so we thought.

Why Won't Anyone Admit That Our Baby Is Sick?

Our story began when our first child, a perfect baby boy, began to get sick. It started benignly enough, with more than just a touch of diarrhea, which his pediatrician attributed to the antibiotics Tyler was taking for ear infections. When time was up on our allotted four-minute office visit, we were told to "keep an eye on it" and call if the diarrhea didn't go away in a couple of weeks.

What we were supposed to "keep an eye on," I'm not sure. The piles of diapers that we had to haul out every afternoon? The lovely rhinoceros-skin texture my hands were assuming because I had to wash them every ten minutes? Or maybe the water bill that had sky-rocketed because of the additional laundry I was doing when the Pampers just couldn't accommodate the excess loads they were being asked to hold? In any case, the doctor *had* told us to call if the diarrhea didn't go away in a couple of weeks, so we did.

Apparently, what he meant to say was, "We tell you to call if it doesn't go away just to get you out of our office feeling like we did something, but really, we'd rather you don't bother us because all we're going to do is listen to you whine for four minutes and then tell you that there's nothing wrong." Why can't people just say what they mean?

Instead, I endured the heavy sighs of the receptionist who took it upon herself to play doctor and say, "You mean you're bringing him in again *just* because of diarrhea?" Well, yeah. That's what I was told to do! Several heavy sighs and even an I-hate-neurotic-new-moms snicker later, we had an appointment—for three weeks out.

Meanwhile, we were buying Pepto Bismol in bulk. I'm the kind of person who gets embarrassed just buying toilet paper, so buying "anti-diarrhea" medications with pictures of happy intestines on the packaging was as difficult as any aspect of this nightmare. But we hoped the magical pink liquid would plug Tyler up while we waited for our follow-up visit to the doctor.

The second visit was, as I alluded to, an obligatory waste of time. After looking in Tyler's ears, nose, and throat (did I lead you, Doctor, to believe that this problem was *above his waist?!*), the doctor concluded that there was nothing to be concerned about. Oh, really? I guess it's *normal* to be changing 22 diarrhea diapers a day? I don't think the doctor was amused when I offered to present him with a stool sample, since I was sure in the next nine minutes we would have one that we could examine together. No, I was sent away and told, once again, to call if the situation didn't improve in the next two weeks. Yeah, right. I'll be sure to do that.

It was with sadness and grief that I realized that this pediatrician whom I had hand-selected after interviewing no less than 12 others in the area, and who had offered a congratulatory hug less than 14 minutes after Tyler was born, wasn't listening to me. It was time to find doctor number two.

Sadly, our experience with the next doctor was a repeat of the one with the first. A quick look in the ears, nose, and throat, followed by a declaration that we had a healthy baby boy, sent my blood pressure skyrocketing. "But what about the diarrhea I mentioned?" I managed to ask with control worthy of the Nobel Peace Prize. "Really, diarrhea is nothing to worry about unless the child is severely dehydrated and losing weight," I was told, as though I had the IQ of an aluminum can. "Well, I've been force-feeding him water to avoid dehydration," I explained, thinking that might make him realize that there was a *reason* Tyler wasn't shriveling up from thirst. "Oh, good," he replied as he raced out the door to his next four-minute appointment. "Keep it up and call me in two weeks if the situation hasn't improved." Ugh.

After a few months, several hundred dollars worth of diapers, and cracked and bleeding hands, we switched to doctor number three. We chose a woman this time, figuring maybe some element of "woman's instinct" or a maternal inkling would alert her to what we believed was a worsening condition. "Well, he's in the 75th percentile for height and weight," she declared after looking in his ears, nose, and throat. "Certainly nothing to worry about with this bruiser," she gloated.

Trying to be patient, hiding the clenched fists, and managing a smile that was as sincere as that of a politician running for office, I replied, "But he used to be in the 98th percentile. Wouldn't that indicate *weight loss*, which could be a sign of something wrong?"

"Oh, honey, don't be ridiculous! What do you *want*, a prizefighter?" Hardy, har-har. I had a real Carol Burnett on my hands. Again, we were sent away and—you know the rest.

And so it was. There was nothing wrong. Never mind that he had been loading up 22 diarrhea diapers a day for the last nine months—apparently he was just a poop machine. Never mind that his belly had grown distended to the point that he couldn't bend over and pick up his toys. Never mind that his arms and legs were skinny—hey, he was still in the 75th percentile for height and weight, and it's not like I was trying to raise a prizefighter or anything.

So it was without a care or a complaint that I dragged my irritable, listless little Biafra baby into the office of doctor number four, a doctor to whom we were assigned when we changed insurance plans. After looking in Tyler's ears, nose, and throat, he laid my little boy down on his back and thumped on his belly like you might thump a honeydew melon to see if it's ripe. "My goodness," he said with that I'm-alarmed-but-I'm-a-doctor-and-don't-want-to-freak-you-out-so-I'll-smile-smugly-and-act-calm voice, "what's going on with his belly? It's very distended." I couldn't answer through the tears of relief.

Relief Turns to Terror

I never thought I'd be so excited to be referred to Children's Hospital. I called my husband with the good news. "Sweetie, guess what?! We have to go to the hospital!" I announced as though we had just won the lottery. Never quite sure how to respond to my usually overly enthusiastic and not always sensical proclamations, he replied, as usual, with caution. "Really? Is that a good thing?" I guess in retrospect it wasn't a dumb question, but at the time it deserved, "DUH! We're going to see the gastroenterologist!"

On the drive to the hospital, Tyler and I sang the "I Love You" song with such glee that we made Barney look like a candidate for Prozac in comparison. "We're going to the hospital to see the nice doctor who's going to help us make you feel better," I sang to the tune of whatever I could come up with on short notice. Tyler, 18 months old then, sang, too, and we practically danced into the waiting room for our first visit with the gastroenterologist.

Somehow a three-hour wait in a doctor's waiting room does a lot to dampen enthusiasm. Our gastroenterologist didn't even look in Tyler's ears, nose, or throat, a small favor for which I could have kissed him, even as tired and hungry as I was. He *did* do the honeydew thump on Tyler's belly, and asked how long he had been experiencing diarrhea. "Oh, about nine months now," I commented. "*Nine months?*" he asked. The large eyes and knitted eyebrows spoke for him, so he didn't have to finish his thought, which was obviously, *Why did you wait so long, you oblivious, inexperienced nitwit?*

The doctor said Tyler would need a variety of tests. He tossed around names such as upper GI, lower GI, ultrasound, serology, endoscopy, biopsy, fecal fat, enzyme panel, WBC, and sweat test. Thinking maybe I had slept through those days during my Biology 101 class in college, and not wanting to admit it, I said, "Oh, right. So that means you're testing for . . . " As though the condition was right on the tip of my tongue and I just couldn't recall it. He saved me the awkward silence that would have ensued and filled in the blanks: "We're going to be looking at a number of possibilities: blood diseases, cancer, cystic fibrosis . . . that sort of thing." I thought I was going to faint.

The Bittersweet Diagnosis

After signing reams of release forms that we never read, and allowing doctors to poke, prod, anesthetize, and "scope" our baby, we finally got a call from the gastroenterologist's office asking us to come in for a consultation. "Well, can't you just tell me what it is on the phone?" I asked. "No, he wants you to come in," the receptionist told me. "But is that a *bad* thing? Wouldn't he just call to tell me nothing's wrong if my baby was okay?" I began to panic.

After a three-day stay in the waiting room (okay, it just *seemed* like three days because hours spent waiting in a four-foot-by-four-foot cubicle with an 18-month-old are automatically quadrupled in value), we finally saw the doctor and heard the words that would change our lives forever: "Your son has celiac disease." Huh? Is that anything like a flu bug? Surely there was a pill we could give him that would make it all better. "It simply requires a dietary change." Okay, so maybe we overdo the goldfish-shaped crackers a little—we can do without for a few weeks. "He won't be able to eat gluten for the rest of his life."

Back up the truck here, Mister. *Rest of his life? Gluten?* Is that anything like glucose? Because we can surely cut down on sugar.

In a state of shock, we were directed down the hall to the hospital dietitian. Without looking up, she put her hand out, presumably wanting the chart that we had been instructed to give to her. Still in a daze, I handed her the chart. Several seconds of silence passed—had she fallen asleep? Was she writing her grocery list in her head? Had she forgotten we were there? Finally, she said, "So you need information on the gluten-free diet, huh? Don't get many of those."

"Really?" I asked. "How many have you had?"

"None."

After digging through her files, she handed me a crumpled blue piece of paper that had writing on both sides. The first side, filled with minuscule type, listed the foods and ingredients we were to avoid. The other side had huge type, presumably in an effort to make the page look full, and was titled, "Acceptable Foods on the Gluten-free Diet." There were six items on the list.

Our First Shopping Trip

Still resembling a zombie, I realized I had an 18-month-old child to consider, and he'd been through as much as I had, so I asked what he wanted to do. "Get a tweat! *Cwackews!*" he replied (translated to "treat" and "crackers" for those of you who don't speak Toddler). Not a bad thought. We had to learn how to shop sometime, so off we went on our first gluten-free shopping expedition.

Armed with our crumpled blue sheet, we started in the cracker aisle. Carefully reading labels, I was amazed and delighted to find that not a single package had gluten in the ingredients list! How *easy* was this going to be! Lest you think that I *do* have the IQ of an aluminum can, you have to remember that I was still in a state of shock, topped off with a touch of denial.

I consulted my trusty blue sheet and realized that flour was, indeed, buried in the list of forbidden ingredients, and put back all the crackers I had tossed into the cart. We went up another aisle. Pretzels . . . nope. Bread . . . not even close. "But Mommy, I just want a *tweat*." Tyler's patience was wearing thin. In desperation, I picked up a bag of Fritos. Could it be? *Really?* Surely I had missed something. No, it was true. Not a single gluten molecule to be found. Hallelujah! I grabbed seven bags and headed for home.

Taking the Fork in the Road

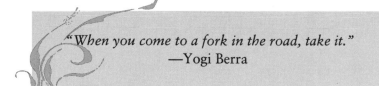

"When you come to a fork in the road, take it."
—Yogi Berra

When we were told that Tyler would have to lead a wheat-free/gluten-free lifestyle, we felt like we'd come to a fork in the road. At first, we felt burdened and overcome with grief and frustration, and we longed for the perfectly healthy little baby we thought we were entitled to. It was easy to focus on what we had lost, and all that we'd have to change in our lives, and initially, we may have found ourselves mired in negativity and bitterness. But we knew that there was another path we could choose. As we learned to live with the diet and its ramifications, we worked hard to find a way to turn the adversity into a positive force in our lives. More than a decade later, I can honestly say that what we once felt was misfortune has grown to become a huge blessing in our lives.

Yes, this diet is a matter of chance, not choice. It's a major change in lifestyle for most people, and it's a difficult adjustment at first. For some, adopting this new way of life feels like a hardship. But if you've come to this fork in your road, as Yogi Berra says, not only do you have to take it, but you might as well make the best of it, because it's the only fork you *can* take to be happy and healthy for the rest of your life.

In the pages that follow, you'll learn not only to live, but to love your new way of eating. More than simply *accepting* this as though it's a life sentence, you can—with a little help from this book—learn to *appreciate* it. In other words, you'll learn to practice what I preach: *Deal with it, don't dwell on it.*

Chapter 2

Digestion 101:
Eating Isn't Supposed to Hurt

*"Man should always strive to have his intestines
relaxed all the days of his life."*
— Maimonides, 12th-century physician

Always strive to have your intestines relaxed. Now *those* are words to live by. That guy was on to something. Because you're reading this book, I'm going to guess that your—uh—intestines (if I may get a little personal here) are a little less than relaxed, maybe even a little uptight lately. That's okay, it happens to everyone—but not on a regular basis (hence the clever term *irregularity*).

Eating isn't supposed to hurt. But when you put things into your body that don't sit well with you, nature has a way of telling you to knock it off. Gas, bloating, diarrhea, constipation, nausea—even subtle signals such as headaches, fatigue, moodiness, and various aches and pains are red flags that shouldn't be ignored.

I'm guessing that you're reading this book because you don't feel well, and you suspect that food may be at the root of your problem. It very well could be, especially if you have any of the following symptoms:

- Fatigue
- Gastrointestinal distress (gas, bloating, diarrhea, constipation, vomiting, heartburn, reflux)
- Headaches
- Inability to concentrate (i.e., ADD/ADHD)
- Inability to gain or lose weight
- Infertility
- Joint pain
- Moodiness or depression
- Muscle aches

If you're thinking, *All those symptoms? What's left?* you're absolutely right. That list covers a lot of ground, but the truth is that when the food you're eating makes you sick, it can manifest itself in all sorts of different ways. That's why it's so hard to pinpoint the cause of your symptoms, and why even doctors often make the wrong diagnosis.

To understand why food doesn't sit well with you, let's start by taking a look at how your digestive system is *supposed* to work.

Don't worry—we're not going to use nine-syllable words that require a refresher course in Latin to understand them, and there won't be a pop quiz. But understanding the basics of digestion will equip you with the knowledge you need to make informed decisions about your diet, and will prepare you for conversations with your physician.

Understanding the Digestive System

The digestive system consists of many parts, including the esophagus, stomach, and the small and large intestines, which are tubular structures where digestion takes place (see Figure 1). Two glands, the liver and pancreas, provide enzymes and other substances needed for digestion. The gallbladder, located just under the liver, stores bile manufactured by the liver.

The food you eat is propelled through the digestive tract by involuntary (automatic) muscular contractions. It is broken down by enzymes into a form that can eventually be absorbed into the bloodstream, and after the nutrients are absorbed, the digestive tract eliminates waste or unwanted material.

Figure 1
The Digestive System

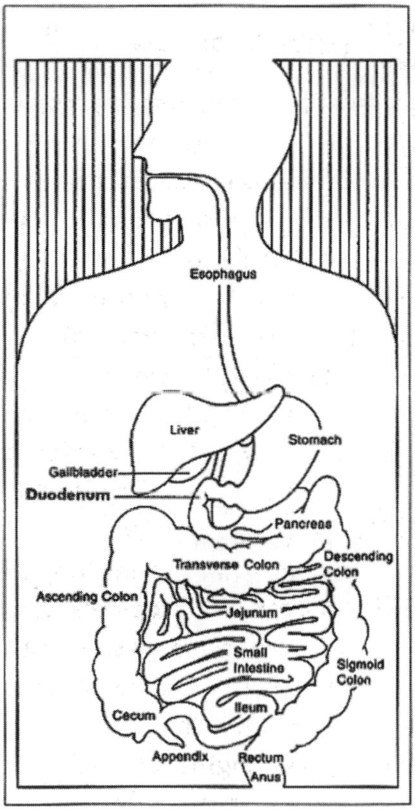

Source: NIH Publication No. 02-2681, March 2002:
http://www.niddk.nih.gov/health/digest/pubs/digesyst/newdiges.htm

A Closer Look at the Small and Large Intestines

Why, you may wonder, would we want to take a closer look at the small and large intestines? Because they're crucial to the digestion process.

The small intestine consists of three parts: the duodenum (closest to the stomach), the jejunum (halfway through), and the ileum (close to where the small intestine joins with the large intestine). The small intestine is amazingly long—nearly 22 feet in adults—and it's here that the nutrients are absorbed from the foods you eat.

The broken-down products of digestion are absorbed into the bloodstream mainly through the lining of the small intestine. This lining has tiny hairlike projections called *villi* (the plural of *villus*). Their purpose is to significantly increase the surface area of the small intestine through which nutrients can be absorbed. To better understand how they increase the surface area, picture yourself driving on a highway from point A to point B. If it's one mile between those two points and the road is flat, you rack up one mile on your odometer. But if there are several tall, pointy hills between point A and B, you'll put more than a mile on your odometer, depending upon how high each hill is. The villi serve to add miles to the odometer, if you will, so that there's more of a chance for the nutrients to be absorbed.

The large intestine (colon) is connected to the small intestine at the ileocecal valve. Waste material, semi-liquid at this point, passes through the valve and into a chamber of the large intestine called the cecum, the beginning of the large intestine. The large intestine looks like a bridge running up one side of the abdomen (ascending colon), across the top (transverse colon), down the other side (descending colon), and halfway across the bottom (sigmoid colon). The sigmoid colon then empties into the rectum.

Almost all nutrients from food are absorbed in the small intestine. Microorganisms in the colon break down some of the dietary fiber and other waste products in the stool that weren't digested by the stomach and small intestine.

Facts about Farts

If you're either (a) 14 years old and under, or (b) male, you're probably giggling at the word itself. Fart. Few words are funnier, and few subjects evoke a response like the subject of flatulence. You know . . . flatus, gas, tooties. *Farts!* Either the topic makes you blush, squirm, and deny that your body has *ever* succumbed to the urge, or you're one of the flagrant farters, generally of the male persuasion, who announces, "Fire in the hole!" before each one, and then boasts of the intensity and duration, time after time, as though each and every one is glorious in its own right. Whichever category you fall into, you do, whether you want to admit it or not, pass gas from time to time.

Passing gas is a normal bodily function, no matter what your mom told you (although she's right that it's not polite to do so at the dinner table). Gas is produced in the gut as a result of bacterial fermentation and as a by-product of food interacting with digestive juices. Some people argue that passing gas produces no healthy benefits, while others believe that it aids in digestion by repositioning the bowels. Certainly few would deny that it feels better once the deed is done.

You've heard the expression "gas bag." Well, some people *are* gassier than others. The amount of gas depends upon how much air is swallowed, the composition of the diet, and the bacteria and microorganisms found in the gut.

People who are gluten intolerant and continue to eat gluten tend to be quite flatogenic. They produce a lot of flatus. Gas. They have gas. Why? Because their food is not being digested properly, nor is it being absorbed. Undigested food makes good feeding ground for bacteria. Like all living organisms, bacteria excrete waste after they eat, and their waste product takes the form of various gases. Excessive flatus is often an indicator of malabsorption or inflammation of the gastrointestinal tract.

The particularly offensive odor emitted by gluten-intolerant people comes from the methane- or sulfur-containing gases produced by bacterial fermentation. Undigested food and bacterial imbalances and overgrowth result in excess gases that are eventually emitted in the stinkiest of forms. The main gases in the gut are nitrogen, oxygen, carbon dioxide, hydrogen, methane, and sulfur-containing gases.

Activated charcoal, which is, as its name implies, burned wood, has been used for thousands of years to treat a variety of diseases, including excessive and smelly gut gas. Activated charcoal binds these gut gases and affords some symptomatic benefit for excessive, smelly gas. Peppermint, fennel, caraway, and ginger can also help relieve gas.

By the way, both Hippocrates and Roman emperor Claudius were fans of farts. Claudius is quoted as proclaiming, "All Roman citizens shall be allowed to pass gas whenever necessary." When in Rome, do as the Romans do.

Digestion Gone Wrong

When something you eat doesn't agree with you, the result can be anywhere from mildly uncomfortable to excruciatingly worse-than-labor painful. It doesn't take a trained medical professional to alert you when your digestive system goes awry.

But discovering the exact *cause* of the problem can be elusive. Symptoms can be hard to pinpoint or articulate. The fact that digestion takes time also adds to the difficulty of making an accurate diagnosis, because sometimes it takes hours or even days for the food you've eaten to manifest into symptoms of discomfort, pain, or abnormal bowel movements.

Disturbances of the gastrointestinal tract may be caused by a variety of problems, including infections, malabsorption conditions, food allergies or intolerances, and disease.

Viral, Bacterial, and Parasitic Infections

In developing countries, diarrhea caused by infection is the leading cause of death in children. Improvements in sanitation and hygiene have had a significant impact on preventing many of these infections, especially those transmitted by contaminated food and water. Infections can be caused by viruses, bacteria, and parasites.

Acute viral infection, also called *viral gastroenteritis,* is quite common, and results in diarrhea, nausea, vomiting, low-grade fever, abdominal cramps, and muscle pains. Many viruses are passed by fecal-to-oral transmission (when people don't wash their hands well enough after using the bathroom), and can be prevented with thorough hand-washing techniques. Rotavirus and Norwalk virus are the two most common causes of viral gastroenteritis.

Bacterial infections are easier to identify than viral infections, and in many cases, antibiotics are useful in their treatment. One of the most common forms of bacterial infection is campylobacteriosis (caused by the bacterium *Campylobacter*), which comes from contaminated food, particularly raw milk and poultry. While symptoms may be abrupt and severe—abdominal pain, nausea, low-grade fever, headaches, and muscle pain—they rarely last longer than a week. For severe symptoms, an antibiotic may be prescribed. Other common bacterial infections are caused by *Salmonella, Shigella,* and *E. coli.*

Parasitic infestations are the least common of the three major causes of gastrointestinal infection in the United States. *Giardia* is one of the most frequently found parasites, and occurs in communities where the water supply is contaminated by raw sewage, or where people drink from lakes or streams that may be used as animal outhouses. *Entamoeba histolytica* and *Cryptosporidium* are other common parasites.

Malabsorption Conditions

Malabsorption simply means that the body doesn't absorb nutrients properly. When this occurs, important nutrients that are supposed to be absorbed into the bloodstream are instead eliminated in the stool. Malabsorption can be caused by a deficiency of pancreatic enzymes, or a problem in the small intestine.

If you or someone you know has been seeing a doctor about a malabsorption condition, chances are you've heard the words "steatorrheal stools." That's because these stools, notably fatty and oily, are a principal sign of malabsorption. The stools are greasy or oily because unabsorbed fat is passed on to the stool. Protein is also not absorbed, resulting in a wasting of the body's tissues.

Malabsorption can cause a deficiency of vitamins A, B12, D, E, and K; as well as folic acid, calcium, and iron. These nutrients are normally absorbed in the small intestine, but in cases of malabsorption they're passed through to the stool.

Common causes of malabsorption include celiac disease, tropical sprue, bacterial overgrowth, scleroderma, AIDS, Whipple's disease, amyloidosis, lactose intolerance, and short-bowel syndrome.

Allergy, Intolerance, Sensitivity, or Disease— Knowing the Difference Is Important

If food isn't sitting well with you, and you've ruled out infections and other problems, the problem could be due to allergy, intolerance, sensitivity, or disease. Which, if any, do you have? You may think you already know the answer to that question, or you may think you don't need to know—but I encourage you to finish reading this chapter and the next one anyway; they contain useful information you may not already have, and they just might help you decide whether you should obtain further testing. The cause of your problems has important implications with respect to the degree to which you may need to alter your diet—and therefore your lifestyle—to feel your best and ensure optimal health.

"I Think I Might Be Allergic"

Yep—you and millions of other people. In fact, one out of three people either says they have a food allergy or modifies the family's diet because they suspect that a family member has an allergy. When people have an unpleasant reaction to something they eat, the first thing they suspect is a food allergy. Yet only about 6 to 8 percent of infants and toddlers have clinically proven allergic reactions to foods. Of the children who experience food reactions, most outgrow these allergies by their third birthdays, dropping the prevalence of food allergy in adults to about one percent of the total population. Strong genetic influences play a part in who will develop allergies.

A food allergy, or hypersensitivity, is an abnormal response triggered by the immune system. In allergic individuals, the presence of

certain proteins called *allergens* prompts the immune system to produce increased amounts of an antibody called *immunoglobulin E*
(IgE). These IgE antibodies bind to the surface of different cells, act-
ing like antennae of sorts. The next time the person eats that specific
protein, the antibodies trigger the release of chemicals throughout the
body. Some of these chemicals, such as histamine, make the person
feel sick, and sometimes result in the sudden onset of symptoms like
throat swelling, skin rashes, wheezing, vomiting, runny nose, diarrhea,
and even a drop in blood pressure. Food allergies usually affect the
skin and intestines, causing rashes, hives, eczema, cramps, nausea, and
diarrhea (some of these symptoms occur in celiac disease and wheat
or gluten intolerance, but usually they occur more quickly with an
allergic response). Respiratory symptoms such as asthma, nasal con-
gestion, and sneezing can also develop, with more serious results. The
most threatening of all is anaphylaxis—a swelling of blood vessels that
causes blood pressure to drop and the throat to close. An anaphylactic
response can be fatal. Approximately 150 people in the United States
die every year from anaphylactic reactions to food.

In an allergic response, symptoms generally develop quite quickly
after an offending food is eaten. Sometimes, people can eat a particular food for years with no problem, and then suddenly have a dramatic
reaction. The top eight food allergens include peanuts, tree nuts (such
as walnuts and pecans), fish, shellfish, eggs, milk, soy, and wheat.

Testing is the best way to determine the existence of a true food
allergy. Allergy tests come in a variety of forms, including skin-prick
tests, blood tests, and "food challenges," in which the patient eats
some of the suspected food in gradually increasing amounts under a
doctor's supervision.

Exploratory new treatments for food allergies include "anti-IgE
therapy," which uses a specially devised molecule that attaches to and
inactivates the IgE antibodies that cause allergic reactions—essentially
stopping the allergic reaction before it starts. Immunotherapy, another
treatment regimen, consists of a series of injections containing small
amounts of an allergen that helps the patient build up an immunity
or resistance to that allergen. Scientists have also learned that delay-
ing the introduction of solid foods to infants until six months of age
and breastfeeding for the first year of life can help prevent food
allergies.

Sensitivity and Intolerance

> "Sensitivity: *The state or quality of being sensitive*"
> "Intolerance: *Inability to withstand; sensitivity, as to a drug*"
> — *Dorland's Illustrated Medical Dictionary,* 28th edition

You may be one of the many people reading this book because you suspect or have been told that you have a wheat or gluten sensitivity or intolerance. But what do those terms mean, how do they differ from an allergy, and most important, can you trust them as a diagnosis?

The terms *sensitivity* and *intolerance* are the source of much confusion. Is it any wonder, when even one of the most well-respected medical dictionaries doesn't provide a clear distinction? Often used interchangeably, both terms basically mean that your body doesn't react well to a particular food, and you should, therefore, avoid that food. Notice that I said "should," not "must."

This fuzzy interpretation of the words *sensitivity* and *intolerance* poses a problem. I don't "tolerate" bratty kids very well, but if my best client's CEO invites his bratty kid to attend our holiday party, I'll tolerate him just fine, thank you very much. In other words, I can stand him if I want to or really have to. Does the same logic apply to a wheat or gluten intolerance or sensitivity? Yes, if that's what you have, and not something more severe. In most cases, though, the terms *wheat* and *gluten intolerance* or *sensitivity* are used when the condition is, in fact, celiac disease.

Celiac Disease: An Autoimmune Disorder

Years of research and talking to people around the world who "don't do well with wheat" have taught me that many people who *think* they have food allergies or sensitivities actually have celiac disease. It's not surprising that people don't know they have it. After all, most people have never heard of it, and doctors rarely diagnose it (you can't diagnose what you don't test for). However, celiac disease is more common than you might imagine, found in approximately one out of every 150 people.

Simply stated, celiac disease is a genetic intolerance to gluten. Unlike an allergy, celiac disease is an *autoimmune* condition, meaning that the body essentially turns against and "destroys" itself. Normally, the cells of the immune system can distinguish between body tissues and foreign organisms such as bacteria, viruses, and other invaders. It's the job of the immune system to fight off these invaders, and it does so with antibodies produced by the body. In the case of an autoimmune disorder, though, the immune system mistakenly interprets the body's own tissues as foreign, and launches an all-out attack on them.

Collectively, autoimmune diseases strike women three times more often than men. According to a recent study, autoimmune diseases are the top ten leading causes of deaths among American women age 65 and younger.[1]

The American Autoimmune Related Diseases Association (AARDA) points out that autoimmune diseases are frequently misdiagnosed or never diagnosed at all. The fact that these diseases often have seemingly unrelated symptoms and unpredictable patterns of flare-ups and remissions, and are often not well understood even by physicians, are cited as reasons for late or misdiagnosis. According to the AARDA, 45 percent of patients who are diagnosed with serious autoimmune diseases are initially written off as "chronic complainers" and not given proper treatment.

The "Compromised" Immune System?

When people are diagnosed with an autoimmune disorder, they often assume that their immune system is compromised, making them more susceptible to colds, viruses, and other illnesses. Not true. Someone who has an autoimmune condition has an over*active immune system, not an* under*active one.*

In most people, gluten doesn't trigger any type of immune response. But in people with celiac disease, certain cells in the intestines react against a toxic portion of the gluten molecule, and launch an attack on the intestinal wall, specifically affecting the villi of the small intestine. As mentioned earlier, the villi are small hairlike projections that act to increase the surface area of the small intestine, providing more opportunity for nutrients to be absorbed and digested into the bloodstream.

When celiacs eat gluten, the villi become damaged, and the harmful effects are cumulative. Damage to the villi begins at the tips, and eventually blunts the villi so much that they become ineffective at absorbing the nutrients from digested food.

Villous blunting generally starts just below the stomach, in the duodenum—the part of the small intestine that connects to the stomach. People diagnosed in the earliest stages of celiac disease have less damage, and therefore generally have several feet of small intestine left to absorb nutrients. The unaffected portion of the small intestine may be large enough that the person never experiences diarrhea or any of the other classic symptoms. This is one of the reasons that diagnosing celiac disease can be a difficult task.

Years ago it was thought that only people with the classic symptoms of diarrhea, abdominal distension, cramping, and other gastrointestinal distress were candidates for a diagnosis of celiac disease. Today we know that the symptoms of celiac disease can be mild or severe, and can be all over the board, including one or all of those listed at the beginning of this chapter. Symptoms may not even include classic gastrointestinal manifestations, and in fact, many people with celiac disease have no symptoms whatsoever. We also know that even in those people without symptoms, internal damage can be serious and can lead to other complications, and that early detection has crucial implications in their future health.

From a lifestyle standpoint, the most important distinction between celiac disease and other conditions is that if you have a food allergy or intolerance and you cheat (assuming you can stand the consequences), you won't cause long-term damage. Not so with celiac disease. Celiacs must adhere to a strict, gluten-free diet for life. If they continue to eat gluten, they put themselves at risk for malnourishment (the consequence of nutritional deficiencies) and a variety of other, sometimes serious, conditions.

Many people who think they have an intolerance or sensitivity mistakenly figure that, since the holiday party comes along only once a year, it's okay to indulge in the pastry puffs, while the bratty kid eats the hosts' pet goldfish. However, with celiac disease, a paltry pastry puff is never okay (but goldfish are gluten-free).

Muddy Waters—The Wheat/Gluten-Sensitivity Spectrum

If you're still confused about the difference between an allergy, a sensitivity, an intolerance, and celiac disease, you're not alone. Even the world's leading medical researchers can't seem to draw clear lines between the four. They do agree that there's a huge (and growing) spectrum of sensitivity, ranging from simple food allergies to celiac disease.

For the purposes of this book, we will use the terms as follows:

- *Sensitivity:* A reaction to wheat/gluten due to an unknown or undiagnosed cause; an umbrella term referring to allergy, intolerance, and disease. In a sensitive person, eating wheat or gluten will cause distress, but because the cause of sensitivity is unknown, long-term consequences are also unknown.

- *Allergy:* A response in which the body identifies wheat or gluten as an allergen, producing IgE antibodies and triggering an allergic response.

- *Intolerance:* An inability to tolerate wheat or gluten, with long-term consequences if wheat or gluten are ingested. Celiac disease is a gluten intolerance.

- *Celiac disease:* A genetic intolerance to gluten. Long-term consequences, sometimes severe, can result if gluten is ingested.

Leaky Gut

All of the conditions that fall within the gluten-sensitivity spec trum have one thing in common: "leaky gut," or increased permeability to gluten. This increased permeability leads to either an allergy, an autoimmune condition (that is, celiac disease), or something in between.

The gut (intestines) has a tough job; it has to protect the body from potentially harmful intruders, but it also has to absorb nutrients. Its challenge is to open pathways to the beneficial and essential nutrients without letting the harmful intruders barge their way in.

The gut usually transports nutrients (the "good guys") to the bloodstream in a relatively passive manner through spaces between cells that are normally kept closed by tight junctions. In a healthy gut, "good" molecules (such as nutrients) can move through the lining cells of the gut, but other biomechanical factors don't allow "bad" molecules (such as toxins) to be absorbed.

The tight junctions between cells in the intestinal lining can get disrupted for a variety of reasons, including inflammation, toxic damage to the lining of the gut (caused by certain drugs or treatments such as radiation therapy), bowel disease, or an excess of certain proteins that are supposed to open these junctions—but which, in excess, seem to hold the door open for the "bad guys." Doctors refer to this syndrome as increased gut permeability, or "leaky gut."

Celiac Disease: The Spectrum Within the Spectrum

Gluten sensitivity spans a huge spectrum, with a line somewhere in there that separates the gluten-sensitive from the celiacs.

One interesting study[2] looked at people who had elevated antibody levels but no blunting of the villi, the minute fingerlike projections of the small intestine that normally help absorb nutrients. Because the villi weren't blunted, those people would *not* be diagnosed with celiac disease by today's standards. Yet two years later, still on a gluten-containing diet, those people showed total villous blunting— they were by then classified as "biopsy-confirmed," or what we call "latent" celiacs (you'll learn more about them later on in this book).

What about those people who have elevated antibody levels, but either don't have an intestinal biopsy done or their biopsy results are negative? What about those who don't show an antibody response, but feel better when they eliminate gluten from their diets? Do they have celiac disease? Not by the clinical definition. *Will* they have celiac disease down the road? Maybe.

Maybe?! We're talking about a lifelong adherence to a strict diet absent of Pop Tarts and beer, and there's a "maybe"? We're talking about a condition that may have a higher risk of all sorts of other conditions, and we're talking "maybe"?

This is what I refer to as "muddy water." Certainly those people who have slightly or moderately elevated antibodies without villous atrophy are gluten-sensitive or gluten-intolerant. But have they crossed the line into the celiac portion of the spectrum? It's hard to know, because without a positive biopsy (one that reveals villous blunting), it's a fuzzy line between gluten sensitivity and celiac disease. It's an important line, but a fuzzy one nonetheless.

This all leads us back to the question posed at the beginning of this section: Gluten intolerance or celiac disease? Which *really* begs the next question: Who cares?

Who Cares What It's Called?

> "I don't know what I have, and I don't really care. I just know that I feel better when I don't eat wheat, so I just avoid it."
> — Cheryl S.

By now, you may be wondering, *Why all this discussion of allergy versus intolerance? Who really cares what it's called, anyway?*

You should care. Celiac disease carries with it three heavy implications that other conditions within the sensitivity spectrum don't:

1. While some people may be okay if they occasionally indulge in wheat or gluten, celiacs must be rigorous in

their adherence to a gluten-free diet, and *never* intentionally indulge.

2.   Celiac disease can have serious associated conditions, whereas other conditions within the sensitivity spectrum may not.

3.   Finally, unlike other conditions in the sensitivity spectrum, celiac disease is a genetic condition, so family members should be alerted to their genetic predisposition.

So I leave you with fuzzy lines and muddy water. You may be wondering, *What else should I know about celiac disease, and how can I find out if I have it?* I'm so glad you asked! While this chapter provided a brief discussion of the differences between allergy, intolerance, and celiac disease, the next chapter goes into a bit more detail about the condition, its causes, symptoms, and treatment. I hope it will help clear the waters, at least a little.

Chapter 3

Celiac Disease—Not You?
You Might Want to Think Again

"Facts do not cease to exist because they are ignored."
— Aldous Huxley

So, you're sure you don't have celiac disease, are you? Would you bet your life on it? Because at the risk of sounding somewhat melodramatic, you might be doing just that.

Just because you haven't been diagnosed with celiac disease, you're not excused to skip ahead to the next chapter just yet. Every day I talk to people about celiac disease, and every day I hear comments like, "Oh, I don't have *that*; I have irritable bowel syndrome." Oh, yeah? Give me a sample of blood and we'll see about that!

Ask yourself if you've ever had any thoughts even remotely close to these:

- *I couldn't have celiac disease, because my doctor didn't diagnose it.*

- *I don't have celiac disease; I just avoid wheat because I feel better when I go wheat-free.*

- *I've already been diagnosed with a different condition (for example, irritable bowel syndrome, chronic fatigue syndrome, fibromyalgia, or gluten intolerance), so I know I don't have celiac disease.*

- *I don't mind eliminating gluten when it's convenient for me, but I sure don't want to be diagnosed with something that would force me to avoid it all the time.*

- *I already asked my doctor about celiac disease, and he said that's not what I have.*

- *I don't have the symptoms of celiac disease like diarrhea—in fact, I have a bigger problem with constipation.*

- *I think I could have it, but I don't feel the effects of gluten, so it doesn't matter if I eat it.*

- *I hardly eat any gluten anyway, so it doesn't matter.*

- *I used to have celiac disease as a baby, but I outgrew it.*

- *I couldn't have celiac disease because I'm very overweight.*

- *Yeah, I might have celiac disease, I guess, but I sure don't want to know it.*

Do any of these thoughts sound even vaguely familiar to you? If so, this chapter is *required* reading.

A Common Condition

As you learned in the preceding chapter, celiac disease is a genetic disorder in which an intolerance to gluten leads to damage of the lining of the small intestine. It's an autoimmune disease, which means that the body turns against itself whenever gluten is ingested. The onset of symptoms can occur at any age, and the disease is usually insidious, gradually getting worse. Treatment is a strict gluten-free diet for life.

Also referred to as gluten-sensitive enteropathy, nontropical sprue, celiac sprue, and coeliac disease (European spelling), the condition was given its moniker in A.D. 100 by Areteaus of Cappadocia, who coined the term *koilika,* which translates to "bellyacher." (Personally, I'd like to see the name changed back to "bellyacher." "Disease" has such an ominous connotation, and this condition, once treated, actually promises restored health and vitality.)

Once considered a rare condition, celiac disease is now thought to be the most prevalent genetic disorder in the world. A lengthy and extremely comprehensive study conducted by the University of Maryland's Center for Celiac Research (CFCR), concluded at the end of 2001, found that even in "healthy" people—those who were not aware of any symptoms whatsoever—the incidence is extremely high, certainly much higher than previously thought.

According to the latest figures from CFCR, approximately one in 150 people has celiac disease. This means that more than 1.3 million Americans have it—yet only about 15,000 have been diagnosed. For every diagnosed celiac, 89 are undiagnosed, and their health and lifestyles may be severely compromised as a result of their undiagnosed condition.

One in 150 people refers to the general population. For people with symptoms, or with relatives who have celiac disease, the likelihood of having celiac disease skyrockets:

- People with "classic" gastrointestinal symptoms: 1 in 40

- People with a celiac first-degree relative (that is, sibling, parent, child): 1 in 20

- People with a celiac second-degree relative (that is, aunt, uncle, grandparent or first cousin): 1 in 40

Symptoms of Celiac Disease

Symptoms of celiac disease may develop at any age, although onset is most commonly seen in children before their second birthday, during puberty, and in adults in their late 40s and 50s. Symptoms are divided into three categories, with varying severity. People with *classic symptoms* (mainly gastrointestinal) experience severe diarrhea, malabsorption, gas, bloating, and weight loss. People with *atypical symptoms* (usually non-intestinal) have no gastrointestinal symptoms whatsoever, but show other manifestations of the disease. *Asymptomatic* people lie somewhere in between or have no symptoms whatsoever, yet damage to the intestinal tract still occurs.

The fact is, symptoms are all over the board, and therein lies the problem with making a quick, definitive diagnosis.

Classic Symptoms—Children

Because "classic" celiac disease often presents itself before a child is about two years old, physicians are taught to look for celiac disease in children with the following symptoms:

- Diarrhea

- Steatorrhea (oily or greasy stools)

- Constipation

- Failure to thrive (not gaining height or weight as expected), weight loss

- Anorexia (lack of desire to eat)

- Distended abdomen (characteristic of malnourishment and gassiness)

- Poor muscle tone

- Irritability

- Dental disorders (lack of enamel formation; ridges and changes in pigmentation in secondary teeth)

- Listlessness
- Short stature
- Delayed onset of puberty/amenorrhea
- Nutritional deficiencies (especially iron and calcium)
- Rickets or osteopenia/osteoporosis (decreased bone density)

If these symptoms are present, a diagnosis is often made quickly, since that's what doctors are taught to look for in medical school. But stray away from *children* with these symptoms, and chances that doctors will miss the diagnosis begin to increase dramatically.

Classic Symptoms—Adults

- Fatigue
- Gastrointestinal distress (gas, bloating, discomfort, nausea, cramps)
- Diarrhea
- Constipation
- Steatorrhea (oily or greasy stools)
- Gastroesophageal reflux (GERD)
- Dyspepsia (indigestion)
- Anemia and/or nutritional deficiencies
- Poor muscle bulk
- Short stature
- Amenorrhea (absence of menstrual cycle)
- Weight loss/weight gain
- Anorexia (lack of desire to eat)
- Clubbing of fingers and toes
- Dermatitis herpetiformis (DH)

- Selective immunoglobulin A (IgA) deficiency
- Associated autoimmune disorders: inflammatory bowel diseases such as Crohn's disease and ulcerative colitis; insulin-dependent diabetes mellitus (type 1 or juvenile diabetes); autoimmune thyroid diseases such as Graves' disease and Hashimoto's thyroiditis; systemic lupus erythematosus (lupus); and autoimmune liver diseases such as primary biliary cirrhosis and autoimmune hepatitis

Cynthia Rudert, M.D., notes that fatigue is the most common symptom shared by all of her celiac patients. Imagine walking into your doctor's office complaining that you're fatigued—surely the response would be, "Really? Well, let's test you for celiac disease, because fatigue is a common symptom in celiac patients." Yeah, right. Unfortunately, many doctors have not yet made the association between celiac disease and fatigue; as a patient, it's your responsibility to manage your health care, which may mean suggesting that you be tested.

Atypical Symptoms and Associated Conditions . . . Also Titled, "Problems That Can Develop If You Don't Go Gluten-Free"

"My daughter has epilepsy, and her doctor said that meant she should be tested for celiac disease. I don't understand; she doesn't have any problems like diarrhea or gas. Why would they say she should be tested for a gastrointestinal problem when we know that what she has is epilepsy?"
— Susan L.

Celiac researchers have identified what they call the "iceberg" theory, which illustrates the fact that the majority of celiacs do not exhibit classic symptoms.

The tip of the iceberg, sticking out of the water, represents the 10 to 30 percent of celiacs who *do* exhibit classic symptoms such as diarrhea, gas, bloating, and nutritional deficiencies. The remaining 70 to 90 percent of the iceberg (the part hidden below the waterline) depicts the majority of celiacs, who have either atypical symptoms or no symptoms whatsoever.

What's scary about this model is its veracity. To exhibit classic symptoms, your body's health must be extremely compromised; only those *very* sick people are considered by most physicians to be candidates for a diagnosis of celiac disease. The majority of celiac patients fall below the waterline of our theoretical iceberg, experiencing chronic ill health and complications of the disease without ever being diagnosed as celiacs.

When celiacs continue to eat gluten, it can wreak havoc on their bodies—not just their intestinal tract, but their entire bodies. While we typically think of celiac symptoms as gastrointestinal, celiac disease is a multisystem condition. It can also affect the neurologic (nervous), endocrine (hormonal), orthopedic (bones), reproductive, musculoskeletal, hepatic (liver), and hematologic (blood) systems.

That's why we see "associated conditions"—those that may develop when a celiac continues to eat gluten. We also call these "atypical symptoms" because sometimes they are the *only* symptoms a person will have. They differ from the classic symptoms mentioned before, yet you need to be aware that these conditions in and of themselves could indicate the presence of celiac disease:

- Attention deficit disorder (ADD)/attention deficit hyperactivity disorder (ADHD)
- Autistic-type behaviors/Asperger syndrome (children)
- Bone "pain"
- Canker sores
- Central and peripheral nervous system disorders
- Chronic fatigue
- Delayed onset of menstrual cycle
- Early menopause
- Emotional and behavioral disturbances such as depression, irritability, lack of ability to concentrate, even schizophrenic-type behaviors

- Epilepsy
- Fibromyalgia
- Headaches
- Infertility (in both men and women), miscarriages, low-birth-weight babies
- Internal hemorrhaging
- Intestinal lymphoma
- Lactose intolerance
- Osteoporosis and bone diseases such as osteomalacia, osteopenia, and rickets
- Pancreatic disease or disorders
- Shortened life expectancy

Some of these conditions are not widely recognized or accepted as symptoms of celiac disease among all doctors, but their possible association has been proposed and in some cases substantiated, and should therefore be considered.

Because some conditions are associated to each other, an astute doctor may realize that the presence of one could indicate the presence of another. Some of these conditions will sometimes disappear completely when a gluten-free diet is adhered to; others, depending upon how advanced they were at the time gluten was eliminated from the diet, will show various levels of improvement.

> *"My husband and I are seeing an infertility specialist. A friend of mine who has celiac disease suggested we be tested for celiac disease, too, and that it could be connected to our difficulties in becoming pregnant. Is there really a connection? Neither of us has any typical symptoms of celiac disease."*
> — Lisa L.

There is a distinction between associated conditions that result *because gluten is being ingested* (those mentioned above, which often improve or disappear when a strict gluten-free diet is adhered to) and conditions that are considered associated *because they are found more often in people with celiac disease.*

This latter category includes Addison's disease, chronic active hepatitis (hepatitis C), diabetes (type 1), Down syndrome, Graves' disease, headaches, myasthenia gravis, Raynaud's disease, rheumatoid arthritis, scleroderma, selective IgA deficiency, short stature (in children, this can be overcome on a gluten-free diet), and Sjogren's syndrome. You'll learn more about these and other associated conditions in the next chapter.

Eczema Medications Not Working?
Consider Dermatitis Herpetiformis

Dermatitis herpetiformis (DH) is sometimes referred to as a "sister" to celiac disease. Everyone with DH has celiac disease, but their primary symptoms are external, rather than internal, presenting as a severe rash on the skin. About 5 percent of celiacs have these external symptoms of DH. People with DH also experience intestinal damage, but generally without the typical gastrointestinal symptoms.

DH is characterized by blistering and intensely itchy skin, and is often misdiagnosed as eczema. The rash is found on the elbows, buttocks, knees, back, face, and/or scalp, and is usually symmetrical, meaning that it occurs in a mirror image from left to right.

Diagnosis is often initially made when it becomes clear that the rash does not respond to eczema medication. To confirm the diagnosis, a small skin biopsy is taken from the normal-looking skin next to a blister site. The presence of IgA antibodies confirms a diagnosis of DH. The treatment for DH is the same as for celiac disease: a strict gluten-free diet for life.

In addition to avoiding gluten, many people with DH find it necessary to avoid iodine and sometimes the related chemical family of bromines. Iodine doesn't cause more IgA to be deposited, but rather causes an inflammation of these deposits in some people with DH, irritating the deposits that already exist. Iodine is often added to salt and vitamins, and is found in high levels of fish and shellfish that come from the ocean (freshwater fish are not a problem). Additionally, iodine is hidden in ingredients such as red dye #3, which is made from red seaweed.

Iodine is important for proper thyroid function. Before eliminating iodine from your diet, consult with a dermatologist or gastroenterologist who thoroughly understands celiac disease and DH.

Misdiagnoses

> *"For six years my husband was told he had irritable bowel syndrome. Then they told him it was Crohn's. Now, 12 years after he first started seeing a doctor, we find out he has celiac disease. He went on a gluten-free diet and all of his symptoms have disappeared. He feels great. I'm just furious that he had to suffer for 12 years with those misdiagnoses. Doctors should be aware that they need to test for this."*
> — Cindy S.

If a person is diagnosed with celiac disease, it's often after years of suffering with a variety of symptoms. In the meantime, he or she is often misdiagnosed as having another condition. According to a study by the Celiac Disease Foundation, the top 20 misdiagnoses before arriving at a biopsy-confirmed diagnosis of celiac disease are:

- Anemia
- Irritable bowel syndrome (IBS)
- Psychological dysfunction (stress, nerves, imagination)
- Diarrhea
- Inflammatory bowel disease (IBD)
- Diabetes
- Spastic colon

- Ulcers
- Virus (viral gastroenteritis)
- Chronic fatigue syndrome
- Weight loss
- Allergies
- Amoebae, parasites, infection
- Gallbladder disease
- Thyroid disease
- Cancer, lymphoma, digestive disorders
- Colitis
- Cystic fibrosis
- Lactose intolerance
- Reflux

Additionally, people are often misdiagnosed with fibromyalgia, carbohydrate malabsorption, recurrent abdominal pain, and other conditions.

The Silent Celiac: No Symptoms Whatsoever

Asymptomatic celiacs show no symptoms whatsoever. Interestingly, to have *no* symptoms can be a symptom in and of itself! While these people may not *feel* the symptoms typically associated with celiac disease, intestinal damage *is* occurring, and the continued ingestion of gluten can result in any number of associated conditions.

You may wonder how we know that some celiacs have no symptoms. Obviously, they were not diagnosed with celiac disease as the result of medical complaints, so why were they tested in the first place? Many of them are first- or second-degree relatives of celiacs who realized the importance of being tested. Others were tested as part of a mass blood-screening research program; they were identified as having antibodies specific to celiac disease and their diagnosis was confirmed with a biopsy of the small intestine.

If I Don't Feel the Effects of Gluten, Why Should I Go Gluten-Free?

> "I was diagnosed with celiac disease, but I
> don't feel anything when I eat gluten. Is it okay
> to have just a little every now and then since
> I don't feel the effects anyway?"
> — David R.

Did the terms *intestinal lymphoma* or *shortened life expectancy*
catch your attention when you read the section on associated conditions? Gastrointestinal lymphoma (cancer) is at least 40 times
more common in untreated celiacs than it is in the general population. New research indicates that the mortality rate for celiacs who
are undiagnosed or who continue to eat gluten is *twice* that of the general population.

Remember, even if you don't feel the symptoms, damage may be
occurring in your intestinal tract, and associated conditions may
develop. *If* you have celiac disease and you currently continue to eat
gluten, I urge you to reread the section on atypical symptoms and
associated conditions.

Death Rate Twice As High for Celiacs

*A thorough study published in 2001[1] showed that the
mortality rate for people with celiac disease is twice as high
as for the general public. The study was done by two Italian
researchers: a professor of statistics and a gastroenterologist.
They followed 1,072 patients who were diagnosed with
celiac disease between 1962 and 1994, as well as more than
3,000 of their first-degree relatives.*

*They then compared the number of deaths through 1998
with the expected mortality rate for the general population.
They found that 53 celiac patients had died, compared to an
expected mortality rate of 25 to 29. A significant number of*

deaths occurred within three years of diagnosis. The death rate for those who failed to adhere to a strict gluten-free diet was six times higher than for those who adhered. The study also found the death rate was 2.6 times higher among those whose diagnosis was delayed for a year, and 3.8 times higher for those who weren't diagnosed for ten years, indicating the more delayed the diagnosis, the higher the mortality rate.

The "Causes" of Celiac Disease

Really, nothing *causes* celiac disease, per se. For someone to have celiac disease, three components must be present: a genetic predisposition; a trigger (something that turns the switch from "off" to "on"), and gluten in your diet. It's interesting to note that you can have the genetic predisposition *and* the trigger, but if you never eat gluten, you will not develop celiac disease.

Genetics

Celiac disease is a genetic condition, but it's only the *predisposition* that celiacs are born with. In other words, they carry a gene or genes that *may* result in celiac disease—or they may never end up with the condition.

People often ask whether celiac disease is dominant or recessive. The answer is neither. It's *multigenetic*, meaning that several genes are involved, each of which may have different strengths of expression, and each of which plays a different part in the development of celiac disease.

In looking at the genetics behind celiac disease, researchers focus on a type of "genetic fingerprint" that each person has, called *human leukocyte antigens* (HLA). These antigens allow the body's immune cells to recognize characteristics of that person that belong only to that person. Because every person has a unique set of HLAs, they can be used in genetic testing to evaluate many different conditions, including celiac disease. The genes that determine susceptibility to celiac disease are found in the HLA region of chromosome six.

Celiac disease *does* run in families, and even if family members don't show symptoms, they should be tested. About 5 percent of first-degree relatives have celiac disease, with or without symptoms. About one in 40 (2.5 percent) second-degree relatives has celiac disease, whether they know it or not. It's important that they be tested properly to avoid associated conditions and complications.

Genetics don't tell the entire story, though. Studies have been done on genetically identical (monozygotic) twins; in 25 to 30 percent of those twins, only one has celiac disease. If the condition was purely genetic, both would have it or both would not. Clearly, there's another mechanism going on here. We call it a "trigger."

Triggers

Some people will go 40 or 50 years without symptoms, and then, *Boom!* they're sicker than they've been in their entire lives. Celiac disease, like many autoimmune conditions, requires a "trigger" to activate the condition. Gluten is the trigger for the autoimmune response in celiacs. Exactly what triggers celiac disease into action is not yet known for sure, although researchers have a few ideas:

- *Gluten exposure in infancy:* New research indicates that early exposure to gluten (less than four months of age)may act as a trigger

- *Loss of tolerance to gluten*

- *Trauma to the body* (for example, infection/virus, surgery, pregnancy, or radiation/chemotherapy)

Sometimes there just isn't an explanation for what triggered the symptoms to appear, or at least nothing that can be pinpointed. More likely, the symptoms may have been there all along, but they were ignored, misdiagnosed, or masked by other conditions. In many cases, people get used to feeling sick, and don't even realize they have symptoms until they reach a point of crisis.

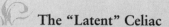

The "Latent" Celiac

The latent celiac is someone with positive blood tests for celiac disease, but a normal-appearing intestinal biopsy. There haven't been enough studies yet to know for sure, but researchers believe that if these people continue to eat gluten, they will eventually develop symptoms and a biopsy that reflects the active phase of celiac disease, showing villous atrophy.

Diagnosing Celiac Disease

The diagnosis of celiac disease is a bittersweet diagnosis, indeed. Not only is it a "label," it's one that sounds so scary and imposing. But remember, it *can* be the key to better health, which is the most compelling reason to confirm the diagnosis.

In Europe, where awareness of celiac disease is much higher than in the United States, the time between onset of symptoms and a diagnosis of celiac disease is four to eight weeks. In the United States, it's an average of 10 to 13 years. Not only does this increase the chance of developing complications and associated disorders, it also can decrease life expectancy, since studies have shown that the more delayed the diagnosis, the higher the mortality rate.

"Nothing in all the world is more dangerous than sincere ignorance and conscientious stupidity."
— Martin Luther King, Jr.

But I Don't Want to Know I Have It!

Not surprisingly, many people don't *want* to know they have celiac disease. Several patients have told me of doctors who said, "I'm not even going to test you for celiac disease, because that's a disease you don't *want* to have." Oh? Well, perhaps I don't *want* to have mousy-brown hair, either, but I do. Somehow a picture of three monkeys with hands over their ears, eyes, and mouths, respectively, comes to mind.

One of the most solid arguments I've heard for not wanting to have celiac disease is higher premiums or even denial of health or life insurance. Some people claim that employers use the results of genetic tests to discriminate. You should know that if your insurance pays for the testing, and your insurance is paid for by your employer, your employer has access to your test results. Discrimination based on those results, however, is against the law. In fact, federal law[2] prohibits insurers from requiring employees to pay more for their health insurance if they have had tests or illnesses. The law does not apply to individuals who purchase their own insurance.

According to Douglas J. Gwilliam, managing partner of employee benefits and insurance for Century Business Services, carriers who underwrite individual health plans and individual life insurance have to take a careful look at any medical records they can find. If someone has been diagnosed and treated for any situation that may have future health implications, the carrier must take it into account.

Gwilliam says that people shopping for life insurance should work with what's called an "impaired risk" broker. This is someone who works directly with faceless underwriters to present additional information regarding treatment, diagnosis, and prognosis in an effort to secure coverage.

For health insurance, Gwilliam recommends a group plan (the smallest "group" is two people) that does not consider preexisting conditions. Coverages are typically pooled with other small companies in an effort to spread risk. Many states also offer state-run plans for people who can't get coverage otherwise. All carriers licensed in that particular state put money into a pool to cover those who can't get coverage anywhere else.

Testing Methods

> *"Facts are stubborn things; and whatever may be our wishes, our inclinations, or the dictates of our passion, they cannot alter the state of facts and evidence."*
> — John Adams, *Argument in Defense of the Soldiers in the Boston Massacre Trials*, December 1770

If you have the symptoms described in this chapter, and if you still refuse to be tested for celiac disease, remember the ancient proverb: "A wise man who walks in dark with blindfold is not much of a wise man." If, however, you decide to be tested for celiac disease, knowing the different types of tests will help you ensure the greatest accuracy and most definitive diagnosis.

What follows is an overview of the different types of testing: blood (serum), intestinal biopsy, genetic, stool, and saliva. For more detailed information about the different types of blood tests and the interpretation of their results (including false positive and false negative), please see the Tech Talk section at the back of this book.

Serum (Blood) Test for Antibodies

The classic and most definitive diagnosis for celiac disease involves a serological (blood) antibody screening followed by an intestinal biopsy, and most experts on the subject agree that a diagnosis of celiac disease is not truly "confirmed" until both tests have been done. The serum antibody test looks for antibodies in the bloodstream that are specific to a celiac's response to gluten. The test is relatively easy, and can be an excellent indicator of celiac disease, but it doesn't confirm the diagnosis or negate the need for an intestinal biopsy.

It's absolutely critical that you be on a gluten-containing diet for at least a couple of months prior to testing. Exactly how long varies from person to person, but it has to be long enough for your body to develop an antibody response. I realize this is sometimes hard to do! Many people put themselves on a gluten-free diet before testing, and then couldn't be *paid* to eat gluten again. But if you have the antibody screening done while you're on a gluten-free diet, you might as well save your blood and your money, because a negative response won't tell you anything about your condition.

Some physicians feel strongly that if you're gluten-free, reintroducing gluten into your diet can lead to serious and severe complications. If you've gone gluten-free for a substantial length of time, genetic testing might be a better option for you.

A negative antibody test doesn't necessarily mean that you do not have celiac disease. Several factors can affect the results of the antibody screening; a negative serology does not definitively rule out the disease.

The Importance of Choosing the Right Lab

You can have your blood drawn at any doctor's office or lab; all you'll need is an order from a physician, nurse practitioner, or physician's assistant. But where the testing is done is extremely important, since even reputable labs often perform these tests improperly.

Until awareness of celiac disease increases, we're still faced with the fact that, relatively speaking, few tests for celiac disease are ordered. In many cases, the labs doing the tests may never have performed this particular test, or may have little experience with it.

It's important to have a competent lab do the testing for three reasons:

First, the reading of the tests is subjective, and results—positive or negative—depend upon the technician's interpretation. With some tests, even experienced and competent technicians may read the same test and arrive at different results.

Second, for the test to provide meaningful results, it must be validated using a large number of clinical documented subjects. In other words, the lab needs to have done many of these blood tests so they know how to interpret test results.

Finally, many labs use antibodies from guinea pigs for testing, but human samples are shown to be much more reliable in testing for celiac disease.

You have a right to know how the test is being done, and to ask that your blood be sent to a specialty lab for testing, although your insurance may not cover the cost of the test if you do so. Sometimes research organizations will do free testing; check with one of the national celiac organizations listed in the Resource Directory to see if there's a free screening in your area.

Remember, your best chances for an accurate assessment are with a lab that's familiar with, or specializes in, these tests. Among those that specialize in testing for celiac disease are Prometheus Labs, the University of Maryland's Center for Celiac Research, and Childrens Hospital Los Angeles. (For contact information, see the Resource Directory.)

The Official Diagnosis: The Biopsy

For now, blood tests are considered a "screening," used only to determine how likely someone is to have celiac disease. If the screen is positive, the diagnosis is confirmed with an intestinal biopsy. Just as was the case with the blood test, it's crucial that you be on a gluten-*containing* diet up until the time of your biopsy.

In some cases, even if the blood test is negative, a biopsy is still a good idea. Most physicians agree that if symptoms are present, a biopsy is warranted, regardless of the blood test results.

Biopsies are usually done by a gastroenterologist. Adults are sedated intravenously with drugs such as Versed and Demerol; children usually receive a general anesthetic so the body is completely relaxed.

The biopsy is performed through an endoscope, an instrument used to visually examine an interior canal or hollow organ. In this case, the endoscope is inserted through the mouth and threaded to the small intestine, where the doctor will clip several (at least four) tissue samples to be sent to a lab for pathological examination.

Specifically, the pathologist will look for any signs of villous atrophy or blunting. In a classic case of celiac disease, there will be partial or total villous atrophy, but any atypical presentations must also be considered prior to ruling out celiac disease.

While many people express concern about the invasive nature of endoscopy, for now it's the only universally accepted form of diagnosis. The procedure itself isn't painful (there are no pain-sensitive nerves inside the small intestine), and the inherent risks of anesthesia and endoscopic complications are relatively minor.

Genetic Testing

Genetic testing for celiac disease involves a blood test that looks at certain human leukocyte antigen (HLA) types.

For celiacs, the HLA types DQ2 and DQ8 on chromosome six are necessary, but not sufficient, for developing the condition. In other words, someone with these two HLA types has a strong genetic predisposition to develop celiac disease, but the predisposition alone is not enough—there must also be a trigger of some sort. However, some people who have these genes do *not* have celiac disease, or have not yet developed it. If someone does not have the DQ2 and DQ8 HLA types, it's about 99 percent sure that they'll *never* develop celiac disease. For that reason, genetic testing is a good way to *rule out* the condition in questionable cases, but it's not a positive predictor of the disease.

Stool Testing

Some labs currently provide home stool testing for the presence of celiac disease, microscopic colitis, and other conditions. Like the blood test, the stool test looks for immunological reactions to gluten by detecting the presence of antigliadin antibodies. Stool samples are taken at home, then sent by overnight mail to a specialty laboratory where the tests are performed.

Some of the labs doing stool testing assert that the stool test is more sensitive than the blood test. They claim that the immune response to food in gluten-sensitive individuals takes place in the intestine, and therefore antibodies are easily detectable in the stool, even before they're detectable in the blood. Therefore, people with slight sensitivities or people in the early phases of gluten sensitivity would show an antibody response in stool testing, even if they don't show a response in serological tests.

There's no question that stool tests are less invasive than a biopsy, and, done in the home, are easier and less cumbersome than having blood drawn and tested. If, in fact, the test is more sensitive than traditional blood screens, it provides people with the ability to be tested even if they haven't been eating gluten recently. This is important, because many people go off of gluten before being tested, and can't be convinced to eat it again.

While stool testing certainly has some exciting and promising implications and offers some logistical advantages over the other testing methods, it's not yet considered "the" standard diagnostic tool for celiac disease.

Saliva Testing

Many people are tested for gluten sensitivity or intolerance with a saliva test. It's fast and easy, and can be ordered by health-care practitioners other than medical doctors (for example, chiropractors, clinical nutritionists, and nurses). It's noninvasive, and it can be done at home and mailed to a lab for testing.

All saliva tests look for levels of antigliadin IgA—the same antibody that traditional blood tests look for. While the saliva test might, in fact, detect intolerance or sensitivity, it's *not* an accepted diagnostic tool for celiac disease. Some warnings about the saliva test include the following:

- *It might detect normal levels of IgA:* A large percentage of the population has elevated IgA levels with no problems whatsoever. Some elevation may, in fact, be a normal response.

- *It doesn't include the entire panel of tests that should be done:* Saliva testing looks at antigliadin IgA, an indicator of gluten intolerance. Elevated levels can also indicate other conditions, and normal levels may not actually rule out celiac disease.

- *There's no standardization, regulation, accreditation, or licensing:* Labs doing saliva testing act independently and without coordination between each other or other researchers. One lab's results may conflict with another's. Furthermore, labs and the practitioners who order the tests can say anything they want—factual or not.

- *Be aware of bad information:* In researching the topic of saliva testing, I talked with several labs and practitioners who order saliva tests and counsel patients. Many of them offered inaccurate information (for instance, their lists of safe and forbidden foods on a gluten-free diet were often inaccurate), and some of the premises that they presented as fact were not factual (I was told by one lab that celiac disease is a result of a compromised immune system, which is not true—it is an overactive immune response).

- *Not all labs are bad:* Most of the labs admitted that the only way to properly test for celiac disease is to do a blood test (antibody screen) followed by an intestinal biopsy. Some labs doing saliva testing are particularly knowledgeable about gluten sensitivity and celiac disease. It's important to assess the competency of your health care practitioner and the lab with which he or she associates.

What if your saliva test is positive? You have three choices. You can ignore it and order a Domino's pizza (tempting, but not advisable); you can seek further testing by having a blood screen and/or intestinal biopsy; or you can try the gluten-free diet and see how you feel. This latter option is not recommended, because if you go gluten-free, you won't be able to have the blood testing or intestinal biopsy until you've done an extended gluten challenge.

Other Tests

Your doctor may refer to other testing methods, such as D-xylose, fecal fat, lactose breath hydrogen, and the sugar absorption test

(SAT). While these tests may be useful in conjunction with other tests, they're far less specific and sensitive for diagnosing celiac disease when used alone. These tests are best used if celiac testing has proven negative and doctors are looking for other diagnoses that may relate to gut malabsorption, or, as in the case of a barium test (contrast radiography), if complications of celiac disease such as lymphoma or strictures are suspected.

Follow-Up Testing

Your doctor will most likely recommend follow-up antibody screenings one year after your diagnosis and maybe periodically after that, for two reasons: (1) to make sure that the diagnosis of celiac disease was, in fact, the *right* diagnosis, and that other conditions weren't causing your symptoms; and (2) to ensure that your diet is gluten-free, with no hidden gluten making its way into your diet.

How often should you have follow-up screenings? If you're still experiencing symptoms, you may want to have more frequent screening to check for hidden gluten and to rule out other conditions. If you're an asymptomatic celiac (someone who doesn't feel the effects of gluten even though you have celiac disease), you won't experience the diarrhea and other symptoms that serve as "friendly reminders" when you mistakenly eat gluten. Checking your antibody levels periodically will help you ensure that your diet stays strictly gluten-free.

R~x~: Gluten-Free for Life

The beauty of this condition is that it requires no drugs, no surgery, no ongoing treatments or side effects. The treatment for celiac disease is simply a dietary modification: the elimination of gluten.

Notice that I didn't say a "simple dietary modification." I said, "*simply* a dietary modification." Those of you who have tried the gluten-free diet may already be acutely aware of the subtle but profound difference.

Celiacs, unlike people who may have slight or moderate gluten sensitivity, must adhere to a strict gluten-free diet for life. In exchange, their condition improves dramatically and rapidly, and the risk of associated conditions subsides. Trade your whole-grain toast for lifelong health? Sounds like a good deal to me.

Improvement on the Gluten-Free Diet: A Diagnosis in and of Itself?

A lot of people put themselves on a gluten-free or low-gluten diet, either intentionally or because they subconsciously tend to avoid foods that make them feel sick. When they then feel better, they say things such as:

- "If I feel better not eating gluten, can't I consider that a diagnosis in and of itself?"

- "I realize that to be properly tested for celiac disease, I need to be eating gluten. But you couldn't pay me to eat gluten again, now that I've been off it and feel so much better."

- "There's no way I want to eat gluten and feel bad again. Can't I just skip the testing?"

- "I don't want my insurance company to have a definitive diagnosis, so I'm not going through with the testing."

One study[3] did a good job of making the point. This study looked at patients who had "explosive, watery nocturnal diarrhea," weight loss, no appetite, and abdominal pain, but no steatorrhea or malabsorption, and normal blood tests (negative for celiac disease). Their biopsy tests showed totally normal villi, although there were some increases in inflammatory cells. Their doctors put them on a gluten-free diet, and all patients improved. Did they have celiac disease?

If it walks like a duck and quacks like a duck, why not just call it a duck? After all, isn't the *real* test whether or not you *feel* better? As you've read, there is ample room for error in all of the testing methods, but feeling better is, after all, the whole idea, isn't it?

There aren't any right or wrong answers, but there *are* some important considerations to take into account.

One of the most solid reasons to know for *sure* is to avoid the temptation to cheat. If you never know for sure that you have celiac disease, you'll be more likely to experience denial at some point, or to conveniently "lose" the condition when, for some reason, you especially want to eat something with gluten in it.

Another important consideration is that your improvement on the gluten-free diet could be coincidental, and another condition causing similar symptoms could be present. In that case, by assuming you have celiac disease when you don't, you could be missing an important diagnosis.

The last good reason I can think of to confirm the diagnosis is family health history. Because celiac disease is a genetic condition, biological family members should be aware if it's in the family, and, in some cases, should be tested themselves.

Who Else Should Be Tested?

Ideally, all first- and second-degree relatives of celiacs should be tested, whether they have symptoms or not. Remember, even in healthy people with no symptoms, celiac disease is quite common—the most common genetic condition that we know. In first-degree relatives, the prevalence is about one in 20 people (5 percent); in second-degree relatives, it's about one in 40. In many cases, these people show no symptoms whatsoever, yet intestinal damage is occurring.

Children who have symptoms, especially in families with a history of celiac disease, should be tested immediately. If the pediatrician refuses to acknowledge the importance of testing, either insist until he or she orders the testing, or switch doctors if you have to.

Asymptomatic kids who have family members with celiac disease should be tested by age three or four. If symptoms develop, even if the original test was negative, further testing should be pursued.

One final group of people who should be tested are those who have conditions that are associated with celiac disease and gluten intolerance, even if they don't have typical symptoms or a family history. The next chapter offers more information on many specific conditions associated with gluten intolerance and sensitivity.

Chapter 4

Associated Conditions:
Is Gluten Putting You at Risk?

"Real knowledge is to know the extent of one's ignorance."
— Confucius

Maybe you're one of those people who has a wheat allergy, celiac disease, or a gluten intolerance, but you don't mind the discomfort you feel from indulging once in a while. Maybe you figure the decadent doughnut is worth the consequent cramping and foul flatulence. But is it worth an increased risk of developing another—sometimes critical—condition?

People who are gluten intolerant are at risk of developing a number of other conditions. If you have a wheat allergy, you may think you're not at risk for these conditions, and you might be right. But what if you *do* have an intolerance that puts you at risk for associated conditions, and you just don't know it yet? Or what if you already have a condition that's associated with gluten intolerance? You may want to at least skim the conditions associated with gluten intolerance to make sure you aren't putting yourself at risk unknowingly.

One of the most compelling reasons to take gluten intolerance seriously is because of the associated conditions that can develop when a gluten-intolerant person continues to eat gluten. The following disorders have been shown to be associated with celiac disease, but because the line between celiac disease and gluten intolerance is fuzzy, you should be aware of these associated conditions even if you consider yourself to be "just" gluten intolerant or gluten sensitive.

There are four categories of associated conditions:

- Conditions that carry a higher risk of celiac disease
- Conditions caused when a celiac or gluten-intolerant person eats gluten
- Conditions that may be associated with celiac disease
- Conditions often confused with celiac disease

Conditions That Carry a Higher Risk of Celiac Disease

People who have certain disorders are more likely to have celiac disease than the general population. For example, some estimates say that as many as 5 percent of people with diabetes have celiac disease, and 5 to 10 percent of people with Down syndrome have it. These conditions don't *cause* celiac disease, but people who have them have an increased risk of having the condition. If you have any of the following high-risk conditions, you should be tested for celiac disease, even if you don't have symptoms:

- Autoimmune diseases
- Addison's disease
- Chronic active hepatitis
- Cystic fibrosis
- Diabetes (type 1 juvenile, insulin-dependent) and diabetic intestinal disorders
- Down syndrome
- Multiple sclerosis
- Myasthenia gravis

- Neurological conditions (including ataxia, epilepsy, and cerebral calcifications)

- Primary biliary cirrhosis (PBC)

- Raynaud's disease (or phenomenon)

- Rheumatoid arthritis

- Scleroderma

- Sjogren's syndrome

> *"I have two daughters, both of whom were diagnosed with other 'associated' conditions. Neither one of them had 'classic' symptoms of celiac disease, but it turned out they both have it. It's scary to think of how much damage could have been done if they had continued to eat gluten; I'm so thankful that my doctor insisted upon testing."*
> — Lisa M.

Can Eating Gluten Cause You to Develop Other Autoimmune Diseases?

Maybe—*if* you have celiac disease. Autoimmune diseases are related, and if you have one, your chances for developing another are higher than for the general population.

In most cases in which celiac disease and other autoimmune disorders are associated, the diagnosis of the other autoimmune disorder was made first. In other words, the other autoimmune disorder developed while the person was still eating gluten (probably because celiac disease had not yet been diagnosed).

A research team at the University of Trieste, Italy, led by Alessandro Ventura, M.D., found that many untreated celiacs (celiacs not on a gluten-free diet) had several organ-specific antibodies, indicating that they may eventually develop autoimmune disorders involving organs other than the intestine. Their findings were reported in *Gastroenterology* (August 1999).[1]

The researchers noted that serum (blood) organ-specific antibodies disappeared when patients were put on a gluten-free diet. Their finding supports the belief that these antibodies are related to the ingestion of gluten. The journal article points out that a gluten-free diet started earlier in life may prevent other autoimmune diseases frequently associated with celiac disease, which is just further evidence of the need for proper testing as early as possible.

If you have celiac disease and have either gone undiagnosed or you cheat on your diet, *how long* you've been eating gluten seems to be an important factor, too, in determining your susceptibility to other autoimmune diseases. Researchers found a clear correlation between the *duration* of exposure to gluten and type 1 diabetes, autoimmune alopecia (hair loss), autoimmune thyroiditis, and epilepsy with calcification (this has not been clearly shown to be an autoimmune condition, but was looked at in the Italian study). As illustrated in Table 1, the association between these conditions and celiac disease had already been recognized, but this report indicated the importance of the duration of exposure to gluten.

Table 1

Duration of Exposure to Gluten and Risk for Autoimmune Disorders in Patients with Celiac Disease

Age at Diagnosis of Celiac Disease *(Eating gluten until this point)*	Chance of Developing Another Autoimmune Condition
4–12 years of age	16.7%
12–20 years of age	27%
Over 20 years of age	34%

Source: A. Ventura, G. Magazzu, and L. Greco, SIGEP Study Group for Autoimmune Disorders in Celiac Disease. *Gastroenterology* 117 (2): 297–303 (August 1999).

Diabetes and Celiac Disease: A Popular Pair

About one in 20 (5 percent) people with type 1 diabetes (insulin-dependent, also called juvenile diabetes) has celiac disease. Diabetes is a chronic disease in which the process of metabolizing carbohydrate, fat, and protein is disturbed. It occurs when the pancreas doesn't produce enough insulin or doesn't properly utilize insulin (the hormone that allows glucose to enter body cells; it is usually released in response to increased levels of sugar in the blood). With inadequate insulin, food isn't properly broken down into glucose (sugar), and glucose builds up in the bloodstream instead of going into the cells.

Glucose is the main source of fuel for the body, so when it can't get into the cells, the body can't use it for energy—even though the amount of glucose in the bloodstream is very high.

Symptoms of diabetes include excessive thirst, frequent urination, and hunger. People may also experience weight loss, nausea, vomiting, fatigue, and bloating. Risk factors include a family history of diabetes, and other autoimmune diseases (for example, celiac disease).

Diabetes, like celiac disease, requires a lifelong modified diet that allows food and insulin to work together to regulate blood sugar levels. Diet plans for diabetics vary, some involving an "exchange system," and newer plans involving carbohydrate counting.

If you've been diagnosed with both diabetes and celiac disease, the gluten-free/low-sugar diet may seem impossible. It's not! Yes, calculating the carbohydrates for gluten-free foods can be difficult at first—and beware—many gluten-free foods will be higher in carbohydrates than "regular" foods. It's probably easiest to start with the diabetic diet, then work to make it gluten-free.

Also, if you're newly diagnosed with celiac disease and only recently gluten-free, your gut may not have healed yet, and full absorption of the food may not yet be occurring. Be aware that as your gut heals, more efficient and reliable absorption will take place, putting even more glucose into your bloodstream, and your insulin requirements may go up. Check your blood sugar levels frequently and consult with your medical practitioner as needed.

You may want to work with a dietitian or nutritionist qualified to counsel you on both the diabetic and the gluten-free diets, and be sure to see the carbohydrate conversion chart for gluten-free flours, which is immensely helpful for diabetics on a wheat-free/gluten-free diet. You'll find recipes later in this book that accommodate both diets.

Diabetic Intestinal Disorders

Because long-standing diabetes can result in decreased function of the nerves that control the muscular activity of the stomach and intestinal tract, diabetics who do not have celiac disease or any other type of gluten intolerance can still suffer from intestinal disorders. As a result, a condition called *diabetic gastroparesis* can occur, resulting in the stomach's diminished ability to mix and propel food and enzymes through the digestive system.

Much like a balloon loses its strength and elasticity, the stomach begins to resemble a limp but enlarged balloon, filled with food that it can't push out. People with this condition may vomit large amounts of fluid and partially digested food that was eaten as far back as two days earlier. Because food isn't properly digested, regulation of the diabetes condition itself is difficult.

When the intestines are affected (rather than the stomach), their propulsive action is impaired. Diarrhea tends to occur at night and, because of damage to the anal sphincter nerves, there may be fecal incontinence during sleep. Some degree of malabsorption may be seen, but this could be a result of other conditions (bacterial overgrowth, for instance).

Drugs can be effective in treating these disorders. Consult your physician for more information on treatment alternatives.

Multiple Sclerosis and Gluten

Several researchers have suggested a link between gluten intolerance or celiac disease and multiple sclerosis (MS). MS occurs when white blood cells attack the myelin sheath that surrounds and insulates the nerve cells of the central nervous system. For years, this has been considered an immune system defect, and MS has been explained as an autoimmune disease.

The big question has been, how do white blood cells get to the myelin to attack it in the first place? Under normal conditions, the blood-brain barrier provides an effective separation between blood cells and myelin. One explanation might be an increased permeability in the blood-brain barrier due to an excess of a protein called zonulin (see the section on zonulin in Tech Talk).

Celiac disease is an autoimmune condition, and we know there's an association between various autoimmune diseases. In addition to the theorized etiology of the two conditions, another commonality between MS and gluten intolerance is that some people with MS seem to improve when gluten is eliminated from their diet. Many patients and researchers tout the benefits of dietary modification for people with MS, and cite improvement in energy levels and sometimes a slowing of the progression of symptoms. Dietary recommendations generally include a healthy diet that eliminates gluten, dairy, animal fat, and processed sugar; and emphasizes fresh or freshly cooked fruits and vegetables, skinless white meat, and seafood.

Because some symptoms of gluten intolerance and celiac disease mimic those of MS, questions arise about why the diet works. Is it because a relatively high number of people with MS have celiac disease (and maybe don't even know it), so their intolerance symptoms disappear? Could it be that because the symptoms of MS and gluten intolerance can be so similar, some people diagnosed with MS actually have celiac disease? Or is it that the symptoms of MS truly do subside when gluten is eliminated from the diet? Further studies need to be done before we can reach a definite conclusion.

Conditions Caused When a Celiac or Gluten-Intolerant Person Eats Gluten

Celiac disease and gluten intolerance in and of themselves don't *cause* any other disorders, but celiacs who continue to eat gluten (intentionally, inadvertently, or because they're not yet diagnosed) are at greater risk for developing certain conditions as a result. These include

- Anemia
- Behavioral abnormalities (schizophrenia, depression, lack of ability to focus)
- Canker sores
- Dyspepsia (indigestion)
- Gastroesophageal reflux (GERD)
- Headaches
- High mortality rate (two times higher than the general population)
- Infertility and difficult pregnancies, miscarriages, low-birth-weight babies
- Intestinal lymphoma (cancer; 40 times higher rate)
- Lactose intolerance
- Neural tube defects (in newborns) due to folate deficiency (that is, spina bifida)
- Nutritional deficiencies
- Osteoporosis, osteopenia, and osteomalacia

Headaches and Celiac Disease

A study published in the journal *Neurology* in 2001[2] found that when celiacs adhered to a gluten-free diet, the number of debilitating headaches they suffered was dramatically reduced.

Dr. Marios Hadjivassiliou and his colleagues at the Royal Hallamshire Hospital in Sheffield, England, reported that MRI brain scans suggest that gluten somehow triggers an inflammatory response in the white matter of the cerebrum, resulting in headaches.

It was a small study, and it has yet to be reproduced. But the *Neurology* report underscores an important point about celiac disease: Its symptoms can be unpredictable and may mimic those of other disorders.

Infertility and Difficult Pregnancies:
The Birds and Bees of Celiac Disease

The inability to have a child can be emotionally devastating. Time-consuming, expensive, draining, and often invasive therapies usually focus on a short list of possible causes of infertility, but rarely is celiac disease considered the culprit. Although published studies have indicated an association between celiac disease, fertility, and pregnancy, many primary-care obstetricians, gynecologists, and perinatologists remain unaware of these important relationships.

It's widely accepted that patients with untreated celiac disease can have delayed onset of puberty and menstruation, earlier menopause, and an increased prevalence of secondary amenorrhea, all of which would be red flags to a physician investigating causes for a couple's inability to achieve or maintain pregnancy. Further research of patients with untreated celiac disease shows higher miscarriage rates, increased fetal growth restriction, and lower birth weights.[3]

When you understand the physiological effects of untreated celiac disease, it's not surprising to find higher rates of miscarriage and infertility. The body needs to be healthy to nurture a developing fetus. If nutrients, especially folate, are not absorbed due to intestinal damage, the body may prevent or abort the pregnancy until it is *itself* healthy enough to support and nurture a fetus.

The beauty of celiac disease is that if a woman with this condition adheres to a strict gluten-free diet, she will have no greater risk for miscarriage and no greater risk during pregnancy than any other woman has.

Oh, and men, don't think you're off the hook here. Men run the risk of becoming infertile if undiagnosed, because celiac disease affects the virility of their sperm.

Milk: Does It Really Do Your Body Good?

Oh, sure, blame the cows. Yes, lactose intolerance is a very real problem, and according to some figures, about 60 percent of the population may, in fact, be unable to digest the principal sugar in cow's milk. But lactose, found only in milk and dairy products, may not be the evil villain it's accused of being. A huge percentage of people with other medical conditions or food sensitivities may *think* they're lactose intolerant when something else in their diet has actually caused the problem. Others may have *developed* lactose intolerance as a result of an untreated condition such as celiac disease.

To be properly digested, lactose requires the enzyme *lactase,* which is produced by the villi, located in the walls of the small intestines. Lactose intolerance occurs when the villi fail to produce enough lactase to break down the ingested lactose.

Small amounts of milk or dairy products usually don't cause problems. But for some extremely sensitive people, or for intolerant people who ingest a lot of milk, the result can be abdominal cramps, bloating, diarrhea, and excessive gas.

People with celiac disease may develop an intolerance to lactose, because the area where lactase is produced—the tip of the villi—is also the area that's damaged when celiacs eat gluten. The ability to produce lactase is therefore diminished, but usually returns after a few weeks or months on a strict gluten-free diet.

Unlike celiacs, who need to eliminate all gluten from their diet, people who are lactose intolerant generally don't need to completely eliminate dairy products. Drinking only small amounts of milk, and drinking it only with meals, can be tolerated by many people who are lactose intolerant. Cheese and yogurt, lower in lactose than milk, are good calcium-rich alternatives; and readily available aids such as Lactaid or Dairy Ease convert lactose into simple sugars that can be easily absorbed.

Conditions That May Be Associated with Celiac Disease

Unlike the conditions that have been studied and shown to have a statistical association with celiac disease, some conditions are related, but exactly how strongly or why may not be known:

- ADD/ADHD
- Autism
- Chronic fatigue syndrome

- Eating disorders (not to be confused with the loss of appetite or weight loss that can occur as a *result* of gluten intolerance)

- Fibromyalgia

- Immune thrombocytopenic purpura (ITP)

- Lupus erythematosus

- Muscle pain and weakness—myositis

- Neurological conditions

Eating Disorders

Eating disorders can be related to gluten intolerance in at least three different ways. First, many people who suffer from gluten intolerance or celiac disease are underweight as a result of being malnourished. Usually, these people eat plenty of food, but because it isn't absorbed properly, their caloric intake is significantly reduced and they have trouble gaining weight. These people are often labeled as anorexic, and are accused of intentionally depriving themselves of food.

A second way that eating disorders play into this picture is when people make a subconscious association between food and not feeling good. They may not know that it's wheat or gluten that makes them feel bad, but they do know that when they eat, they get sick. They stop eating or eat substantially less, and in that sense are anorexic, simply because they don't feel good when they eat.

The third way in which eating disorders are associated with wheat or gluten intolerance is the more classic presentation of anorexia nervosa, a psychological disorder in which people intentionally starve themselves. Being consumed with food doesn't always mean wanting to eat it in massive quantities; in fact, anorexia nervosa sometimes has its roots in an obsession with food. In this case, it usually involves an intense desire to lose weight. When some people realize their food intolerance can have a laxative effect, or they assume they'll lose weight because their food isn't being properly absorbed, they intentionally eat the offending food to induce weight loss.

This is anorexia nervosa with a psychological pathology, and should be taken seriously. Teenage girls are especially prone, and parents need to watch carefully to make sure their daughters don't fall into this dangerous trap. Many parents have told me of their teenage celiac daughters embarking upon weight-loss plans that involve intentionally eating gluten, just to induce diarrhea and lose weight. Professional intervention is highly recommended.

Muscle Pain and Weakness

Muscle pain (myalgia) is a common complaint, usually associated with overuse or an injury, and it's cause is usually pretty obvious. But muscle pain *can* be a symptom of many other conditions such as infectious disease, autoimmune disease, parasitosis, or other problems, and if chronic and unexplained, should be taken seriously.

Celiacs often complain of muscle pain, but it usually goes away after they start the gluten-free diet. A serious condition called *myositis,* though, may be associated.

Myositis is a broad term meaning inflammation of a voluntary muscle; it encompasses a number of conditions called *inflammatory myopathies* (a group of muscle diseases involving the inflammation and degeneration of skeletal muscle tissues). They're thought to be autoimmune disorders, because inflammatory cells surround, invade, and destroy normal muscle fibers as though they were foreign to the body. The result is muscle weakness, which can develop slowly over weeks, months, or years.

There are several forms of myositis. Each results in muscle weakness, but is unique in its development and treatment. Early diagnosis and treatment are crucial.

Lupus: More about Aches and Pains

I remember being little and wondering why "growed-ups" were always talking about aches and pains. It seemed like such a whiny, waste-of-time subject. That was a few decades ago. Today I find myself sheepishly reaching for a bottle of ibuprofen more often than I care to admit. Most of us experience aches and pains, but for some, they could be the early signs of a life-threatening disease called *lupus*.

Systemic lupus erythematosus is a chronic disease that can affect virtually any organ in the body. As in all autoimmune conditions, the lupus-affected immune system produces antibodies that attack healthy tissue instead of the foreign invaders they're supposed to repel. Like celiac disease, the symptoms vary, ranging from mild skin or joint pain to life-threatening damage of internal organs.

Thought to affect more than 1.4 million Americans, lupus is not rare. It affects women nearly ten times more often than men, and is more prevalent among African Americans, Native Americans, Asians, and Latinos.

Because it's an autoimmune disorder, lupus is considered to be associated with celiac disease; people with lupus should be tested for celiac disease and watch for symptoms.

Neurological Conditions

The idea that neurological conditions may be and probably are associated with celiac disease isn't a new one. More than 40 years ago scientists described neurological symptoms associated with celiac disease, including the following:

- Ataxia (gluten-sensitive, with IgG response)
- Cerebellar ataxia (resulting in disjointed, clumsy movements)
- Dementia
- Epilepsy and cerebral calcifications: Epilepsy is 20 times more common in people with celiac disease than in the general population
- Optic myopathy
- Peripheral neuropathy

Researchers at Columbia and Cornell universities are currently studying the relationship between celiac disease/gluten sensitivity and peripheral neuropathy, which is one of the more commonly seen neurological complications accompanying celiac disease. It's characterized by pain, numbness, weakness, and loss of reflexes in the arms and legs; and has many causes, including nutritional, inflammatory, and autoimmune response.

In the cases of neuropathy related to the immune system, some people are found to have antibodies to "ganglioside molecules." These molecules are found in abundance in the human nervous system and are important for normal cell function. The fact that the body launches an attack against them in the form of antibodies is typical of an autoimmune response, in which the body attacks itself.

In the initial phase of the current study, researchers looked for ganglioside antibodies in people known to have celiac disease. More than one-quarter of the patients studied had these antibodies, and subsequent neurological examination revealed that more than 80 percent of these patients had peripheral neuropathy. Interestingly, the ganglioside antibodies weren't found in any of the healthy controls.

According to Armin Alaedini, Ph.D., of Cornell University,[4] the results of this study point to a possible autoimmune etiology for the peripheral neuropathy suffered by some celiacs. He explains that for these people, anti-inflammatory medications, in addition to the gluten-free diet, may be beneficial in treating the disease.

Further research on the relationship between ganglioside reactivity and celiac disease is under way in joint studies between Columbia and Cornell universities.

Conditions Often Confused with Celiac Disease

Several conditions have symptoms that mimic those of celiac disease. In some cases, the conditions coexist, but usually a diagnosis of one of the following conditions is made when, in fact, the person has celiac disease instead:

- Bowel obstruction
- Colitis (chronic ulcerative colitis)

- Common variable hypogammaglobulinemia (an immune deficiency)
- Cow's milk allergy (in kids)
- Crohn's disease (regional enteritis)
- Diverticulitis
- *Giardia* infection
- Hemochromatosis
- HIV enteropathy
- IgA deficiency
- Intestinal bacterial overgrowth
- Irritable bowel syndrome (IBS)
- Lactose intolerance
- Pancreatic insufficiency
- Protein-losing enteropathy or lymphangiectasia
- Scleroderma
- Tropical sprue
- Whipple's disease

Bacterial/Yeast Overgrowth and the Candida Controversy

Bacteria, as you know, grow like weeds in our gastrointestinal tract. Often referred to as *flora,* the microorganisms of the gut have vigorous chemical and transformation reactions that significantly impact several important components of healthy gut and body function.

Like any good movie, the story of the flora has good guys and bad guys. The good guys are bacteria such as *Lactobacillus* and *Bifidobacterium*, which are used in dairy products to produce fermented foods such as yogurt, fresh cheese, desserts, and buttermilk. These and other "good" bacteria are sometimes referred to as *probiotics,* and when consumed live and in sufficient quantities, they promote healthy function of the lining of the intestines, aid in digestion, and prime the immune system so that it's better able to fight the disease and infectious organisms that can cause bowel problems.

Although they work hard to maintain a healthy environment for the gut, probiotics are sometimes challenged by menacing bacteria trying to undermine their good deeds. Enter *Candida albicans* stage left. *Candida*, as it's usually called, is a naturally occurring yeast thought by some to wreak havoc on intestinal well-being, especially when it grows out of control and outnumbers the good bacteria. Other bacteria, such as *Clostridium* and other types of coliforms (bacteria commonly found in the bowels), can rot or putrefy food and produce toxic products (toxic amines) from protein in the diet. The good bacteria, *Lactobacillus* and *Bifidobacterium,* have been shown to prevent the formation of these toxic amines.

In most cases, the friendly bacteria win out over the bad guys, and a healthy balance is kept in check. But healthy bacteria can be destroyed by the overuse of antibiotics; birth control pills; hormonal changes; a sugar-rich diet; steroids; or prolonged or acute exposure to chemicals, pesticides, or molds.

When the good bacteria are destroyed, yeast such as *Candida* can grow unchecked, giving rise to a variety of medical conditions. This condition is called *candidiasis, yeast syndrome,* or *yeast-related illness.* The significance of candidiasis in the story of the healthy gut is the subject of controversy; some say its importance is overrated, and others say it's key.

Like all yeasts, *Candida* thrives in a carbohydrate-rich environment. Many experts recommend removing as much sugar from the diet as possible, as well as yeast that's found in many bread (wheat- and gluten-containing) products, and fermented and aged products.

Usually, *peristalsis,* or the constant muscular movement of the intestine, eliminates bacteria in the form of waste. In some cases, bacterial overgrowth results from impaired peristalsis, or after bowel surgery where small portions of the bowel are removed or bypassed.

Diagnosing bacterial or yeast overgrowth is relatively simple; usually testing is done on a culture of blood, a breath test to measure hydrogen produced by bacteria, or a stool test. Some doctors don't test their patients; instead, they experiment with a one- to two-month trial of antifungal medication.

Crohn's Disease and Ulcerative Colitis:
Inflammatory Bowel Disease

Inflammatory bowel disease (IBD) refers to a group of chronic diseases that cause inflammation of the small and/or large intestines. It's often confused with celiac disease because diarrhea, weight loss, abdominal cramps, and pain are common symptoms. But bleeding is a symptom of IBD that's not usually associated with celiac disease.

Scientists still don't know the exact cause of IBD, but know that it runs in families. Two types of IBD that occur are Crohn's disease and ulcerative colitis. Crohn's disease causes inflammation deeper into the walls of the intestines, and usually occurs in the lower part of the small intestine (ileum). It can, however, occur in any part of the digestive tract, and can extend deep into the lining of the affected area. Ulcerative colitis causes inflammation and ulcers in the surface of the lining of the large intestine (colon) and the rectum.

To test for Crohn's disease or ulcerative colitis, an endoscopy, sigmoidoscopy, or colonoscopy examines the small bowel and large intestine. A stool sample will show occult (hidden) blood, and blood tests will check for anemia and a high white blood cell count, signifying inflammation and/or infection.

While the exact cause of IBD is not known, there may be a relationship between bacteria in the gut and mutated genes. Specifically in Crohn's disease, a mutation in a gene called Nod2 may increase someone's susceptibility. Nod2 and another gene called Nod1 are involved in the immune system's response to bacteria in the gut.

Yet another theory lies with a bacterium called *Mycobacterium paratuberculosis*. Some researchers believe that there may be a link between Crohn's disease and this bacterium, which is found in a small percentage of both raw and pasteurized milk.

IBS: Common, or Commonly Misdiagnosed?

Ask many gastroenterologists how many IBS patients they have, and they'll usually tell you it's the most common condition they see. Ask how many celiac patients they have, and most will say they have only a few, if any. Hmmm . . . something doesn't figure. If celiac disease is the most common genetic condition that we know of (one in 150 people, and one in 40 with symptoms—the people who are, after all, *in* the gastroenterologists' offices), how is it that many gastroenterologists don't have any celiac patients? The answer is that some patients are diagnosed as having IBS when they may actually have celiac disease.

Two primary sets of criteria are used to identify IBS: the Manning and the Rome criteria. The Manning criteria have been used since they were developed in the 1970s by a team of English researchers led by Adrian Manning, M.D. They establish an IBS diagnosis based on abdominal pain occurring more than six times in the previous year in combination with the following symptoms:

- Visible abdominal swelling
- Relief of stomach pain as a result of bowel movement
- Increased bowel movements with the onset of stomach pain
- Loose stools accompanying stomach pain
- Passage of mucus from the rectum
- Feeling that the bowel has not been completely evacuated after bowel movement

The Rome criteria for IBS diagnosis were developed more recently by a team of researchers in Rome. They establish an IBS diagnosis based on two important criteria:

1. At least three months of chronic or recurrent symptoms of abdominal pain or discomfort, generally in the lower abdomen, that is:

   - relieved by a bowel movement;
   - associated with a change in the frequency of bowel movements (increase or decrease); and
   - associated with a change in stool consistency (softer or harder).

2. Two or more of the following symptoms occurring every few days:

- Altered stool frequency (more than three bowel movements a day or fewer than three in a week)

- Altered stool form (hard or watery)

- Altered stool passage (straining or difficulty during stool passage; urgency—the sudden need to rush to the bathroom for a bowel movement; or feeling that the bowel hasn't completely emptied after a bowel movement)

- Passage of mucus during a bowel movement

- Bloating or a feeling of abdominal distension or fullness

Do any of these symptoms sound familiar? You probably recognize them from the chapter on celiac disease. No wonder so many celiacs are told they have IBS.

A recent study[5] looked at patients who met standardized criteria for having IBS. They were then tested for celiac disease. While nearly 75 percent were confirmed to have IBS, 20 percent had "organic abnormalities" (for example, diverticulitis), and 5 percent were found to have celiac disease (confirmed by intestinal biopsy).

Differentiating between IBS and celiac disease can be a profound distinction because there's no cure for IBS, and no known treatment. Patients are sent away and told basically to "live with it," or even worse, to "eat a high-fiber diet." Celiac disease, on the other hand, is fully treatable, and health is usually completely restored. Most important, if celiacs are misdiagnosed as having IBS, they're not advised to eliminate gluten from their diets, and gluten continues to wreak havoc on their bodies.

Dueling Diagnoses: When You Have More Than One Condition

As is all too apparent from the long list of "associated conditions" in this chapter, many of these disorders go hand in hand, which means there's a better-than-average chance of having more than one. While one diagnosis and its accompanying treatment (or lack thereof) can be difficult, being diagnosed with more than one condition can seem overwhelming. (In an attempt to add levity to an otherwise solemn subject, I'll compare it to having kids—having one is a job in and of itself. Having more than one increases the responsibilities exponentially.)

Yvonne Schwalen of Illinois was devastated to discover that her son, Danny, had not one but two chronic diseases.

It was April of 1997 when we received the news that our 17-month-old son had diabetes. The words "no cure" and "injections for the rest of his life" resounded in our heads. We tearfully started blood testing and giving shots to our tiny, frightened son who did not understand why we were doing these things. Life was a challenge, and our family had many adjustments to make. Fortunately, time has a way of making things easier without noticing. Blood tests, injections, carbohydrate counting, and checking for ketones became part of our daily routine. Gradually our son returned to his old self, approaching challenges with endless excitement and zeal. We felt like we had conquered the monster and had regained our lives.

This was not to be our last trial. Danny then started experiencing "tummy aches" and would cry during the nights with leg pains. Doctors felt growing pains and blood-sugar fluctuations were the cause. It seemed logical until unexplained low blood sugars, which didn't respond to juice treatments, started appearing. We felt like we were losing control. It wasn't until a diabetes education class discussed symptoms of celiac disease that it all came together. Testing was done, and our suspicions were confirmed. We eagerly started the gluten-free diet, anxious to see our son return to health. We were surprised to find out that the results would not be immediate. It took a frustrating four to six months of cutting back insulin and holding injections until the meals "soaked in" before we started noticing a great change. In that time, we did learn the diet. Sticking to fresh and homemade foods seemed the easiest

*for us. We also learned that the carbohydrates seem a bit
higher on the gluten-free starches. (That issue surfaced
once the carbohydrates started absorbing like they should.)*

*Bit by bit we adjusted ourselves to the new routine, and
finally I can say we are here . . . and it feels good! Let's just
hope we don't have any more changes for quite a while.*

It's common for someone with celiac disease to be diagnosed with
one or more *other* conditions, such as diabetes, Down syndrome,
lupus, arthritis, and thyroid disease. Often, these other conditions were
diagnosed *before* celiac disease, so the diagnosis of celiac disease can
be especially painful, begging the questions, "What now?" or "Why
me (or my child)?"

While it may seem at first as though having two diagnoses (or
more) is insult upon injury, the truth of the matter is that once you
begin the gluten-free lifestyle, you'll likely find that symptoms aris-
ing from other conditions begin to diminish, if not disappear completely. It's much easier, for instance, to manage blood-sugar levels
when your body is properly digesting nutrients. Certainly you will
have more energy, and your body, finally able to absorb important
nutrients, will be stronger and better equipped to withstand stress and
trauma.

Speaking of stress and trauma, most people know the term *comfort foods,* and will seek out their favorite indulgences when they feel
uptight, anxious, stressed, or depressed. But what many people don't
know is that sometimes, rather than relieving the stress, food can actually cause it. In fact, food can have a tremendous impact on your
behavior in many different ways—both positive and negative. In the
next chapter, we'll explore the relationship between wheat, gluten,
and behavior.

Chapter 5

Wheat, Gluten, and Behavior:
The Bagel Made Me Do It!

"Our character is what we do when we think no one is looking."
— H. Jackson Brown, Jr.

You may be wondering what behavior has to do with what you eat. Remember the Twinkie Defense? If you're old enough to remember dancing raisins singing, "I Heard It Through the Grapevine," you probably remember the famous case in 1978 when Dan White, a former San Francisco supervisor who had recently resigned his position, climbed through a window in the basement of San Francisco's City Hall and shot and killed both Mayor George Moscone and Supervisor Harvey Milk.

When White was absolved of responsibility for his actions, the facts were convoluted into the story of a slick lawyer who got White off with the now-famous Twinkie Defense, which most people believe represents the idea that junk food can cause people to commit (and get away with) the most heinous of crimes. Actually, White's lawyers claimed that White, who had once been a healthy eater, had begun eating Twinkies, which they claimed as *evidence* of his depression and altered state, not as the *cause* of it.

But the story *sounded* good: Attorneys for a sugar-shoveling, carbo-craving criminal claimed he was thrust into a hypnosis of Hostess homicidal hysteria, a virtual victim of sugar-induced insanity.

Could there be a way to blame our food for our behaviors? Hold your fire there, Rambo; I'm not suggesting you use wheat or gluten as an excuse for bad behavior. But as crazy as it sounds, if you're gluten intolerant, or even if you're not intolerant, but you process gluten differently from other people, there may be justification in blaming the bagel.

You Are What You Eat

Why do people have a hard time believing that nutrition and behavior are inextricably linked? It's easy to buy into the fact that if you use a higher grade of gasoline, your car will run better. So why do people think their behavior is completely independent of the nutrients they put into their bodies?

For decades, psychobiologists have studied the effects of our biology on our behavior. Of particular interest to people with gluten intolerance are the abnormally high hormone levels in people who suffer from malabsorption, as in the case of gluten-intolerant people who continue to eat gluten. People with malabsorption often have high levels of circulating adrenocorticotropic hormone (ACTH) and acetylcholine (ACh), often referred to as stress hormones. These high levels of ACTH and ACh interfere with learning and create anxiety, the desire to escape, a fear of new or unfamiliar things, and poor conditioning response. Experimental evidence suggests that people with malabsorption act similarly to people who have lesions in the hypothalamus (which regulates body processes) and the hippocampus (part of the limbic system, which affects mood and motivation). Studies done on the psychiatric characteristics of gluten-intolerant people have generalized some as turned inward, difficult in temperament, negative, schizoid, paranoid, rigid, stereotyped, and repetitious in behavior. Brain disturbances have been reported, including fuzzyheadedness, disorganization, irritability, and memory impairment.

While there are not many long-term, well-supported, scientific studies on the effects of gluten on behavior, researchers have definitely noted connections. Specifically, researchers have examined the association between gluten and schizophrenia, autism, and ADD/ADHD.

Schizophrenia

While some celiacs are characterized as having abnormal behaviors as described above, others suffer from true schizophrenic-type behaviors. Is it coincidence that they suffer from both conditions, or are celiacs more susceptible to schizophrenia? Or are some *symptoms* of untreated celiac disease similar to symptoms of schizophrenia?

Some researchers believe that in gluten-intolerant people, gluten may be broken down into small peptides (gliadinomorphins) that cross the blood-brain barrier and interact with receptors intended for endorphins and other endogenous (natural) opiates produced by the body. (See the section on zonulin in Tech Talk for more information about the mechanism that may allow this to occur.)

Some investigators have even noted that the incidence of schizophrenia is higher in places where wheat is the staple grain than where non-gluten-containing grain consumption is the norm. In one study done in the highlands of Papua, New Guinea, where little or no grain is consumed, only 2 people out of 65,000 adults could be identified as overtly insane, chronic schizophrenics. In the coastal area, where wheat is consumed more, the prevalence of schizophrenia was about three times higher.[1]

One of the first and most recognized researchers to link gluten intolerance and schizophrenia is F. Curtis Dohan, M.D., of the University of Pennsylvania. As early as the 1960s, Dohan reported that children with celiac disease "more often than by mere chance" become schizophrenic adults. He also reported that gluten can induce common behavioral disturbances in both children and adults who are celiacs, and that these agitations subside after introduction of a gluten-free diet.[2]

Interestingly, Dohan noted that casein was a culprit as well. His recommended diet, then referred to as CFMF (cereal-free/milk-free), proved effective in helping hospitalized schizophrenics earn discharges. Twice as many discharges were given to the group on a CFMF diet as to those who were not.

More recently, researchers Kalle Reichelt, M.D.; M. M. Singh, M.D.; and S. R. Kay, M.D., have studied the relationship between schizophrenia and gluten. While most of their research has been on small subject groups and for short periods of time, they have found significant relationships between diet and behavior. Future research will undoubtedly reveal even more along these lines.

Autism: Gluten-Free, Casein-Free Dietary Intervention

The stories that people tell about improved health on a gluten-free diet are astounding. Some people, while still sick and eating gluten, feel so ill that they must quit their jobs and go on disability, only to find the gluten-free lifestyle offers them restored health and vitality. Few stories can compare, however, to the amazing reports of autistic children who have improved—sometimes dramatically—on the gluten-free/casein-free dietary intervention program.

Autism is one of several conditions in a spectrum that includes Asperger's syndrome and pervasive development disorder—not otherwise specified (PDD-NOS). The incidence of autism is rising at alarming rates throughout the country; in California, for instance, the state's Department of Developmental Services reported a 273 percent increase in diagnosed cases of autism between 1987 and 1998. Studies in Illinois, Florida, England, Iceland, and Japan have all recorded rates of autism much higher than previously assumed, too. Ten years ago, it was estimated that 4 to 6 children in 10,000 would become autistic; now that number is 1 in 500 or less.

Usually symptoms appear between the ages of 18 and 36 months, typically erasing behaviors that had been learned and personality traits that were just beginning to emerge. Some children may appear perfectly normal until two or three years old, at which time they seem to "fade away."

Autistic children are often unresponsive to other people, communicate poorly, do not appear to enjoy being cuddled or touched, and in fact sometimes pull away from physical contact—even when it comes from their own family. Stereotypical, monotonous body movements such as finger-flicking in front of their eyes, spinning, and head-banging seem to accompany the withdrawn behavior. Fascination with parts of objects (that is, fixating on one part of a toy rather than the toy itself) is also characteristic, as is the distress associated with small changes in the environment. Autistic kids tend to be unusually insistent on routines.

What causes this condition begs the age-old question: Is it nature or nurture? Is it a simple case of genetics, or is it provoked by something in the environment such as a toxin or virus? There's little doubt that genetics plays a part. A family with one autistic child has a 5 to 10 percent chance of having another child with the disease. In contrast, a family with no autistic children has only a 0.1 to 1.2 percent chance of having an autistic child. Three out of four autistic people are male.

The brains of autistic people are different. One recent study at the University of Rochester's Embryology Department describes structural abnormalities in an autistic brain suggesting developmental abnormalities that occur weeks after conception—a time most women don't even know they're pregnant.[3] Other researchers point to the fact that autistic brains have smaller memory, emotion, and attention/learning centers (amygdala, hippocampus, and cerebellum) than normal, which would suggest developmental problems during the third trimester of gestation or shortly after birth. (Interestingly, though, autistic people often have extremely good memories, and can even tell you exactly what was said and done on a particular date several years ago.)

Scientists believe that genetics and brain development only predispose children to autism. Other factors must come into play for the condition to be "triggered." A subject of hot debate, those factors might include chemicals, antibiotics, and childhood vaccines.

Most pertinent to this book are some interesting theories about how food may act as a catalyst for the stereotypical autistic behaviors. The premise behind dietary intervention for autism is based on what is now called the "opioid excess theory" of autism, led today by researchers Paul Shattock and Dr. Reichelt.

Jaak Panksepp, Ph.D., observed in the 1980s that some "autistic traits" resembled those of people addicted to opioid drugs. Opiate addicts often are "in their own world," are insensitive to pain, exhibit repetitive behaviors (for example, rocking), and—here comes the red flag for those of us reading this book—experience serious gastrointestinal problems. Panksepp proposed the idea that autistic children may have elevated levels of *naturally* occurring opioids, resulting in the behaviors that are typical of both autistic people and opiate users.

Why autistic people have an excess of these naturally occurring opioids is not thoroughly understood. But the fact remains that people with autism often have abnormal opiate-like peptides in their urine, and these peptides are not found in non-autistic control subjects. How do the peptides get there? Several theories abound, the most relevant of which seem to point to the proteins gluten and casein (found in milk products).

The theory rests on the premise that our bodies metabolize gluten and casein into peptides called *gliadinomorphin* and *casomorphin,* respectively. In non-autistic people, these peptides are further broken down into constituent amino acids, but in autistic people they are not. These peptides, which can function as opioids much like opiate drugs, are usually excreted in the urine, and in fact, autistic people often have elevated levels of these peptides in their urine.

Behavioral issues may arise if these peptides escape the gut, enter the bloodstream, and cross the blood-brain barrier. Exactly how this mechanism occurs—and even *if* it truly occurs—is not yet known.

Some authorities on the subject recommend complete elimination of all gluten and casein from the diet. At first, this can be difficult. Like opiate addicts, autistic people sometimes seem almost *addicted* to foods with gluten and casein, and taking those foods away or forbidding their ingestion can be the catalyst for some serious battles.

Reichelt believes that removing casein from the diet is most significant for children who display autistic traits in infancy, whereas children who appear to develop normally until around two years old and then "fade away" are probably more sensitive to gluten. Elimination of both casein and gluten is the recommended protocol for people experimenting with a dietary intervention program.

Autism and Celiac Disease

So what is the relationship, if any, between autism and celiac disease? Researchers have noted for decades that children classified as severely autistic often have gastrointestinal problems. Could they have celiac disease? Maybe. Could the malabsorption that's characteristic of celiac disease actually result in a deficiency of important neurotransmitters in the brain, and therefore in resulting autistic behaviors?

Possibly. What about the other way around? Could it be that children who are diagnosed with celiac disease at a very early age and therefore are put on a gluten-free diet "prevent" autistic behaviors from emerging by being gluten-free?

Few studies have been done on the relationship between autism and celiac disease, but some are currently under way; it is with eager fascination that we await the results.

Antibiotics: Do They Play a Role in Autism?

Well now, there's a can of worms for you. Many children in the United States have consumed more than their fair share of antibiotics, for everything from runny noses to sore throats. For years, scientists have warned that the flagrant overuse of antibiotics can have dangerous long-term repercussions in at least two ways: creating antibiotic-resistant bacteria, and killing off the "good" bacteria in the gut.

When they were originally developed, antibiotics were useful for fighting bacterial infection. But bacteria are living organisms, able to mutate or change enough so that the "ammunition" we use against one particular strain becomes ineffective in fighting a new, mutated strain. The more antibiotics we use, the more strains of resistant bacteria develop, and some people believe there will be a time in the not-too-distant future when the antibiotics we currently use become pretty much useless in treating general bacterial infection.

The rampant use of broad-spectrum antibiotics (antibiotics that target several strains of bacteria) has resulted in even more bacterial resistance. But it's creating another problem, too. Using broad-spectrum antibiotics is somewhat akin to using a great big net to catch fish because you aren't quite sure which lure works best. You could try to guess which fish are lurking underneath your fishing boat, and drop the lure that works best to attract and catch those fish. But what if those fish aren't in that spot? Wouldn't it be easier to toss a net and see what you find? Surely you'll get the fish you're looking for, and maybe others as well.

The problem is, you can catch dolphins, too. The dolphins, in this analogy, are the "good" intestinal flora and fauna—the bacteria that aid in digestion, provide protection against infection, and produce beneficial vitamins. Antibiotics can virtually wipe out the friendly flora and fauna, allowing yeast overgrowth to develop into a serious problem.

Yeast overgrowth is a generic term referring to any types of "bad" bacteria that are allowed to take over, basically shoving out the "good" yeast. The ultimate bad guy (or one of them) in this scenario is *Candida albicans*, which can flourish into a condition called candidiasis.

The subject of just how sinister *Candida* is can generate hot debate among physicians. Some believe it presents a variety of toxic components from its own structure, or as a consequence of its own chemistry-producing toxins. Some also believe that *Candida* infections can damage the gut wall, allowing large molecules like gluten and casein to cross into the bloodstream and maybe even to cross the blood-brain barrier. It could be *Candida* overgrowth, they hypothesize, that contributes to the opiate excess that may be at least partially responsible for some autistic behaviors.

So Long to Soy, Too?

Recently scientists have begun looking at soy as another possible catalyst of autistic behaviors. There's a high association between milk and soy allergies; many people who react to milk also respond to soy. Furthermore, soy is one of the top eight allergens, and may even affect behavior.

Lisa Lewis, Ph.D., and Karyn Seroussi of the Autism Network for Dietary Intervention (ANDI) suggest that all kids on the gluten-free/casein-free diet should have a two- to three-week no-soy trial, documenting behavior in a daily diary during the trial period. They then recommend rotating soy back into the diet, with a total soy immersion day (every meal and snack), and then no more soy for four days. During those four days, they suggest watching for poor conduct; changes in activity level; discomfort; and sleep, skin, or bowel problems. A strong intolerance will show up quickly; allergies can take a few days for the reaction. If there are no reactions during the no-soy days, they believe it's okay to put soy back in the diet on a regular basis. They do advise that for kids who are highly allergic and/or reactive to foods, it's best to keep all foods on a rotating basis, since they believe anything eaten on a daily basis could begin to cause problems. Fortunately, they point out, this is a small minority of kids.

Autism and Food: A Missing Piece of the Puzzle?

Ted Kniker, M.D., of the San Antonio Autistic Treatment Center in Texas, has been working with colleagues to study the theory that opioid-like peptides somehow leak from the gut into the blood, resulting in the opioid excess theory described above.

In a recent (2001) study,[4] Kniker found that 5 out of 28 children and adults with autism showed improvement in their symptoms after gluten and casein were eliminated from their diets. When he expanded the study and eliminated several other foods, including buckwheat, soy, tomato, pork, food colorings, and grapes from their diets, he noted that symptoms changed "dramatically in 39.3 percent of patients." Eight out of 28 patients showed clear improvements when measured for disruptiveness, alertness, retentiveness, and improved sociability and cognition.

In the first half of the study (just gluten and casein eliminated from the diets), five patients deteriorated, but two of those returned to baseline levels in the last month of the study. In the second half of the study (with more than just gluten and casein eliminated), three patients deteriorated, but Kniker hopes that they, too, will return to baseline levels. He believes that those who deteriorated may still have been eating potentially allergenic foods.

Kniker postulates that extraneous factors such as diet, immune dysfunction, infections, or toxins cause the brain dysfunction of autism. He notes that future studies will improve upon previous ones by identifying all potentially troublesome foods through blood tests, dietary elimination, and challenge procedures, rather than imposing an "arbitrary" diet.

Reading, Writing, and Ritalin:
Alternative Thinking for ADD/ADHD

In the old days, moms trying to rush their kids out of the house to catch the school bus asked, "Did you brush your teeth? Do you have your lunch? Did you do your homework?" These days many have a new item on the checklist: "Did you take your Ritalin?"

Attention deficit disorder (ADD)/attention deficit-hyperactivity disorder (ADHD) is the number-one psychiatric disorder among kids. The prevalence of ADD/ADHD is said to be 5 to 10 percent of school-aged children.[5]

Diagnosis is usually made when children exhibit behaviors such as inattention, hyperactivity, impulsivity, academic underachievement, or behavior problems, and parents seek medical attention to manage these behaviors. The Diagnostic and Statistical Manual of Mental Disorders (DSM) contains specific criteria, guidelines, and practice parameters established by groups including the American Academy of Pediatrics, so a diagnosis (even one that is made on the basis of subjective behaviors) is usually believed to be definitive.

Some people believe the label is too quickly slapped on a child. First-, second-, and third-grade boys are often deemed as having ADD/ADHD because they're impulsive and squirmy, with a lack of motivation or ability to concentrate. (Imagine! An eight-year-old boy who's impulsive and squirmy!) There may or may not be truth to the assertion that too many kids are being labeled as ADD/ADHD without sound substantiation, but some children legitimately fall into the DSM category of ADD/ADHD, and can benefit from medical treatment.

The usual treatment protocol for ADD/ADHD is stimulant therapy. Stimulants such as Ritalin (methylphenidate) and Cylert (pemoline) are often prescribed, and are considered safe and "highly effective" for managing core symptoms of ADD/ADHD in most children.[6] Studies suggest that stimulant therapy may also increase a child's capacity to follow instructions, while reducing the level of emotional overreactivity—improvements that may help the child facilitate better relationships with parents, teachers, and peers.

Obviously, parents are "buying into" the idea that stimulant therapy may be the answer for their children. Prescriptions for Ritalin have increased more than 600 percent over the past five years, according to the U.S. Drug Enforcement Agency.

But what if—just what *if* those behaviors were caused by a metabolic malfunction—one that could be short-circuited by eliminating offending proteins from the diet? Wouldn't it be interesting to at least *try* eliminating those proteins before or instead of initiating stimulant therapy? It seems as though the best way to treat children or adults with ADD/ADHD would be to treat the underlying *cause.*

Some speculate that nutrition may play a part in ADD/ADHD. Some people point to hypoglycemia, or low blood sugar, while other researchers believe that the same opioid peptides that may be culprits in autism (gliadinomorphin and casomorphin), may also be responsible for ADD/ADHD behaviors.

The core symptoms of ADD/ADHD—inattention, restlessness, and impulsivity—are also symptoms of celiac disease. Could people who have celiac disease be misdiagnosed as having ADD/ADHD? Certainly. Could some people with ADD/ADHD simply be metabolizing gluten and casein into endogenous opiates and suffering the "narcotic" effects? Possibly. Could a gluten-free/casein-free diet benefit these people and possibly even replace the need for stimulants? Maybe. Sure seems like it might be worth a try.

More Information on Dietary Intervention

To date, double-blind, placebo-controlled, peer-reviewed studies to prove the opioids excess theory have not been completed, although several are under way. Anecdotal evidence and data from "open studies" done in the United States and Europe, however, is compelling, and many people believe that dietary intervention *could* work and is well worth the effort involved in giving it a try.

For more information on the mechanisms involved, or on the diet itself, see:

Websites: **www.autismndi.com**
                            www.gfcfdiet.com

Books/literature: *Special Diets for Special Kids* (books 1 and 2), by Lisa Lewis, Ph.D., published by Future Horizons, Inc.

The Journal of NIH Research

I hope that the first several chapters of this book have left you well armed with a thorough understanding of how food may affect the way you feel, both physically and emotionally. So now what? If you do nothing with that knowledge, it's like being all dressed up with nowhere to go. You need to put that knowledge to work and find out whether you have a medical condition that *requires* a wheat-free/gluten-free diet. If you haven't done so already, your first step should be to see a doctor. In the next chapter, you'll learn how to make the most of your efforts to get good medical advice.

Chapter 6

Talking to Your Doctor:
Discussing Diarrhea and Other
Fates Worse Than Death

"I've learned that life is like a roll of toilet paper.
The closer it gets to the end, the faster it goes."
— Andy Rooney

Most of the people who read this book have probably suffered some type of discomfort, usually for quite some time. For the majority, it has been discomfort of the most embarrassing kind: gastrointestinal. People would rather discuss their sexual dysfunction than their—er—uh—bowel movements. So it isn't a surprise that people hesitate to seek medical attention for their—ahem—gastrointestinal distress. It can be embarrassing, awkward, uncomfortable, and humiliating . . . and that's how we feel just making the appointment!

It gets worse from there. I'm pretty sure the first class taught in med school is called "How to Intimidate Your Patients," and the first hour is dedicated to the golden rule: Make them strip. Naked patients are far less chatty (HMO allowable chitchat has decreased 40 percent in the last year), and in fact, in their nakedness, they often forget to ask the tough questions that force doctors to utter the words they are never allowed to say: "I don't know."

Personally, being naked makes me, oh, I don't know, a little self-conscious. Even donning a swimsuit in public is dicey, since I'm one of those moms who would have to pull on a pair of shorts before jumping in the ocean to save my drowning kids. I'd rather deny just about any medical problem than go through the inevitable naked interrogation required for diagnosis and treatment.

So the very first thing they make you do is strip naked and put on a large paper towel–sandpaper hybrid that's supposed to tie closed, but no one, including the inventor, is sure how it works. Sitting with the straightest posture you've had since grade school, atop a sheet of tissue paper that you're sure is sticking to your butt, you nervously await the nurse or physician's assistant.

Since you're there to talk about your bowel movements, the nurse will, by law, be young and attractive, especially if you're of the male persuasion. "What seems to be the problem today?" she'll chirp. At that moment you wish you had any condition involving a "normal" part of your body: blindness, a brain tumor, gangrene, ingrown toenails . . . anything but *this*.

Feeling awkward and humiliated, and wishing you could trade places with someone in the middle of an IRS audit, you attempt to sound nonchalant as you force yourself to discuss your most intimate and disgusting bodily functions or lack thereof. Then you wait in agony for the doctor who, you know, sooner or later, will want to investigate the scene of the crime.

At some point, it's important to realize that a trip to the doctor—albeit one that will probably involve nakedness and probing—is less than optional. Sometimes the strip search is the easy part. It's dealing with the intimidation that can be tough.

Dealing with Doctors

> "*If a hammer is the only tool in your toolbox,*
> *then every problem begins to look like a nail.*"
> — Abraham Maslow

I have a great deal of respect for doctors, especially those who enjoy their work and dedicate themselves to improving the lives of their patients. I've met a lot of doctors like that, and have several in my own family. Unfortunately, I've also come across more than my fair share of doctors who refuse to take their patients seriously, or to think outside the box.

Too many people, regardless of profession, know how to use only the tools they have in their toolbox. As Maslow so profoundly points out, if all they have is a hammer, then they'd better hope the only problems they encounter are nails that need to be pounded in or pulled out. But what if *your* health concern requires a screwdriver? Your doctor *can* hammer a screw in, and the ultimate result might—or might not—be a good one.

After reading this chapter, you will better understand your body, learn how to articulate your health concerns, and be prepared to discuss some conditions your doctor may not know about. You'll be able to, in essence, hand your doctor a screwdriver.

For me, one of the scariest parts of being a patient is that my body—my future—is at the mercy of this one individual who may or may not *really* be competent or educated in the precise area that I need. It's a lot like taking my car to a mechanic to be worked on. Is that mechanic *really* an expert on all of my car's features and inner workings? Why is he always able to find another $450 worth of problems I didn't even know existed? If I take my car to another mechanic, will he agree with the first one's diagnosis? If not, what does *that* tell me? The bottom line is, the last time I tried to change my engine oil by myself, my husband stopped me just as I was unscrewing the cap to the *transmission* fluid—not even close to the engine oil plug that I should have been loosening. So I'm at the mercy of mechanics, competent or not. And most of us are at the mercy of our doctors.

Talking the Talk: A Quick Lesson in Medicalese

When you, as a patient, seek the opinions and guidance of physicians and other health-care professionals, you expect them to provide you with accurate information and advice. It's important for you to be educated so you can ask the right questions and—sometimes this can be difficult—understand the answers.

Does it seem as though they're speaking Greek? They are! If medical terminology sounds Greek to you, that's because a lot of it is . . . Greek. Much of today's medical terminology is derived from Greek and Latin words. But if you understand how the word is broken down, and if you can understand each part of the word, then you will be able to speak medicalese.

For instance, *cardio* means "heart," *nephro* means "kidney," *phleb* means "vein," and *odont* or *dont* means "tooth." These root words are combined with other root words, or with prefixes or suffixes that further explain a condition or procedure.

Procedure and condition words sometimes include *algia,* which means "pain"; *ectomy*, which means "to remove"; and *itis,* which means "inflammation of." So *odontalgia* is just a fancy word for "toothache"!

Medical words that end in "y" usually refer to a procedure, such as *endoscopy* (literally translated to mean "scope inside"). Adding "ly" generally refers to an act or process.

Be Prepared

The key to getting the information you need from your doctor is to make sure you're prepared before the visit. If you wait until you get there to think of your questions, you're likely to be nervous or intimidated, and you probably won't get the answers you need.

Here are some tips that will help you be better prepared to talk to your doctor:

- *Do your homework before you go:* If your doctor or someone you know has suggested that you may have a particular condition, research it before your appointment. If necessary, bring this book, or print out information that may be valuable for the physician. Be sure you don't sound like you're telling your doctor how to do his or her job, but *do* be persistent. If you suspect you may have celiac disease, this is especially important, because researchers have learned a lot about the condition in the last few years, and what doctors learned in medical school years ago may no longer be fact.

- *Write down your questions before you get to the doctor's office:* The only dumb questions are the ones that don't get asked. Be as clear as you can in your questions, and ask as many as you'd like. It's your body (or your child's), and you have a right to understand what's going on with it.

- *Repeat the doctor's answers:* The safest way to ensure that you have understood someone is to repeat their answers back to them. If you don't understand the terminology, make sure you ask for clarification.

- *Refer to family history:* If you're related to someone who has been diagnosed with allergies, intolerances, or celiac disease, be sure to mention that you have a family history of that condition. In the case of celiac disease, remind your doctor that in first-degree relatives of celiacs, about 1 out of 20 people (5 percent) has the condition; in second-degree relatives, it's about 1 in 40.

- *Don't allow yourself to be intimidated or bullied:* This is your body, and you have the right to ask for testing, and to thoroughly understand your state of health.

- *Bring a translator:* If you feel that you just can't understand what the doctor says, bring a friend or family member to help you understand and remember.

- *Don't leave until every question has been answered:* Sometimes we feel rushed when we're in the doctor's office, as though we're imposing if we take more than the allotted 3, 5, or 15 minutes. Don't succumb to this intimidation; ask every question, and don't leave until you fully understand your condition and treatment.

- *Know how to follow up:* Make sure you have the name of a nurse, physician's assistant, or other appropriate person who can get answers for you if you have questions later. It can be difficult to get to the right person when you call, so sometimes e-mailing or faxing your questions to the doctor's office will be most effective. Make sure you also include your own contact information on any communication you send so that someone from the doctor's office can get back to you with the answers.

Convincing Your Doctor to Test

"My nephew was diagnosed with celiac disease, so I know I should be tested, too. But I can't convince my doctor to test me, because he says I don't have classic symptoms. How can I get the test done?"
— Maria N.

From the patient's standpoint, the tests themselves are a breeze. Getting your doctor to *order* the tests could be the tricky part. While convincing your doctor to test you for allergies may not be difficult, getting him or her to test for other conditions can be. For instance, many physicians believe that, to justify testing for celiac disease, the patient (usually a child, they're taught) must show signs of severe diarrhea, malnourishment, and a distended belly. After reading thus far, you know that this thinking is not only inaccurate, but that a delayed diagnosis can lead to severe complications. The issue is probably going to be convincing your doctor to do the test, and to do the *type* of test that you believe is best for you.

Any primary-care physician, nurse practitioner, or physician's assistant has the authority to order the initial tests. If you find that your doctor is reluctant about testing, be prepared, be respectful, and be assertive. Most important, don't give up until you're satisfied that you've been thoroughly and accurately tested for anything you suspect you might have.

Is Your Doctor the Right *Doctor?*

Your doctor may be a wonderful physician—for someone else. Not all doctors are created equal, and not all doctors understand, want to understand, or will take the time to understand wheat allergy, gluten intolerance, and celiac disease. If that's the case, it may be necessary to switch doctors, as emotionally difficult and logistically cumbersome as that can be.

Chances are, if you've been sick for a prolonged period of time, you're seeing a specialist. If your symptoms are classic, you're most likely seeing a gastroenterologist, or "GI" specialist. Just because someone is a gastroenterologist doesn't make them an expert on celiac disease or any other condition; in fact, they may know very little about wheat allergy, gluten intolerance, or celiac disease, and much of their information could be out of date.

If you suspect that you have a gastrointestinal disorder and you feel that your doctor isn't knowledgeable on the subject, provide information and ask if he or she will take the time to learn more.

In the case of many gastrointestinal disorders, proper diagnosis and ongoing monitoring are important, and you have the right to ask as many questions as it takes for you to feel comfortable with your doctor's knowledge on the subject. If you suspect that you may be gluten intolerant or have celiac disease, you should ask your physician some of the following questions:

- Can you explain gluten intolerance and its symptoms? How many patients with gluten intolerance or celiac disease have you seen? (If the answer is none, that's okay, as long as you feel your doctor truly understands the condition and keeps up with recent research.)

- Do you currently have any patients with celiac disease? (If the answer is no and your doctor is a gastroenterologist, you may want to consider this to be a red flag. If the prevalence of celiac disease occurs in one in 40 people who have symptoms, how could a gastroenterologist have *no* patients with the condition?)

- What is your knowledge of celiac disease? (This is an intentionally open-ended question. Sit back and let the doctor talk.)

- Do you have any subspecialties? (Many gastroenterologists subspecialize in conditions of the gut such as malabsorption. Since celiac disease is a malabsorption condition, someone who specializes in this would most likely be more knowledgeable.)

- Ask questions that you know the answer to, not to be challenging or smug, but to see how knowledgeable your doctor is:

  — How is celiac disease diagnosed? (See the section on testing.)

  — Isn't celiac disease a childhood disease? (The answer should be no.)

  — How rare is it?

  — What causes it?

  — Is it okay to have just a little gluten from time to time? (The correct answer is no.)

  — Will my family members have it? (Remember, about 1 in 20 first-degree relatives has celiac disease; about 1 in 40 second-degree relatives has it.)

If you find that your doctor won't or doesn't want to learn about the condition, request a new physician immediately. If you're reluctant to believe that your doctor isn't the right doctor, or you hesitate to accept the fact that you may need to make a change, please read the following section carefully. It was written by Michelle Maria Pietzak, M.D., a pediatric gastroenterologist and one of the country's leading researchers and experts on celiac disease. She has taken a bold and courageous stand, and makes an eloquent case for why doctors are reluctant to test for celiac disease. Her essay is based on education, experience, and her passion to help a vast number of people whose health could be greatly improved if they were properly diagnosed.

Why Your Doctor Won't Test You for Celiac Disease
by Michelle Maria Pietzak, M.D.

As Danna Korn elegantly recounted in an earlier chapter, patients with celiac disease (or parents of children with celiac disease) often go from doctor to doctor for several years in this country before being diagnosed correctly. However, in Europe, the disease is often correctly diagnosed within weeks of seeing a general practitioner. Why is this? Isn't our health-care system the best in the world? Don't people from all countries come to train in our medical schools and residency programs to learn all there is to know about the practice of medicine? Well, there's a key word in that last sentence, and it is *practice*.

When we graduate from medical school and residency (the three to nine years or more spent after medical school, training in a specialty under the guidance of senior physicians), we do not know "all there is to know" about medicine. Unfortunately, some of us think that we do!

My story of how I got involved doing research in celiac disease reflects this. I had finished four years of college during which I earned a bachelor's degree in biology, and went through four years of medical school and three years of residency in pediatrics. During that time, I had never seen, heard of, or taken care of a patient with celiac disease.

True! My only exposure to this disease was for about five minutes out of my four years in medical school in a class called Pathology. There, I learned that "gluten-sensitive enteropathy" was a rare condition, treated by diet, and that it classically presented in the first two years of life as a short, malnourished, Caucasian child with a big belly (the picture showed a starving, Third World-looking child).

Since I had not seen any patients who looked like this, I didn't test any for celiac disease. And since I never tested anyone for this "rare" disease, I hardly thought about it at all—even when a patient may have looked a little bit like that "Third World" baby.

That all changed for me on May 20, 1995. I was doing the last rotation of my pediatric residency at Childrens Hospital Los Angeles in the Pediatric Intensive Care Unit. Almost done with my residency! I had already decided that after my residency, I was going to do a fellowship (another three years of training and sleepless nights) in pediatric gastroenterology and nutrition.

On that fateful day, my future boss, Dan W. Thomas, M.D., called me and said, "There's a doctor who is going to speak about celiac disease today over at the university, and I think you should go." My first thought was, I *have a wedding to plan! I can't afford the time to go to this talk!* My second thought was, I'*m soooo tired, I should just go home after work and take a long nap.*

I would like to say that my third thought was not equally selfish, but it was. I realized, *Hey, Dr. Thomas is going to be my boss for the next three years, so I better do this and make him happy.* The afterthought was, *Gee, I'm going to do a fellowship in GI and nutrition, and I know nothing about celiac disease. I better go to this and learn something about it so I don't look stupid.* So, while I would like to say that I went to this talk out of pure scientific interest, I really went for selfish reasons.

Little did I know that this talk would change not only the direction of my academic career, but my life in general as well.

And so off I went to hear the then-relatively-unknown-but-still-charismatic Alessio Fasano, M.D., from the University of Maryland speak about celiac disease in his thick Italian accent. The talk was held in a very small room, where not more than ten people sat around an oval table. Not exactly a large turnout, and I initially thought perhaps I was wasting time better spent picking out appetizers for my wedding. But once the talk began, I was mesmerized.

Dr. Fasano spoke of all the different ways this disease could present (things I had never heard before, such as anemia and joint pain and type 1 diabetes), and about the "celiac iceberg" that existed in this country, with the majority of celiac patients located "below the surface" of the water. He spoke of how common the disease was in his native Europe, and how both the genes and the grains necessary to have this disease existed here in my country. He spoke of the thousands of people who are chronically tired and ill, and whose doctors are unable to figure out what's wrong with them. Within an hour, I was both appalled by and converted to the "celiac cause."

I became formally involved with the Center for Celiac Research in 1998. CFCR was founded by Drs. Fasano and Karoly Horvath in 1996 to address the specific question of "where have all the American celiacs gone?" CFCR quickly became a leader in both patient and laboratory-based research on celiac disease in the United States, and I, now fresh from my fellowship, was eager to participate on any level they would allow.

Patients often tell me that their doctors refuse to test for celiac disease. What other disease can you possibly think of that a physician will tell you "you don't have," without doing a history, physical exam, or any tests to rule it out? Parents of celiac kids tell me their doctor won't test the other kids in the family because it's a rare disease. One teenager with biopsy-proven celiac disease told me she went to her pediatrician's partner for a minor illness (while her regular doctor was on vacation), and he told her to go off her gluten-free diet, because she "looked too healthy" to have celiac disease. Would a physician tell a patient with a high cholesterol level to go out and have a bacon double cheeseburger because she didn't "look" like her cholesterol was high? Preposterous!

Why is this happening in this country? Is celiac disease really rare here, or is some other factor at play? Unfortunately, through our research, we have discovered that celiac disease is not rare in the United States. What is rare are doctors who know how to diagnose and treat the condition.

What follows are my top ten reasons why your physician won't test you for celiac disease. This is based on personal experience, and the horror stories the celiac community has shared with me over the past six years. Hopefully, when we understand the root of this problem, we can better educate our American colleagues, so the perception of celiac disease as "rare" will no longer be an issue.

The Top Ten Reasons Your Doctor Won't Test You for Celiac Disease

1. ***Physicians are "imprinted" by their experiences in medical school and residency training:*** As I alluded to in my personal account, medical school and residency are critical learning periods during which future doctors are molded. If physicians are not exposed to celiac disease during training, it's unlikely that they will ever look for it once graduated from medical school or residency.

2. **Routine blood tests will not make the diagnosis of celiac disease (although an astute clinician will be able to find "clues" there):** The routine blood tests done during an annual "healthy" checkup, or even when a patient is sick, rarely include a specific celiac test. Instead, they consist of a complete blood count (CBC) and chemistry panel. In a patient with untreated celiac disease, the CBC may reveal anemia, or a low red blood cell count. If the red blood cells are small (called a microcytic anemia), this can be due to iron deficiency. If the red blood cells are immature and large (called a macrocytic anemia), this can be due to vitamin B12 or folate deficiency. Iron, B12, and folate can all be malabsorbed in patients with celiac disease. However, many physicians will just prescribe iron or vitamin supplements to treat the anemia, without looking for a cause. The chemistry panel in a patient with untreated celiac disease may also show abnormalities, such as low potassium, bicarbonate, or protein levels, which can be seen with long-standing diarrhea. The chemistry panel can also show high liver enzymes, but this finding is more likely to cause the doctor to look for liver disease (such as hepatitis) than celiac disease.

3. **Celiac disease can present with symptoms outside of the gastrointestinal tract and can also be "silent":** Since celiac disease is a multisystem disorder (affecting many different organs, not just the gastrointestinal tract), the patient with celiac disease may see many different specialists for a variety of different complaints. In such cases, rarely does any one physician recognize that multiple symptoms (for example, anemia, infertility, joint pain, and rash) can all be due to one disorder. We're taught in medical school to find the simplest explanation for the patient's symptoms, which in this case would be one disease (celiac disease). On the other hand, we're also told, "When you hear hoofbeats, think of a horse and not a zebra" (meaning common diseases are more common than rare ones!). Unfortunately, celiac disease is still considered a "zebra," so many physicians don't even think about it. Even more confusing

to health-care practitioners is the fact that celiac disease can be "silent": Although they have no symptoms, some patients have positive blood tests and biopsies consistent with celiac disease. On a gluten-free diet, they report less fatigue and fewer gastrointestinal complaints, meaning that they weren't really asymptomatic—they just weren't bothered enough by their vague symptoms to seek medical attention.

4. **Physicians think that people who complain of multiple symptoms affecting many different parts of the body are either hypochondriacs or just plain crazy:** Patients who have multisystem disorders, such as an autoimmune disease like celiac disease, often have problems with many different parts of the body. Some physicians may perceive this long list of complaints as hysteria and exaggeration, as opposed to looking for one disease that might explain it all. These physicians are also more likely to label such patients as depressed, "crazy," or having a "secondary gain" (such as missing school or work), rather than doing a more thorough history and physical exam, blood tests, x-rays, or biopsies to find the true etiology of the problems.

5. **Physicians feel uncomfortable when a patient knows more about a disease than they do:** Many doctors have what is referred to as a paternalistic attitude, a kind of "doctor knows best" philosophy. When a patient questions their clinical opinions, these doctors may feel as if they're being challenged by someone "less knowledgeable," and may not take it seriously. They may even have a hostile reaction to being challenged by a patient who comes in having done research on a disease that they know nothing about. Most physicians are also most comfortable diagnosing and managing diseases with which they're familiar, such as irritable bowel syndrome, lactose intolerance, and depression (three of the most common diagnoses that celiac patients receive). Celiac disease, on the other hand, is often a condition that they don't know how to test for or treat, which makes them uneasy.

6. **Some doctors are just not good listeners:** This is a sad but true statement. Only recently have courses in doctor-patient communication been added to the medical school curriculum. And sometimes these things just cannot be taught! Often a patient will have to "shop around" to find a doctor who takes complaints seriously and with full attention.

7. **Physicians generally get their continuing medical education from medical journals and conferences:** Again, since celiac disease is perceived as rare in this country, it is not often written or spoken about in American medical journals or conferences. This is finally starting to change.

8. **Routine endoscopies and poorly done biopsies won't discover celiac disease:** Patients with gastrointestinal complaints often undergo endoscopies (in adults, this is done mostly to look for cancer), but if the intestine appears normal, biopsies may not be routinely obtained during endoscopy. Since the intestinal changes seen with celiac disease are microscopic, the gastroenterologist cannot diagnose celiac disease just by looking through the endoscope camera. To confirm or rule out celiac disease, biopsies must be obtained from multiple locations; because celiac disease affects the intestine in a "patchy" manner, some areas may appear normal, and other areas may appear abnormal. The biopsy also has to be performed correctly; if the villi are cut at an angle, they may appear improperly short. Also, many people with celiac disease have various degrees of villous atrophy (shortened villi) that can sometimes be misinterpreted if the pathologist is not familiar with all the possible biopsy changes found in the early stages of this disease.

9. **Cost containment in the era of managed medical care sometimes prohibits testing:** I often hear from patients that their health plan will not pay for a biopsy because it's not "cost effective," even if the patient has symptoms and blood tests consistent with celiac disease. These health-plan providers

do not understand that diagnosing celiac disease early is actually preventive medicine. Patients with untreated celiac disease have twice the mortality at any given age as patients who do not have the disease. This is likely due to the increased incidence of other autoimmune disorders as well as higher rates of small bowel lymphoma (an intestinal cancer) in individuals not adhering to a gluten-free diet. Treating celiac disease early will also prevent osteoporosis, a huge burden to the healthcare system.

10. **If you don't look for it, you won't find it:** When I ask physicians if they have any patients with celiac disease, they usually say no. When I ask if they test any patients for celiac disease, I usually get the same answer. Because of the perception that celiac disease is rare is this country, physicians rarely test for it. Because they don't test for it, they never diagnose it, resulting in a medical practice with no celiac patients (unless they come in with a diagnosis from another doctor, which tends to be doubted). To me, this is equivalent to a doctor saying, "I have no patients with hypertension in my practice," when they never check a blood pressure. Seek and you will find!

Author's note: If you think you detect a little frustration from both Dr. Pietzak and me, you're right! It's a helpless feeling to hear story after story of people who suffer needlessly because doctors don't—and sometimes won't—understand celiac disease and gluten intolerance. Awareness is growing, and diagnoses are on the rise, but patients must still take responsibility for their health and do what they can to ensure their condition is properly assessed and that the advice they're given is based on current knowledge and research.

Some people prefer not to deal with traditional medical practitioners at all, and would rather discuss their health issues with a naturopath, chiropractor, nutritionist, or other alternative health-care professional. The next chapter will introduce you to some nontraditional approaches to the wheat-free/gluten-free diet that aren't typically discussed by medical doctors.

Chapter 7

Complementary Medicine: Unconventional Approaches Might Be Right for You

"He who joyfully marches in rank and file has already earned my contempt. He has been given a large brain by mistake, since for him the spinal cord would suffice."
— Albert Einstein

There was a time when I would scoff at terms such as *alternative, naturopathic, holistic,* and *complementary.* I figured that pursuing therapies such as acupuncture, chiropractic, and traditional Chinese medicine (TCM) was akin to wearing crowns of aluminum foil to keep the extraterrestrial beings away.

Yes, I admit it, I tend to sway toward conformity and conventionalism. Worse yet, I can't even blame my parents for this particular trait. One might assume that my father, an M.D., or my mother, a well-educated author who researches and writes about health-related topics, might be responsible for this right-wing tendency. Suffice it to say that conformity and conventionalism aren't even in their vocabularies.

When I was a little girl I remember curling up with a coloring book and crayons, carefully outlining each illustration and filling it in with appropriately complementary (and always vivid, of course) colors. My mom would glance over my shoulder and say, "That's beautiful, sweetheart, but try not to stay in the lines so much." Try *not* to stay in the lines? I had worked so hard to impress her with my ability to be controlled and detailed—and she thought I should color *outside* the lines? What did she think I was, a preschooler?

My tendency to buy into accepted norms is deeply ingrained and well entrenched, in spite of my parents' early attempts to keep me from falling into the trap of such mundane conformity. In recent years, though, I've learned that in most aspects of life, thinking "outside the box" offers a fresh perspective with unlimited opportunities for happiness and success.

In terms of medical conditions, "the box," as I see it, is traditional Western medicine and conservative thinking. I still embrace this box for the core of my beliefs; for instance, I believe that if you think you might have an allergy or intolerance to any food, you should be properly (oops, there's my bias peeking through) diagnosed.

So far, this book has focused on the box. All the information on allergy, intolerance, and disease has been based on universally accepted, published, medically proven fact and theory. But in my extensive research and passion to learn more about the etiology of these conditions, and testing and treatment options, I've learned that there's a lot to be learned by thinking outside the box. For some, traditional testing methods, enduring a gluten challenge, and accepting diagnostic results as gospel are not acceptable or preferential alternatives.

Understand that I still advocate taking a hard look at what you hear—ridiculous claims and theories are often proclaimed in the name of science, and some of them are as fictional as the tales of Paul Bunyan (we all know his ox wasn't really blue). But I have also heard the most amazing stories about unconventional approaches to various conditions, and I now realize that hard science isn't always the only criterion in judging the merit of an idea or hypothesis.

The Evolution Revolution: The Paleolithic Diet

In an attempt to understand why our bodies respond better to some types of foods than others, some scientists have looked at the evolution of humans and the correlating evolution of our diets. One of the most popular evolutionary diets is the Paleolithic diet.

The Paleolithic diet is based on a diet similar to that of humans in the Paleolithic period, which began with the manufacture of stone tools and ended shortly before the development of agriculture about 10,000 years ago. During this agricultural revolution (after the Paleolithic period), humans shifted from being hunter-gatherers to food *producers*, and their diets changed dramatically as wheat and other grains were introduced.

But remember, that occurred only 10,000 years ago. That's *yesterday* in evolutionary terms. Genetically speaking, we've changed very little in the ensuing years, and are nearly identical to our late Paleolithic ancestors.

The basic premise of the Paleolithic diet is that our diets today are unnatural for humans, resulting in conditions such as heart disease, cancer, diabetes, obesity, and autoimmune diseases. In contrast, proponents of the diet believe that humans who lived in Paleolithic times as hunter-gatherers followed a more natural diet of meat, fish, leaves, berries, and nuts—and that they rarely, if ever, developed the conditions we see today.

Believers in this theory maintain that our genetic adaptation has been unable to keep pace with cultural progress. In other words, our diets have changed dramatically since the development of agriculture 10,000 years ago—and even more dramatically since the Industrial Revolution—but our bodies haven't changed and evolved at the same pace.

The introduction of agriculture radically changed our nutritional intake. Over the course of a few millennia, the proportion of meat in our diets declined drastically, while vegetable foods came to comprise as much as 90 percent of our intake. One of the most noticeable changes that occurred in humans as a result is that they were, on average, six inches shorter than their preagricultural ancestors. Animal-protein content of Western diets has since increased and is more nearly adequate now, and we're now nearly as tall as were the first biologically modern human beings.

Our diets are still very different, though, than they were in Paleolithic times. Today's diet is generally divided into the six basic food groups shown on the Food Pyramid: meat and fish; fruit; vegetables;

milk and dairy products; breads and cereals; and fats and sweets. We're taught that servings from all six groups provide a well-balanced diet, but our Paleolithic predecessors ate from only the first three groups. They rarely or never ate cereal grains, and had no dairy foods whatsoever.

Although they're few and far between, some hunter-gatherer societies still exist today. One of the ways scientists have studied their theories about the Paleolithic diet is by looking at the diets of the few surviving hunter-gatherer populations, whose way of life and eating habits closely resemble those of preagricultural human beings.

The conditions that have emerged in Western society (for example, coronary heart disease, hypertension, diabetes, and cancer) have evolved mostly in the past century, and are virtually unknown among the hunter-gatherer populations. Of course, longer life expectancy in industrialized countries is one reason that chronic illnesses are pertinent; but even young people in the Western world develop asymptomatic forms of these conditions, whereas hunter-gatherer youths do not. Furthermore, even "older" members of primitive cultures— those over the age of 60—remain relatively free from these disorders.

When hunter-gatherers are brought into modern society and begin to eat a diet filled with processed grains, oils, sugars, and dairy products, they develop the same conditions that are so prevalent in modern humans.

Most relevant to this book is that proponents of the Paleolithic diet emphasize the avoidance of two Neolithic foods common to our diets today: gluten and milk. Among the many conditions they say are improved on the diet are autism, multiple sclerosis, and rheumatoid arthritis.

To learn more about the Paleolithic diet, an excellent Website can be found at: **www.paleodiet.com**.

Raw Is Rare

How much food do you eat in its raw, natural form? No, I don't mean unpackaged, and "raw" sugar doesn't count. For most of us, our food must be cooked, soaked, or otherwise processed before we eat it. In fact, some of the foods we eat—certain grains, legumes, and tubers—are actually poisonous if eaten raw, yet as a society we eat huge amounts of them in their highly processed forms. These highly processed, convenience foods are also high in easily digestible carbohydrates, which raise blood sugar levels and are easily stored as fat.

Raw, natural foods are inherently healthy, but the cooking process eliminates many of the benefits these foods provide. Heat, oxidation, and other chemical reactions that occur during cooking can destroy vitamins (especially B and C), amino acids, and enzymes. Boiling or blanching foods can cause important vitamins and minerals to leach out, and microwaving can create hot spots that damage or eliminate nutrients. Even steaming can cause nutritional loss.

Most raw, natural Paleolithic foods, on the other hand, are low in carbohydrates, and the carbohydrates they do have are complex as opposed to simple. They are also high in protein, which is vitally important to our diets. The upshot? You might want to reconsider "raw" in your regular refreshments!

The Blood-Type Diet

The blood-type diet is based on evolutionary theories that have their roots in the same time period as the Paleolithic diet—about 10,000 years ago. This diet theorizes that blood types evolved in response to the dietary changes that resulted when agriculture was born and grains were introduced into human civilization.

According to the theory, type O is the oldest blood type, and at one point in time everyone was type O. One of the most popular books on the subject, *Eat Right 4 Your Type* by Dr. Peter J. D'Adamo (with Catherine Whitney), explains that type A's, for instance, evolved after the introduction of agriculture, when grains were introduced into the diet. Type A's can, according to this theory, better tolerate and absorb cultivated grains and other agricultural products because a mutation in their digestive tracts and immune systems occurred as a result of eating these new grain products.

The blood-type diet theory claims that your blood type reflects your internal chemistry, and can determine your susceptibility to illnesses. It suggests that your blood type can also be used to determine which foods you should eat or avoid for optimal health. *Eat Right 4 Your Type* refers to gluten, saying that it "binds to the lining of the small intestine, causing substantial inflammation and painful irritation in some blood types—especially type O." It goes on to say that type O children are unusually sensitive to wheat and dairy products, and that type O's in general do not tolerate whole-wheat products at all; wheat products should be completely eliminated from their diet.

Since the author of this book suggests that type O's avoid gluten (but then gives permission to eat barley, rye, and spelt—an inconsistency that should not be overlooked), many people have suggested that the diet is a good one for celiacs and others avoiding gluten in their diets.

While I have read some well-supported reviews in the scientific literature about the blood-type diet that raised concerns in my mind about its merit, judging the credibility of this diet—or any other, for that matter—is not the venue of this book. It *is* important to note that the "type O" diet as outlined in the book is not a celiac diet, nor does the author claim it to be. And while he also doesn't specifically say the diet is gluten-free, he does say that type O's should avoid gluten. To someone unfamiliar with the diet, it would be easy to infer that the diet he outlines is gluten-free. It is not. Barley, rye, and spelt are considered in *Eat Right 4 Your Type* to be "neutral" foods, which the author defines as "food that acts like a food" (versus food to be avoided, which "acts like a poison"), and are therefore permitted on the type O diet. They are not, of course, permitted on a gluten-free diet.

A Closer Look at Research: Does Coffee Cause Car Accidents?

"It has just been discovered that research causes cancer in rats."

Ridiculous claims can be veiled in the name of science, so don't believe everything you hear, even if it's a "scientific study." Not all science is good science; how studies are conducted is a critical factor in determining the difference.

It wouldn't be hard, for instance, to make a "scientific" case for the theory that coffee causes car accidents. After all, if you look at every person who has ever been in a car accident and you ask them about the day of the crash, you're likely to find that more than 90 percent of them drank coffee that morning. Cause and effect? Does coffee cause car accidents? Obviously not—and that's my point.

Ask anyone who has ever been on a debate team and they'll tell you it's easy to make a convincing argument for just about anything—especially if you're armed with enough knowledge to sound as though you know what you're talking about. Use enough big words, make enough sense to appeal to the average person, and you're likely to win them over.

With the proliferation of mass media and our country's unquenchable thirst for information that will help us look and feel better, hypotheses about health—often self-serving or contrived—are perpetuated faster than gossip on a cheerleading squad. Sadly, these conclusions can be broadcast in the form of infomercials, printed in books and magazines, and are assumed to be based on credible information. Soon they're accepted as fact, but often with very little basis.

It's your responsibility to take a hard look at what you hear. Does it make sense? That's important, but it's not enough. Is the source credible? Again, vital, but not enough. Be a tough critic of things you hear, especially when they concern your body.

Remember, 42.7 percent of all statistics are made up.

Now that you've read the first part of this book, you've added quite a few tools to your toolbox. You've learned some of the many different reasons people have for giving up wheat or gluten, and how to discuss your concerns with your doctor. You know you'll feel better on the wheat-free/gluten-free diet, and you're ready to begin reaping the rewards of the hard work you've put into finding out what was wrong in the first place.

The next part of this book will give you even more tools, and help you handle the day-to-day aspects of living on a wheat-free or gluten-free diet. Are you ready? Then turn the page and let's talk about how, what, and where you can eat!

Part II

Weaning from Wheat and Bootin' Gluten: How, What, and Where to Eat

Now that you've had the chance to determine whether you should give up wheat or gluten, and why, it's time to get started on the diet. You're probably hungry by now! This part of the book will guide you through the everyday aspects of life on a wheat-free/gluten-free diet. It lists safe and forbidden foods and ingredients, and answers some common questions about grains and other wheat substitutes. You'll find suggestions for shopping, menu planning, and cooking, as well as helpful hints for preparing your kitchen and purging your medicine cabinet of ingredients that might make you sick. As a special bonus, you'll find an entire chapter of delicious and easy-to-make recipes by cookbook author Connie Sarros, targeted specifically to those who combine their wheat-free/gluten-free diet with casein, diabetic, and vegetarian restrictions.

For many people on the wheat-free/gluten-free diet, the fear of eating out becomes imprisoning. In the next few chapters, you'll learn the importance of not living your life in a bubble, and you'll discover some helpful hints for accommodating yourself when you travel, entertain guests, eat at restaurants, and attend social functions.

Chapter 8

What Can You Eat?
Safe, Forbidden, and
Questionable Ingredients

"What is food to one, is to others bitter poison."
— Lucretius 99 B.C. – 55 B.C.

Wheat is often referred to as the staff of life, but if you have an allergy or intolerance, wheat may seem more like the *sap* of life, sapping you of energy and important nutrients. Worse yet, this common grain is everywhere. Even "America the Beautiful" sings of "amber waves of grain," as though wheat was at the very core of our country—and sometimes it seems as though it is, especially to someone trying to do without.

Believe me, I understand how hard it is to sort through the foods that are allowed and those that aren't. There's a lot of information to (if I may be forgiven the pun) digest! Especially when you throw into the mix the fact that some foods are okayed by some groups, but forbidden by others, and that some people need to avoid wheat, while others need to avoid all foods that contain gluten.

Which may beg the questions, what *are* wheat and gluten, and how can you tell the difference?

> *What can I eat, free of gluten or wheat?*
> *It seems like there's nothing for me as a treat.*
> *I read all the labels on crackers and bread;*
> *I know of ingredients you've never read.*
> *It's hidden in products like seasonings . . .*
> *Why can't they just label these questionable things?*
> *Oh, please tell me something that I can just eat*
> *that doesn't have any gluten or wheat!*
> — Danna Korn

Why We Eat Wheat

Cooking vessels dating back to 6700 B.C. have been found containing remnants of cooked wheat in one form or another, and archeologists have uncovered grinding tools used for wheat 50,000 years before that. But it wasn't until the end of the Paleolithic era that agriculture "took root," and wheat-growing changed the complexion (and presumably the digestive systems) of the ancient world. The Tigris and Euphrates Valley, now dry as a bone, but known then as the Fertile Crescent, was once covered with endless rows of golden grain.

While the advent of agriculture had a profound effect on our diets, thanks to the introduction of cereals, the Industrial Revolution had an important effect, too. As people began to move away from agricultural communities and into large cities, they realized they had to make flour last long enough to feed large masses of people. The grain processor was the answer to their problems, by removing some of the things that made flour spoil: the nutrient-rich oil, outer-bran, and germ layers of the wheat berry. These layers contain most of the important lipids (fats), sterols, vitamins, and minerals found in wheat. (By the way, these vitamin- and mineral-rich outer layers such as bran are sold to ranchers as livestock feed, which means in some respects, that cattle eat better than we do.)

What remains after most of the nutrient-rich portions of wheat are removed is unbleached flour. It still contains nutrients, but most flour is then usually bleached, oxidizing proteins and extending shelf-life. To make up for sapping flour of its nutrients, it's synthetically "enriched," but usually at much lower nutritional levels than were present in the unmilled food.

Fortunately, wheat is usually well labeled, but beware of aliases. There are several varieties of wheat, sometimes labeled as flour, semolina, spelt (which some people on a wheat-free—not gluten-free—diet can tolerate), frumento, triticale (a man-made wheat-rye cross), bulgur, kamut, and trigo.

Interestingly, the word *trigo* is used by the Portuguese, who didn't like the word *wheat,* because it's derived from the old English *hwit* ("white"), referring to the fact that flour is often bleached. Health-minded Portuguese instead called it *trigo,* which—ironically—means "hard to handle."

What Is *Gluten, Anyway?*

Gluten (GLOO-ten): Noun. A substance found in nearly every food on this planet. When found to be present in one's favorite food, it can elicit sudden tears of frustration; when found to be absent from one's favorite food, it can elicit sudden tears of joy.

Okay, I admit it; I made that definition up. Serious students of linguistics would tell you that there are two additional and completely different definitions of *gluten.* One is simple, commonly accepted, and most frequently used—but technically incorrect. The other is a complex but technically correct definition. I'll give you both. I'll also give you a brief history of how the term evolved, because this evolution led to the newly revised, incorrect, but widely accepted definition.

Historically, gluten comes from wheat, and only wheat. It's what scientists call a "storage protein," and what bakers call the dough-forming ingredient in wheat. Bakers, botanists, and even celiacs agree that gluten is the component that makes breads doughy and elastic. Because of these properties, and due to its high protein content, gluten is added to some foods and promoted as a healthy additive.

For the intolerant, however, it is anything but.

At some point in our not-so-distant history, the association was made between wheat (specifically gluten) and celiac disease. It became widely accepted that gluten makes celiacs sick, which is true. Soon, physicians realized that barley and rye make celiacs sick, too, and people started saying, "Celiacs can't eat gluten. They can't eat wheat, barley, and rye, either; therefore, wheat, barley, and rye all have gluten, right?" Not really.

But the "Wheat, barley, and rye all have gluten" theory stuck, and even though it isn't technically correct, it's widely accepted today. For the purposes of this book, we'll stick with it, too.

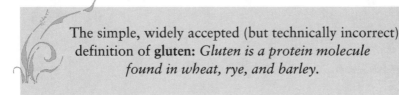

The simple, widely accepted (but technically incorrect) definition of **gluten:** *Gluten is a protein molecule found in wheat, rye, and barley.*

Technically speaking, gluten is the general name for *prolamins* (also referred to as "prolamines"), a protein fraction found in a variety of grains. The prolamins that cause damage to celiacs include gliadin (found in wheat), secalin (found in rye), and hordein (found in barley).

People often refer to gliadin as the offending part of gluten, and it is—for wheat. But secalin and hordein also cause an immunological response in celiacs. Other grains have prolamins, too (corn's prolamin is called zein, and rice's prolamin is orzenin), but their prolamins are not toxic to celiacs.

To be even more specific, only a part of the gliadin, secalin, and hordein proteins are harmful. Proteins are made from long chains of hundreds of amino acids, sort of like beads in a necklace, forming something called a peptide. If the sequence of amino acids changes, the result is a different peptide. Parts of the long chain of a protein are also called peptides. Researchers have identified at least one particular peptide as the culprit in gluten sensitivity, although there may be more.

For years, there has been controversy over whether or not oats contain gluten, but we now know that the peptide they contain (avenin) does not affect people who are gluten intolerant. There is, however, some concern about contamination of oats (we'll address this further in the next chapter), so many people on a gluten-free diet choose to play it safe and avoid them altogether.

In addition to the question about oats, there are ongoing controversies about other grains, and whether or not they harm people who are gluten intolerant or have celiac disease. Some people may have reactions to these grains, but they're probably due to characteristics of the grains that aren't related to gluten content (or lack thereof). In this book, you'll find grains classified as safe or forbidden, based on the most recent research available. Regardless of whether or not a food contains gluten, always remember the golden rule: *If it makes you sick, don't eat it.*

Safe and Forbidden Foods

At first glance, the lists of safe, forbidden, and questionable foods may seem lengthy, and you may wonder if you'll ever be able to shop without a cheat sheet. You may also be concerned because the lists have names of ingredients you've never heard of. Don't worry. With time, you'll start recognizing most, if not all, of the ingredient names, and you'll be able to readily identify them on food labels as either safe or forbidden.

Remember, if you're trying to follow a wheat-free (but not necessarily gluten-free) diet, everything on the safe list is okay for you, because the gluten-free diet is, by definition, wheat-free.

Table 2 Safe Foods		
Acacia gum	Agar	Arrowroot
Acorn quercus	Algae	Artichokes
Alcohol (some spirits—specific types)	Almond nut	Astragalus gummifer
	Annatto	Baking soda
Alfalfa	Apple cider vinegar	Balsamic vinegar
Amaranth	Arabic gum	Beans
Adzuki bean		

Besan

Bicarbonate of soda (some contain gluten)

Buckwheat

Butter (beware of additives)

Canola oil

Carrageenan chondrus crispus

Carob bean

Carob bean gum

Carob flour

Cassava manihot esculenta

Cellulose[1]

Cellulose gum

Cheeses (except blue and chilton)

Chickpea

Corn

Cornmeal

Corn flour

Cornstarch

Corn syrup

Cowitch

Cowpea

Cream of tartar

Distilled vinegar

Eggs

Fish (fresh)

Flaked rice

Flax

Fruit (including dried)

Gelatin

Gram flour (chickpeas)

Grits, corn

Guar gum

Herbs

Honey

Hyacinth bean

Job's Tears

Kasha (roasted buckwheat)

Kudzu root starch

Lentils

Locust bean gum

Maize

Maize, waxy

Maltodextrin[2]

Manioc

Masa flour

Masa harina

Meat (fresh)

Methyl cellulose[3]

Milk

Millet

Milo

Mung bean

Nuts (except wheat, rye, and barley)

Nut, acorn

Nut, almond

Oats[4]

Oils and fats

Peas

Pea—chick

Pea—cow

Pea flour

Pigeon peas

Polenta

Potatoes

Potato flour

Prinus

Psyllium

Quinoa

Ragi

Rape

Rice

Rice flour

Rice vinegar

Romano bean (chickpea)

Sago palm

Sago flour

Saifun (bean threads)

Scotch whiskey

Seaweed

Seeds (except wheat, rye, and barley)

Sesame seeds

Soba (be sure it's 100% buckwheat)

Sorghum

Sorghum flour

Soy

Soybean

Spices (pure)

Spirits (some specific types)

Starch (made in the U.S.)

Succotash (corn and beans)

Sunflower seeds

Sweet chestnut flour

Tapioca

Tapioca flour

Tea

Tea-tree oil

Teff

Teff flour

Tepary bean

Tofu-soya curd

Tragacanth

Tragacanth gum

Turmeric (*Curcuma*) Whey Xanthan gum
Urad beans White vinegar Yam flour
Urad dal (peas) vegetables Wines Yogurt (plain, unflavored)
Wine vinegars (and balsamic)
Urad flour
Vinegars (some specific types) Wild rice

Source: Excerpted with permission from **www.celiac.com,** 2002.

---

[1]Cellulose is a carbohydrate polymer of D-glucose. It is the structural material of plants, such as wood in trees. It contains no gluten protein.

[2]Maltodextrin is prepared as a white powder or concentrated solution by partial hydrolysis of cornstarch or potato starch with safe and suitable acids and enzymes.

(a) Maltodextrin, when listed on food sold in the U.S., must be (per FDA regulation) made from corn or potato. This rule does NOT apply to vitamin or mineral supplements and medications. [Federal Register (4-1-96) 21 CFR. Ch. 1, Section 184.1444.]

(b) Donald Kasarda, Ph.D., of the United States Department of Agriculture, a research chemist specializing in grain proteins, found that all maltodextrins in the U.S. are made from cornstarch, using enzymes that are NOT derived from wheat, rye, barley, or oats. On that basis, he believes that celiacs need not be too concerned about maltodextrins, though he cautions that there is no guarantee that a manufacturer won't change their process to use wheat starch or a gluten-based enzyme in the future. [From the CELIAC Listserv archives, on the Internet, Donald D. Kasarda, posted November 6, 1996.]

(c) "Additives Alert," an information sheet from the Greater Philadelphia Celiac Support Group, updated early in 1997. This specific information comes from Nancy Patin Falini, dietitian advisor. [May 1997 Sprue-Nik News.]

[3]Methyl cellulose is a chemically modified form of cellulose that makes a good substitute for gluten in rice-based breads, etc.

[4]Cross-contamination with wheat is a slight possibility.

Table 3
Safe Additives (Gluten-Free)

Adipic acid

Acacia gum

Agar

Algin

Alginate

Allicin

Aluminum

Annatto color

Arabic gum

Aspartame (can cause IBS symptoms)

Aspic

Ascorbic acid

Benzoic acid

Betaine

BHA

BHT

Beta carotene

Biotin

Butylated hydrox-yanisole

Butyl compounds

Calcium carbonate

Calcium chloride

Calcium phosphate

Calcium silicate

Calcium stearate

Camphor

Caprylic acid

Carboxymethyl-cellulose

Carnauba wax

Carob bean gum

Carrageenan casein

Castor oil

Cellulose gum

Cetyl alcohol

Chlorella

Chymosin

Citric acid (made in the U.S.)[1]

Collagen

Corn sweetener

Corn syrup solids

Cortisone

Cotton seed oil

Cysteine, L.

Demineralized whey

Desamidocollagen

Dextrimaltose

Dextrose

Dioctyl sodium

Elastin

Ester gum

Folic acid—Folacin

Formaldehyde

Fructose

Fumaric acid

Gelatin

Glutamine (amino acid)

Glutamic acid

Glycerides

Glycerol monooleate

Glycol

Glycolic acid

Guar gum

Hemp

Hydrogen peroxide

Hydrolyzed soy protein

Iodine

Invert sugar

Keratin

Lactic acid

Lactose

Lanolin

Lecithin

Lipase

Locust bean gum

Magnesium carbonate

Magnesium hydroxide

Malic acid

Maltitol

Microcrystalline cellulose

Mineral oil

Mineral salts

Monosodium gluta-mate (MSG; made in the U.S.)

Monopotassium phosphate

Musk

Niacin—Niacinamide

Oleyl alcohol/oil

Paraffin

Pepsin

Peru balsam

Petrolatum

Phenylalanine

Polyethylene glycol

Polyglycerol

Polysorbates
Potassium citrate
Potassium iodide
Pristane
Propolis
Propylene glycol
monostearate
Propyl gallate
Pyridoxine
hydrochloride
Rennet
Reticulin
Rosin
Royal jelly
Sphingolipids
Sodium acid
pyrophosphate
Sodium ascorbate

Sodium benzoate
Sodium citrate
Sodium erythrobate
Sodium hexam-
etaphosphate
Sodium lauryl sulfate
Sodium nitrate
Sodium silicoalu
minate
Sodium stannate
Sorbic acid
Sorbitol-mannitol (can
cause IBS symptoms)
Soy lecithin
Stearates
Stearamide
Stearamine
Stearic acid

Sucrose
Sulfosuccinate
Sulfites
Sulfur dioxide
Tallow
Tartaric acid
TBHQ (tetra- or trib-
utylhydroquinone)
Thiamin
hydrochloride
Tolu balsam
Tragacanth gum
Tri-calcium phosphate
Tyrosine
Vanillin
Vitamin A (retinol)
Whey
Xanthan gum

Source: www.celiac.com, 2002

[1]All the citric acid produced in the U.S. is made from corn. Outside the U.S. the acid can also be derived from other sources of dextrose, including cane sugar and wheat. Some of the citric acid used in the U.S. is imported from other countries, such as China. Imported citric acid may be made from corn, sugar, or wheat. U.S.-made citric acid capacity remains stable. There are three domestic producers of citric acid—Archer Daniels Midland, Cargill, and Haarmann and Reimer—with total capability of 460 million lb./yr. of citric acid. All three produce citric acid through the fermentation of corn-based dextrose.

Table 4
Forbidden Foods

Alcohol (some spirits, specific types)

Artificial color[1]

Artificial flavoring[2]

Baking powder[3]

Barley (*Hordeum vulgare*)

Barley grass (can contain seeds)

Barley malt

Beer

Bleached flour

Blue cheese (made with bread)

Bran

Bread flour

Brewer's yeast

Brown flour

Bulgur (bulgur wheat/nuts)

Calcium caseinate (contains MSG)

Caramel color[4]

Cereal binding

Chilton

Citric acid[1]

Coloring

Couscous

Dextrins[5]

Edible starch

Einkorn (*Triticum monococcum)*

Farina graham

Filler

Flavoring[2]

Food starch

Fu (dried wheat gluten)

Germ

Glutamate (free)

Graham flour

Granary flour

Gravy cubes[1]

Groats (barley, wheat)

Ground spices[1]

Gum base

Hydrolyzed plant protein (HPP)[1]

Hydrolyzed vegetable protein (HVP)[1]

Inulin[1]

Kamut (pasta wheat)

Malt

Malt extract

Malt flavoring

Malt syrup

Malt vinegar

Matzo semolina

Miso[1]

Modified food starch[1]

Modified starch[1]

Mono- and diglycerides[3]

MSG (made outside the U.S.)[1]

Mustard powder [1]

Natural flavoring[2]

Pasta

Pearl barley

Rice malt (contains barley or Koji)

Rye

Seitan

Semolina

Semolina *(Triticum)*

Shoyu (soy sauce)[1]

Small spelt

Soba noodles[1]

Sodium caseinate (contains MSG)

Soy sauce

Spelt *(Triticum spelta)*

Spirits (some specific types)

Sprouted wheat or barley

Starch[1]

Stock cubes[1]

Strong flour

Suet in packets

Tabbouleh

Teriyaki sauce

Textured vegetable protein (TVP)

Triticale X triticosecale

Udon (wheat noodles)

Vegetable starch

Vinegars (some

specific types)

Vitamins[1]

Wheat germ (oil)

Wheat grass (can contain seeds)

Wheat nuts

Wheat starch[6]

Wheat, Abyssinian hard (*Triticum durum*)

Wheat, bulgur

Wheat, common (*Triticum aestivum*)

Wheat, club (*Triticum aestivum* subspecies

compactum)

Wheat, durum (*Triticum durum*)

Wheat, Einkorn (*Triticum monococcum*)

Wheat, hard

Spelt (*Triticum spelta*)

Emmer (*Triticum dicoccon*)

Emmer, wild (*Triticum dicoccoides*)

Wheat, Poulard (*Triticum turgidum*)

Wheat, Polish (*Triticum polonicum*)

Wheat, Persian (*Triticum carthlicum*)

Wheat, macha (*Triticum aestivum*)

Wheat, Vavilovi (*Triticum aestivum*)

Wheat, shot (*Triticum aestivum*)

Wheat, Oriental (*Triticum turanicum*)

Wheat, Timopheevi (*Triticum timopheevii*)

Wild Einkorn (*Triticum boeotictim*)

Whole-meal flour

Source: **www.celiac.com**, 2002

---

[1]Can utilize a gluten-containing grain or by-product in the manufacturing process, or as an ingredient.

[2]According to 21 CFR S101, 22(a)(3): "[t]he terms 'natural flavor' or 'natural flavoring' means the essential oil, oleoresin, essence or extractive, protein hydrolysate, distillate, or any product of roasting, heating, or enzymolysis, which contains the flavoring constituents derived from a spice, fruit or fruit juice, vegetable or vegetable juice, edible yeast, herb, bark, bud, root, leaf or similar plant material, meat, seafood, poultry, eggs, dairy products, or fermentation products thereof. Whose significant function in food is flavoring rather than nutritional."

[3]Mono- and diglycerides can contain a wheat carrier in the U.S.. While they are derivatives of fats, carbohydrate chains may be used as a binding substance in their preparation, which are usually corn or wheat, so this needs to be checked out with the manufacturer. According to a Sept./Oct. 2001 article titled "Know the Facts" in *Gluten-Free Living,* probably all mono- and diglycerides made in the U.S. are gluten-free.

[4]The problem with caramel color is it may or may not contain gluten, depending on how it is manufactured. In the U.S., caramel color must conform with the FDA standard of identity from 21CFR CH.1. This statute says: "the color additive caramel is the dark-brown liquid or solid material resulting from the carefully controlled heat treatment of the following food-grade carbohydrates: dextrose (corn sugar), invert sugar, lactose (milk sugar), malt syrup (usually from barley malt), molasses (from cane), starch hydrolysates and fractions thereof (can include wheat), sucrose (cane or beet)." Also, acids,

alkalis, and salts are listed as additives which may be employed to assist the caramelization process.

[5]Dextrin is an incompletely hydrolyzed starch. It is prepared by dry heating corn, waxy maize, waxy milo, potato, arrowroot, wheat, rice, tapioca, or sago starches, or by dry heating the starches after (1) treatment with safe and suitable alkalis, acids, or pH control agents; and (2) drying the acid- or alkali-treated starch. Therefore, unless you know the source, you must avoid dextrin. According to a Sept./Oct. 2001 article titled "Know the Facts" in *Gluten-Free Living,* probably all dextrins made in the U.S. are gluten-free.

[6]Most celiac organizations in the U.S. and Canada do not believe that wheat starch is safe for celiacs. In Europe, however, Codex Alimentarius Quality wheat starch is considered acceptable in the celiac diet by most doctors and celiac organizations. This is a higher quality of wheat starch than is generally available in the U.S. or Canada.

Wheat-Free/Gluten-Free Diet by Food Groups

Sometimes, when getting started on the wheat-free/gluten-free diet, it's helpful to have a list of safe and forbidden foods arranged by food groups. That way, you can quickly determine whether your favorite snack or food item is okay or not, without having to read an ingredients label. The chart that begins on the next page outlines safe and forbidden foods by food groups.

Table 5
Wheat-Free/Gluten-Free Diet by Food Groups

Food Products	Foods Allowed	Foods to Question	Foods Not Allowed
Milk	Milk, cream, most ice cream, butter-milk, plain yogurt, cheese, cream cheese, processed cheese, processed cheese foods, cottage cheese	Milk drinks, flavored yogurt, frozen yogurt, sour cream, cheese sauces, cheese spreads	Malted milk, ice cream made with ingredients not allowed
Grain Products	**Breads:** Bread and baked products containing amaranth, arrowroot, buckwheat, corn bran, corn flour, cornmeal, cornstarch, flax, legume flours (bean, garbanzo or chickpea, garfava, lentil, pea), millet, potato flour, potato starch, quinoa, rice bran, rice flours (white, brown, sweet), sago, sorghum flour, soy flour, sweet potato flour, tapioca, and teff	Buckwheat flour	Bread and baked products containing wheat, rye, triticale, barley, oats, wheat germ, wheat bran, graham flour, gluten flour, durum flour, wheat starch, oat bran, bulgur, farina, wheat-based semolina, kamut, einkorn, emmer, faro, and imported foods labeled "gluten-free that may contain ingredients not allowed" (e.g., wheat starch)
	Cereals: **Hot:** Amaranth flakes, cornmeal, cream of buckwheat, cream of rice (brown or white), hominy grits, rice flakes, quinoa flakes, soy flakes, and soy grits	Rice and corn cereals, rice and soy pablum	Cereals made from wheat, rye, triticale, barley and oats; cereals with added malt extract or malt flavoring

Food Products	Foods Allowed	Foods to Question	Foods Not Allowed
Grain Products, cont'd.	**Cold:** Puffed amaranth, puffed buckwheat, puffed corn, puffed millet, puffed rice, rice flakes, and soy cereals		
	Pastas: Macaroni, spaghetti, and noodles from beans, corn, pea, potato, quinoa, rice, soy, and wild rice	Buckwheat pasta	Pastas made from wheat, wheat starch, and other ingredients not allowed
	Miscellaneous: Corn tacos, corn tortillas	Rice crackers, some rice cakes and popped corn cakes	Wheat flour tacos, wheat tortillas
Meats & Alternatives	**Meat, fish, poultry:** Fresh	Prepared or preserved meats such as luncheon meat, ham, bacon, meat and sandwich spreads, meat loaf, frozen meat patties, sausages, pâté, wieners, bologna, salami, imitation meat or fish products, meat product extenders	Fish canned in vegetable broth containing hydrolyzed vegetable protein (HVP) or hydrolyzed plant protein (HPP)*; turkey basted or injected with HVP/HPP; frozen chicken containing chicken broth (made with ingredients not allowed)
	Eggs: Eggs	Egg substitutes, dried eggs	
	Others: Lentils, chickpeas (garbanzo beans), peas, beans, nuts, seeds, tofu	Baked beans, dry roasted nuts	
Fruits & Vegetables	**Fruits:** Fresh, frozen, and canned fruit juices	Fruit pie fillings, dried fruits, fruits or vegetables with sauces, French-fried potatoes (esp. those in restaurants)	Scalloped potatoes (containing wheat flour), batter-dipped vegetables
	Vegetables: Fresh, frozen, dried, and canned		

Food Products	Foods Allowed	Foods to Question	Foods Not Allowed
Soups	Homemade broth, gluten-free bouillon cubes, cream soups, and stocks made from ingredients allowed	Canned soups, dried soup mixes, soup bases, and bouillon cubes	Soups made with ingredients not allowed, bouillon, and bouillon cubes containing HVP or HPP* or wheat
Fats	Butter, margarine, lard, vegetable oil, cream, shortening, homemade salad dressing with allowed ingredients	Some salad dressings, some mayonnaise	Packaged suet
Desserts	Ice cream, sherbet, whipped toppings, egg custards, gelatin desserts; cakes, cookies, pastries made with allowed ingredients; gluten-free ice cream cones, wafers, and waffles	Milk puddings, custard powder, pudding mixes	Ice cream made with ingredients not allowed; cakes, cookies, muffins, pies, and pastries made with ingredients not allowed; ice cream cones, wafers, and waffles made with ingredients not allowed
Miscellaneous	**Beverages:** Tea, instant or ground coffee (regular or decaffeinated), cocoa, soft drinks, cider; distilled alcoholic beverages such as rum, gin, whiskey, vodka, wines, and pure liqueurs; some soy and rice beverages	Instant tea, coffee substitutes, fruit-flavored drinks, chocolate drinks, chocolate mixes, flavored and herbal teas	Beer, ale, and lager; cereal and malted beverages; soy or rice beverages made with barley or oats
	Sweets: Honey, jam, jelly, marmalade, corn syrup, maple syrup, molasses, sugar (brown and white)	Spreads, candies, chocolate bars, chewing gum, marshmallows, and lemon curd	Licorice, Smarties®, and other candies made with ingredients not allowed
	Snack foods: Plain popcorn, nuts, and soy nuts	Dry roasted nuts, flavored potato chips, tortilla chips, and soy nuts	Pizza, unless made with ingredients allowed

Food Products	Foods Allowed	Foods to Question	Foods Not Allowed
Miscellaneous, cont'd.	**Condiments:** Plain pickles, relish, olives, ketchup, mustard, tomato paste, pure herbs and spices, pure black pepper; vinegars (apple or cider, distilled white, grape or wine, spirit), gluten-free soy sauce	Seasoning mixes, Worcestershire sauce	Soy sauce (made from wheat), some mustard, pickles (made from wheat flour), malt vinegar
	Other: Sauces and gravies made with ingredients allowed, pure cocoa, pure baking chocolate, carob chips and powder, chocolate chips, monosodium glutamate (MSG), cream of tartar, baking soda, yeast, brewer's yeast, aspartame, coconut, gluten-free communion wafers	Baking powder	Sauces and gravies made from ingredients not allowed, hydrolyzed vegetable/plant protein (HVP/HPP*), communion wafers

Source: Excerpted with permission from *Gluten-Free Diet: A Comprehensive Resource Guide* © Shelley Case, B.Sc., R.D., second printing 2002.

---

[1] If the plant source in HVP/HPP is not identified, or if the source is from wheat protein, HVP/HPP must be avoided.

Additional Things to Be Aware Of

- Rice and soy beverages (that is, Rice Dream), because their production process sometimes utilizes barley enzymes

- Bad advice from health-food store employees (for example, that spelt and/or kamut are safe for celiacs)

- Cross-contamination between food store bins selling raw flours and grains (usually via the scoops)

- Wheat-bread crumbs in butter, jams, toaster, counter, etc.

- Lotions, creams, and cosmetics (primarily for those with dermatitis herpetiformis)

- Stamps, envelopes, or other gummed labels

- Toothpaste and mouthwash (major brands in the U.S. are safe)

- Medicines: many contain gluten

- Cereals: most contain malt flavoring, or some other non-gluten-free ingredient

- Some brands of rice paper

- Sauce mixes and sauces (for example, gravy, soy sauce)

- Some ice creams

- Packet and canned soups

- Dried meals and gravy mixes

- Some laxatives

- Grilled restaurant foods (gluten-contaminated grill)

- Fried restaurant foods (gluten-contaminated grease)

- Ground spices: wheat flour is sometimes used to prevent clumping

Why Some Foods Are Questionable

> *The golden rule:*
> *When in doubt, leave it out!*

Many people who must eliminate wheat from their diets due to allergies don't realize that wheat can be "hidden" in additives and ingredients—at this time, manufacturers aren't required to identify them as wheat on the label. If you're eliminating gluten from your diet, you've probably already run into several examples of ingredients being called safe on one list and forbidden on another. Why is there any debate? Shouldn't it be a simple matter of asking, "Does it have gluten or not?"

The simple answer is that sometimes there isn't a simple answer. Some ingredients have been in question for years, simply because they cause some type of negative reaction in some people—but it's not necessarily a wheat or gluten reaction.

Distilled vinegar, for instance, has been at the heart of this type of controversy for more than a decade, and has prompted more recounts than the 2000 presidential elections. But, like the election, no matter how many times the votes are counted, the final answer has always been the same: There's no gluten in distilled vinegar (malt vinegar does have gluten). This is great news, because mayonnaise, mustard, and many salad dressings that were once suspect because of their vinegar content are no longer questionable.

Buckwheat, quinoa, amaranth, and canola oil have for years been accused of causing a gluten reaction in celiacs, yet they don't contain gluten. Another type of reaction may be occurring, such as an allergy, or something specific to the food itself. Buckwheat, for example, is said to contain a photosensitizing agent that can cause a skin rash in some people who eat it and go into the sun. Quinoa and amaranth have high concentrations of oxalate (also found in spinach), which, in and of itself, may cause problems in some people, especially in high doses.

The safe and forbidden lists concur with new guidelines established by the American Dietetic Association (ADA) in its sixth edition of the *Manual of Clinical Dietetics* (2001). In the new manual, an entire chapter is devoted to the treatment of celiac disease, providing dietitians with information on celiac disease and the gluten-free diet. It clearly states that some foods once thought to be questionable are, in fact, safe for celiacs. These formerly "questionable" (but no longer questioned by most people) foods include distilled vinegar, buckwheat, quinoa, amaranth, teff, distilled alcoholic beverages (including rum, whiskey, gin, and vodka), and canola oil.

Table 6
Questionable Foods

Category	Food Products	Notes
Milk Products	Milk drinks	• Chocolate milk and other flavored drinks may contain wheat starch or barley malt
	Cheese spreads or sauces (e.g., nacho)	• May be thickened/stabilized with wheat; flavorings and seasonings may contain wheat
	Flavored or frozen yogurt	• May be thickened/stabilized with a gluten source; may contain granola or cookie crumbs
	Sour cream	• Some low-fat/fat-free may contain modified food starch
Grains	Buckwheat flour	• Pure buckwheat flour is gluten-free; sometimes buckwheat flour may be mixed with wheat flour
	Rice cereals, corn cereals	• May contain barley malt extract; may contain oat syrup or barley malt extract
	Buckwheat pasta	• Some "soba" pastas contain pure buckwheat flour, which is gluten-free, but others may also contain wheat flour
	Rice cakes, corn cakes, rice crackers	• Multigrain often contains barley and/or oats; some contain soy sauce (might be made from wheat)
Meats/ Alternatives	Baked beans	• Some are thickened with wheat flour
	Imitation crab	• May contain fillers made from wheat starch
	Dry roasted nuts	• May contain wheat
	Processed meat products	• May contain fillers made from wheat; may contain HPP or HVP (from wheat); may contain flavorings made from wheat
	Meat analogs/ "imitation"	• Often contain wheat or oats
Fruits & Vegetables	Dried fruits	• Dates and other dried fruits may be dusted with oat or wheat flour to prevent sticking
	Fruits/vegetables with sauces, fruit pie fillings	• Some may be thickened with flour
	French fries	• May contain wheat as an ingredient

Category	Food Products	Notes
Soups	Canned soups, dried soup mixes	• May contain noodles or barley; cream soups are often thickened with flour; may contain HPP or HVP (from wheat); seasonings may contain flour
Fats	Salad dressings	• Seasonings may contain flour
Desserts	Milk puddings/mixes	• Starch source may be from wheat
Miscella-neous	Beverages	• Some instant teas, herbal teas, coffee substitutes, and other drinks may have grain additives
	Lemon curd	• Usually thickened with flour
	Potato, tortilla chips, soy nuts	• Some potato chips contain wheat; seasoning mixtures may contain flour
	Baking powder	• Contains starch, which may be from wheat
	Seasoning mixes	• May contain wheat flour or hydrolyzed wheat protein
	Worcestershire sauce	• Some may contain malt vinegar

Source: Excerpted with permission from *Gluten-Free Diet: A Comprehensive Resource Guide* © Shelley Case, B.Sc., R.D., second printing, 2002.

Questionable Ingredients

With the new ADA dietary guidelines in place, hopefully we have put to rest once and for all the questions about distilled vinegar, buckwheat, quinoa, amaranth, millet, and teff. With any luck, labeling laws will become more stringent, and future labels will clearly identify any gluten-containing foods. Until we can rely upon better labeling, there are still some ingredients that you should question, whether you're wheat-free or gluten-free. The following is an attempt to tease some elements of fact out of the tangle of conflicting information we've gotten on these ingredients.

The following information is compiled from various resources; primarily from *Gluten-Free Living,* published by Ann Whelan; and *Gluten-Free Diet: A Comprehensive Resource Guide,* by Shelley Case.

Wheat Starch: It would seem by its name that wheat starch would be off-limits, but actually there is some question, and some Europeans believe that, in some forms, it is permissible on the gluten-free diet. Proponents say that most of the protein in wheat starch is "starch granule protein," rather than gluten, and several studies have corroborated its safety for celiacs. Some scientists are skeptical, however, and warn against its use; most groups in the United States and Canada have not accepted it as being safe for the gluten-free diet.

Modified Food Starch: Modified food starch can be derived from many sources: corn, tapioca, potato, *wheat*, or other starches. Most modified food starch in North America is derived from non-gluten-containing sources. It is still prudent, however, to check with the manufacturer, asking from what source the modified food starch is derived.

Natural Flavors: Most natural flavors don't contain gluten (wheat isn't a very good "flavor enhancer"). Manufacturers are getting better about clear labeling, and usually call out if they've used a flavor that contains wheat/gluten, but to be 100 percent certain, you must call the manufacturer and ask.

Malt: Malt is almost always derived from barley, and therefore not allowed on the gluten-free diet (it *is* allowed on a wheat-free diet). Malt extract is made when malt is mixed with water and heated to very high temperatures. The enzymes break down the starches into sugars. Sometimes, however, malt is made from corn, and is usually specified as such on the ingredients label. If not specified, it is most likely made from barley and is therefore not gluten-free.

Hydrolyzed Vegetable Protein (HVP) or Hydrolyzed Plant Protein (HPP): Hydrolyzed proteins may be derived from a gluten-containing source, but must be listed as such on the ingredients label.

Dextrin: Dextrin, a hydrolyzed starch, is usually made from non-gluten-containing sources, but it *can* be made from wheat. Also, because wheat starch is used more commonly in Europe than in the United States, imported foods or additives are suspect. You should call the manufacturer to determine the source.

Mono- and Diglycerides: Mono- and diglycerides are simply fats made from oil and used in baked products as a preservative, and in "wet" foods as a stabilizer, improving consistency. They show up in the "to be questioned" column of most lists, *not* because they contain gluten—they don't, in and of themselves—but because they could, usually only in wet form, contain wheat as a binding agent, or "carrier." It's important to emphasize, though, that wheat is almost *never* used (those who have looked into it haven't found a company that uses it). Most manufacturers would list wheat if it was included as a carrier, but for now the FDA doesn't require it.

Spices, Herbs, Seasonings: Spices themselves do not contain gluten, but sometimes a filler, carrier, or anti-caking ingredient is added, and those can contain gluten. Most labels specifically name all of these additional ingredients, so you can determine whether they're gluten-free or not; if it's not clear, call the manufacturer to be sure. Spices do not contain gluten, but seasonings sometimes contain a carrier made from wheat or wheat starch.

Candy Bars Coated in Flour?

For years, some people have asserted that candy bars are questionable because they are, they claimed, coated in flour to prevent them from sticking to the packaging. According to Alison Bodor, Director of Technical and Regulatory Affairs at the National Confectioners Association/Chocolate Manufacturers Association, if a candy bar were to be coated in flour, the manufacturer would have to list it on the ingredients label.

"Any substance that contains one of the 'big eight' allergens (wheat, milk, fish, shellfish, eggs, peanuts, tree nuts, soy) must be labeled on the ingredient statement of a candy product or other food product," she explained. Bodor further clarified that if wheat flour were sprinkled on candy prior to wrapping, it might be considered a processing aid instead of an ingredient, and processing aids may be exempt from labeling, but not if they're one of the top eight allergens. Wheat flour, whether used as an ingredient or a processing aid, would have to be listed on the ingredients label. How sweet it is!

Yet Another Can of Worms: Is Less Than 100 Percent Gluten-Free Okay?

The correct answer is no, and as a respected spokesperson in the field of celiac awareness, I say that anything less than 100 percent gluten-free is not acceptable. But to expect, much less demand, perfection isn't reasonable, especially in light of the contamination issues we've pointed out that are a matter of fact, even with "safe" grains such as rice and corn.

Some people worry about contamination at manufacturing facilities, and avoid any products made at the same facilities as gluten-containing foods. While this is certainly a safe way to go, it may (or may not, if I may be so wishy-washy) be overkill. American companies have to follow Good Manufacturing Practice (GMP) regulations. GMPs are regulations issued by the Food and Drug Administration (FDA) as *minimum* requirements, and are used by pharmaceutical, medical device, and food manufacturers as they produce and test products that people use. Equipment and utensils must meet stringent guidelines on sanitation and cleanliness, and specific mention is made of contamination issues: "Food-contact surfaces shall be maintained to protect food from being contaminated by any source, including unlawful indirect food additives."[1]

Whether or not you choose to feel that these guidelines are acceptable safety measures is a personal judgment that you need to make.

Contamination: Is It an Issue?

It's only an issue if you breathe. Without a doubt, the risk of contamination exists in gluten-free foods. Contamination can occur in flour mills, processing plants and manufacturing facilities, bulk bins, and even when food is prepared or cooked. The opportunities for contamination abound. How to deal with it is a purely subjective matter.

I know of people who won't eat beef unless they know the cows were fed uncontaminated corn—no wheat—while they were living. I'm not making this up! And I have to say, I admire their diligence and determination to be as gluten-free as possible. But to the uninitiated, let me just tell you that, as far as gluten and wheat are concerned, there's no reason to avoid beef (just watch the seasonings).

It's important to be diligent, but in my opinion it's just as important for maintaining your sanity not to go overboard. Avoid obvious contamination risks such as bulk bins and fries cooked in oil that was used to deep-fry breaded foods. You can *see* the breading floating in that stuff—yes, it's contaminated!

The issue of contamination is the same for all grains, since for the most part, they're all made in the same types of mills (although there are some designated gluten-free grain facilities). So if you choose to avoid buckwheat or quinoa because they're reputed to have high contamination risks, you might want to avoid corn and rice, too.

Foods you eat *will* be contaminated. And as hard as you try, you *will* make mistakes. You may even cheat on purpose from time to time (although if you're tempted, you need to reread the section on what can happen to some people who continue to eat gluten). Someone who cooks for you will surely use the same knife to butter your toast as he used to butter the Wonder Bread. But don't live your life in a bubble to avoid the micron of gluten that may have found its way into otherwise gluten-free foods.

Beware of Jumping to Conclusions

When Tyler was six years old, his class went on a field trip to, of all places, a bagel shop to see how bagels were made. For some reason, I couldn't chaperone, so I was mortified to get a call from his teacher saying that he was violently ill, having thrown up several times.

As I rushed to pick him up, I cursed myself for letting him go—surely, all the flour dust floating around was the problem—and I reached deep into my guilt-ridden soul to berate myself for being a terrible mother and not attending the field trip.

When I got there, he was feeling great, and I was shocked to see a gluten reaction pass so quickly. As I took him from his teacher, I said, "I guess the flour was flying all around in there and made him sick."

"Oh, no," she said apologetically. "I guess I should have clarified on the phone. He got car sick, and was throwing up before we even arrived!"

Labeling and Labeling Laws

Shopping one day for pizza-makings, I absently picked up a package of pepperoni and, out of habit more than anything else, began reading the ingredients label. I thought I was hallucinating when I read "Gluten-Free" clearly marked on the label. I reread it seven or eight times, clutched it to my bosom like it was a prized possession, and danced my way through the store, stopping several people I didn't even know to show them the precious words inscribed on the package. I will forever have a fond spot in my heart for that thoughtful action by Hormel.

Many of us dream of products labeled clearly as being "gluten-free," and in some wild fantasies, we can even imagine a gluten-free logo that would be stamped on all allowable foods, which would, of course, then be displayed in the huge "gluten-free aisle" of all grocery stores. We're just not there yet, although thanks to some activists in the celiac community, we're getting closer.

In the United States, products that are more than or equal to 2 percent meat and poultry fall under the jurisdiction of the USDA. If they contain products other than meat and poultry, or if the meat or poultry has additives, for instance, the products (or additives) come under the regulations of the USDA *and* the FDA.

The USDA has clear-cut guidelines (Codes of Federal Regulations or CFRs) about natural flavorings and spices, and states clearly that hydrolyzed proteins, beef and poultry stocks (which can have gluten), and natural flavorings must clearly list their source, and that flavorings can only be listed as a flavoring if "there are no health concerns linked to them" (see **www.fsis.usda.gov**).

The FDA has some loopholes in its regulations, allowing wheat and other allergens to be added to ingredients in the form of carriers or other additives without clearly specifying their presence on labeling.

Representatives from the FDA are aware, however, that labeling laws should be more specific, and are working to improve the situation. During the summer of 2001, the FDA held a daylong workshop on labeling food allergens, specifically what are called the "big eight" allergens. These foods are said to cause 90 percent of allergic reactions. The list includes wheat, so efforts to effect better labeling of these allergens help those who have celiac disease as well as those with wheat allergies or intolerances. For celiacs, wheat, of course, is not the only problem, but it's a very big one.

Among those representing the wheat-free/gluten-free contingent was one of the most active and informed proponents of better labeling, Ann Whelan, editor/publisher of *Gluten-Free Living*. This independent publication contains articles designed to help readers make intelligent, safe decisions about the foods they purchase, in addition to general information of interest to celiacs or anyone else on a wheat-free or gluten-free diet. It's the best source of information on ingredients and food labeling.

Whelan summarized the proceedings and conclusions of the FDA meeting:[2]

Food labeling is not currently adequate enough for the needs of those who follow a gluten-free diet. One of the biggest stumbling blocks is modified food starch. Since the "food" is not specified, you must call the processor to see if it's safe. As it happens, most modified food starch is corn-starch, but there is no way to know for sure without calling.

Years ago, the FDA helped us out by regulating the labeling of what previously had been declared as "hydrolyzed plant protein" or "hydrolyzed vegetable protein," which often were indicated by HPP or HVP. The Administration said processors had to identify the vegetable or food in ques-tion, so you should read "hydrolyzed soy protein" or "hydrolyzed wheat protein," for example. If they would pass the same regulation for modified food starch, celiacs would be spared a lot of phone calls.

During the workshop held in the summer of 2001, the FDA was looking at three specific aspects of food labeling:

1. *Source or plain English labeling.*
2. *Use of advisory labeling such as "may contain peanuts."*
3. *Labeling of ingredients currently exempted from declaration (that is, common or usual names for flavorings, spices and colors, and incidental additives).*

At the workshop, representatives from consumer groups and industry discussed the three aspects, while officials from the FDA listened. There was every indication that the FDA would move forward in trying to put some of the recom-mendations from that meeting in effect.

Then the tragedies of September 11, 2001 happened, followed by anthrax scares, and better labeling was moved to the FDA back burner as concern for preventing bioter-rorism via the food supply moved front and center.

Celiacs, of course, are intensely interested in this issue, too. But until the FDA is able to redirect its efforts, we will be left to our own devices in figuring out what food labels mean and in calling food processors to ask them to explain their labels.

Fortunately, strictly on a volunteer basis, manufacturers have begun to clarify labeling, often specifying the source of the ingredient (for example, "modified *corn* starch" instead of "modified *food* starch").

Codex Alimentarius Commission

The Codex Alimentarius Commission, an international committee formed in 1962, acts as a united effort on behalf of the Food and Agriculture Organization (FAO) and the World Health Organization (WHO). Its mission is to ensure consumer protection as it pertains to food safety and quality by developing internationally agreed-upon standards and regulations based on scientific principles and fair trade practices. It currently encourages involvement by developing countries, but has active participation from the United States; Canada; and most European, Latin American, African, and Asian countries. Within the United States, Codex activities are coordinated by officials from the U.S. Department of Agriculture (USDA), the Food and Drug Administration (FDA), and the Environmental Protection Agency (EPA).

Codex has developed international standards for gluten-free foods that specify if a product has 500 parts per million (ppm) milligrams per kilogram (mg/kg) or less of gluten, it can be considered "gluten-free." New standards are being considered that would lower that limit to 200 ppm, which is what the United States follows. Canada has adopted a policy that considers 20 ppm "gluten-free," while 200 ppm and below is considered "low-gluten" or "gluten-reduced"; Sweden has proposed the same policy.

In Europe, this tolerance of some gluten (albeit very low levels) for celiacs is widely accepted, and a stamp of "Codex Alimentarius Quality" deems a product acceptable for people on a strict gluten-free diet. Codex-quality wheat starch, with a gluten content of less than 200 ppm, is used widely throughout Europe in "gluten-free" products. Studies have corroborated its safety for celiacs, but many scientists warn that they are skeptical of the long-term effects of wheat starch, and advise against its use.

By the way, the Codex commission hasn't categorized oats as being safe or unsafe, and is waiting for further studies.

Codex standards and contamination controversies aside, most experts agree that even a little bit of gluten can harm a celiac, especially if ingested on a regular basis. If you're a celiac and you do get gluten in your diet, if you're lucky, you'll feel terrible. That will help you pinpoint the culprit, and will serve as a friendly reminder the next time you're tempted to cheat. Those of you who have mild reactions or none whatsoever have a more difficult challenge finding and avoiding the bad stuff. All you can do is be as diligent as possible, use common sense, read labels carefully and frequently, show a lot of restraint, and live by your new motto: *When in doubt, leave it out.*

Home Testing Kits for Gluten/Casein Content in Food

For the more-than-ten years I've been doing this diet, I've been wondering, "Why can't we just *test* food for gluten? Either it has it or it doesn't!" It seemed so logical to have a test—you know, like the kind we used in junior-high chemistry class to test the pH of a particular liquid, or like a home pregnancy test.

Such a test *does* exist. Made by ELISA Technologies, it's fast, reliable, and highly sensitive, detecting levels of 100 to 200 ppm or less. The company has other testing methods in its lab that are even more sensitive, detecting levels down to 8 ppm; and the home test of the future may detect as little as 20 ppm.

The company's laboratory versions of the tests are called ELISA (enzyme-linked immunosorbent assay), and other ELISA tests are available for testing for casein, whey, peanuts, sesame, soy, and egg. Home versions for casein (milk protein) and peanut are in development and will be available in 2002.

The Gluten Home Test uses a format similar to a home pregnancy test. According to ELISA president Bruce Ritter, it is best used on foods that you think are gluten-free, but you're just not sure. "One example of how you might use this test is if you go out to dinner and the chef assures you the sauce is gluten-free, but you want to make sure before you eat it," said Ritter. "Another use would be to test 'gluten-free' products you have purchased for use in the home to see if they really are gluten-free."

The test is easy to do, and takes just over five minutes. The home kits offer three levels of detection. Very low gluten or gluten-free tells you the level is "not detectable," or below 100 to 200 ppm. If the sample contains "some" gluten, it is measured as "detectable," above 50 to 200 ppm. A third level indicates very high levels of gluten, above about 10 percent.

The test is considered most reliable when it detects gluten, rather than when it doesn't. If the test detects gluten, that's the end of the story. But if it doesn't detect any, you have to wonder about three possibilities: first, there's no gluten; second, the test missed it; or third, the gluten was destroyed, and whether or not it will be harmful to a celiac is uncertain.

At around $80 for a kit that includes five tests, it's probably not something you'll do before every meal. But in questionable situations, it's nice to know you have a way to check your food before you eat it.

Bathroom Items and Medications: A Peek in the Medicine Cabinet

We've given a lot of thought to the ingredients in the food items in our kitchen cabinets, but what about the things in our bathroom cabinets? It's important to pay attention to the ingredients in anything you put in your mouth, even if it's not what you'd typically think of as food.

Nutritional supplements: Many supplements, in an attempt to promote their wholesome goodness, declare "wheat-free" or "gluten-free" on the label. Ingredients are generally well defined, and there aren't usually many chemicals or preservatives added to the list of ingredients. If it's not labeled wheat- or gluten-free, check for questionable ingredients such as flavorings, stabilizers, and starch, and contact the manufacturer for clarification if necessary. Remember, wheat-free isn't the same as gluten-free.

Makeup, lotion, and hair-care products: Cosmetics are defined by the Federal Food, Drug, and Cosmetic (FD&C) Act as articles intended to be applied to the human body for cleansing, beautifying, promoting attractiveness, or altering the appearance without affecting the body's structure or functions. Included in this definition are skin-care creams, lotions, powders and sprays, perfumes, lipsticks, fingernail polishes, eye and facial makeup, permanent waves, hair colors, deodorants, baby products, bath oils, bubble baths, mouthwashes, and materials intended for use as a component of a cosmetic product.

Ingredients for these products are not required to undergo approval before they're sold to the public, and may contain gluten sources. The question, though, is, does it matter if someone who's sensitive to gluten uses hair and skin products with gluten in them?

The short answer is that there isn't a short answer. If the product is lipstick, or if you eat your shampoo or lotion, gluten as an ingredient can be ingested and cause a response. But gluten can't be absorbed through the skin, because the protein molecules in gluten are too large. People who have dermatitis herpetiformis, a form of celiac disease, may be an exception.

That's not to say that you won't have a response to topical lotions or makeups. People with celiac disease and people with allergies often have other sensitivities as well. Furthermore, some people are extremely sensitive, and millions of people—even those without wheat or gluten allergies and sensitivities—respond to these products. If you fall into one of those categories, it's a good idea to select products that are nontoxic and non-allergenic.

Toothpaste: You're not supposed to swallow your toothpaste, and if it's not ingested, it's not a problem for the type of sensitivities we've discussed throughout this book. But most people, especially children, use too much toothpaste, sometimes to the point of ingesting unsafe amounts of fluoride. If you're an enthusiastic paste user, and if you tend to swallow while you brush, you may want to be careful about the toothpaste you buy. Most toothpaste is gluten-free, but check with the manufacturer to make sure the type you're using doesn't have hidden sources of unsafe ingredients.

Your New Vocabulary

After reading this far, you're sure to be the hit of the party with all the cool new terms you can banter about, such as *villi, Codex Alimentarius Commission* (say that one after you've had a couple glasses of wine), and *antigliadin antibody response*. If you think that's impressive, your vocabulary will increase even more when you begin to read labels and discover the myriad unpronounceable ingredients contained in your food.

So while you may be able to impress your friends at parties by saying things such as, "Isn't it interesting that mono- and diglycerides assume different chemical structures in wet versus dry forms that actually alter their chemical composition?" it's important to learn alternate terminology for everyday foods, and to learn the names of foods you may never have heard of but can eat on the diet. Masa, for instance, refers to corn flour, and is gluten-free. Tamari is a type of soy sauce and is usually gluten-free (but not always; check the label for wheat). Milo is sorghum. Other allowable things you may not have heard of include tofu, kudzu, poi, chickpea, taro, groats, kasha, and glutinous rice (sticky rice; no gluten).

On the other hand, for stimulating party conversation, you might want to stick to sports. Or if sports don't float your boat and you're still looking for conversation clinchers, check out the next chapter, where you'll learn everything you ever wanted to know about grains, but didn't even know to ask.

Chapter 9

Grains:
Everything You Need to Know
and Didn't Even Know to Ask

"The flower is the poetry of reproduction.
It is an example of the eternal seductiveness of life."
— Jean Giraudoux

If you're an adventuresome eater, you're in for a treat. In searching for alternatives to wheat, rye, or barley, you'll discover a variety of wheat-free/gluten-free grains you may never have heard of before, many of them loaded with nutrients and robust flavors not found in typical American grains such as wheat and rice. If you're not the adventurous type, and you just long for the ease of a few tried-and-true favorites, you're sure to find them in the pages of this chapter.

Perhaps you fall into still another category . . . you've been eating a wheat- or gluten-free diet for a while and you think you already know everything there is to know. Okay, what's quinoa, and how the heck is it pronounced? Is teff wheat-free? Do Job's Tears have religious significance? If you don't know the answers to these questions, or if you think ragi is a spaghetti sauce and sorghum is what you get when you have your teeth cleaned, it's time to move on to lesson one.

Whole Grains: A Kernel of Truth

*Raise your right hand and repeat after me: I'll eat
the grain, the whole grain, and nothing but
the grain, so help me gluten.*

Fiber. Grains. Whole grains. What *is* all the hoopla about, anyway, and how do we know what's *really* important? While we've known for many years that fiber is a necessary part of our diets, we're learning that there's a lot more to whole grains than just their fibrous content. The latest research focuses on an array of vitamins, minerals, and phytonutrients (disease-fighting, protective substances) found in whole-grain foods.

What does *whole grain* mean? Just as the name implies, it's the entire edible part of a grain or seed. A grain consists of three parts: the germ, which is the sprout of a new plant; the endosperm, which is where the seed stores its energy (and where 90 percent of the protein is found); and the seed's outer layer, the bran, which contains most of the grain's nutrients and fiber. Whole-grain foods contain all three parts.

If whole-grain foods are at one end of the spectrum, "refined grains" are at the other end. Refined grains have been stripped of their bran and germ layers during processing. Even refined grains have fiber, and are assumed to be nutritionally valuable. But compared to whole grains, they're diminished in their nutritive value.

Some people believe that the individual components of whole grains—the vitamins, minerals, fiber, and disease-fighting phytochemicals—seem to work together to help protect against chronic diseases such as diabetes, heart disease, and certain cancers. The components appear to be synergistic, meaning that each individual component is important, but the value of the whole grain is greater than the sum of its parts.

Packed with vitamins, minerals, and fiber that you just don't find in plain white bread or white rice, whole grains are now being recognized by governmental agencies. The United States Department of Agriculture (USDA) came out with guidelines in 2000 that, for the first time, included a recommendation targeting whole grains.

It says, "Choose a variety of grains daily, especially whole grains." The Food and Drug Administration (FDA) extols the virtues of whole grains, too, citing the healthful nature of whole-grain products. If a product has 51 percent or more whole grains, its packaging can contain a statement that touts the positive role of whole grains in fighting heart disease and cancer.

While studies are relatively new, some credit whole grains with improving all sorts of health conditions. For people with diabetes, eating more whole grains can help control blood sugar levels and reduce fasting insulin levels. Whole grains may also help alleviate a syndrome called *insulin resistance,* in which the body's cells become desensitized to the effects of insulin. Eating more whole-grain foods has been credited with a lower incidence of type 2, or adult-onset, diabetes (this is not the same as the autoimmune disease, type 1 diabetes, associated with celiac disease). Whole grains are also an excellent source of phytonutrients, which are found in fruits and vegetables, but they're even more concentrated in whole-grain foods.

The indigestible fiber in whole grains helps keep bowel movements regular by contributing to stool bulk. The fiber also absorbs toxic and harmful molecules and eliminates them with the stool, providing them less opportunity to harm the bowels.

Getting enough whole grains is tough for anyone; estimates indicate that only 7 percent of Americans eat the recommended three servings per day. But it's especially tricky for someone on a wheat- or gluten-free diet, because wheat is *the* grain in most people's diets. Obviously, labels touting "100 percent wheat," "cracked wheat," "whole wheat," and "multigrain" are off-limits (and may not be whole-grain, anyway). When we cut those out, we turn to rice and corn, but where can we go from there? I'm so glad you asked.

Alternative Grains and Non-Grains

Even if you can't eat wheat, rye, barley, or oats, there are several other grains, fruits, and legumes that are not only acceptable alternatives to wheat, but they're loaded with flavor and nutrients. Brown rice is whole-grain and wholesome. Some of the lesser-known and often ancient grains and non-grains are great tasting, and particularly high in protein, vitamins, and minerals. With so many great alternatives available, there's no need to get stuck in a rut.

Here are some of the many choices available to you on a wheat- or gluten-free diet:

(WF = wheat-free; GF = gluten-free)

- Amaranth (WF/GF)
- Barley (WF)
- Buckwheat/groats/kasha (WF/GF)
- Cassava (arrowroot) (WF/GF)
- Chickpea (garbanzo) (WF/GF)
- Job's Tears (WF/GF)
- Millet (WF/GF)
- Montina (WF/GF)
- Oats (WF/GF, but oats in the United States can be contaminated with wheat and other grains)
- Quinoa (WF/GF)
- Ragi (WF/GF)
- Rice (WF/GF; only brown rice is whole grain)
- Sorghum (WF/GF)
- Soy (WF/GF)
- Tapioca (WF/GF)
- Taro root (WF/GF)
- Teff (WF/GF)

Many of the proteins found in these alternatives are a great source of complex carbohydrates. The fuel from these carbs, found in plant kingdom starches, produces what nutritionists call a protein-sparing effect, which means the body can meet its energy requirements without dipping into its protein reserves.

Several of these alternative grains and non-grains are high in lysine, an amino acid that controls protein absorption in the body.

Because this amino acid is absent from most grains, the protein fraction of those grains is utilized only if eaten in conjunction with other foods that *do* contain lysine. For example, the proteins from spelt, teff, wheat, and other grains are better utilized when eaten with high-lysine foods such as peas, beans, amaranth, or buckwheat. Remember, though, to be careful about the wheat or gluten content of the grain you're eating (that is, spelt is a form of wheat).

A Note about Spelt

Spelt is a type of wheat, but some people with wheat allergies claim to tolerate spelt better than wheat because it's more soluble than other types of wheat. They say that when ingested, the nutrients are quickly dissolved and easily absorbed. It should be noted that at least one grain expert has searched for evidence to substantiate these claims and has been unable to find any well-done studies to support them.

Amaranth (WF/GF): Loaded with fiber and more protein than any traditional grain, amaranth is nutritious and delicious, with a pleasant peppery flavor.

For centuries, the Aztec culture depended upon amaranth, and believed it had mystical powers. They believed that a single spoonful would bring strength and power to even the weakest of men. On holy days, Aztec women pounded amaranth with honey and human blood into a dough that they baked into the form of snakes, birds, and other animals. The Aztec ate these delicacies as a way of keeping their faith, strength, and fitness.

It was this spiritual ritual that caused the demise of amaranth for the Aztec. In 1521, Hernán Cortés, the Spanish conquistador, discovered the holy-day ritual and thought it blasphemous, a mockery of the Christian communion he'd been raised to revere. He commanded his troops to burn every square inch of amaranth that bloomed between the Gulf of California and the Bay of Campeche, and ordered them to cut off the hands of anyone found with a single seed in his possession.

The plant nearly vanished from the earth until 1972, when a botanical research team found wild amaranth growing in a remote region of Mexico. The researchers collected some seeds and took them to Pennsylvania, where they thrived and eventually made a comeback.

The name means "not withering," or more literally, "immortal." While it may not make you immortal, it *is* extremely healthful, especially with its high lysine and iron content.

Barley (WF): While barley is *not* gluten-free, it is well tolerated by people with *wheat* sensitivities. A hardy perennial, able to withstand drought, flood, frost, and pests, barley can be harvested from the upper reaches of the Arctic to the tropic plains of the equator. The Chinese, who seem to have been the first to discover most foods, are credited as being the earliest barley eaters, starting around 1520 B.C.

Each kernel of barley is protected by three layers of skin: two inedible husks and a delicate covering known as the aleurone, which protects the endosperm (or pearl). Polished or pearl barley, which consumers generally find on their grocery store shelves, is refined barley with the husks, aleurone, and embryo washed away, leaving only the endosperm. Sadly, most of barley's protein, fiber, and vitamins are found in the aleurone and washed away. But even polished barley has as much protein as a glass of milk, as well as substantial amounts of niacin, thiamin, and potassium.

If you think barleycorn is a malt drink that will give you a nasty hangover, you're only half right. Barleycorn was once a standard measure of length. In the early 14th century, a royal decree stated, "All metric units be standardized as one inch being equal to three grains of barleycorn, laid end to end." That same decree designated the running foot equal to 39 barleycorns, and the linear yard equal to 117 barleycorns. Interestingly, barleycorn remained the basis of all metric calibration in Great Britain and America for the next 400 years.

Most malt, by the way, is derived from barley, and must be avoided by people who are sensitive to gluten.

Buckwheat (groat; kasha) (WF/GF): It sounds as though it would be closely related to wheat, but buckwheat is not a wheat at all. In fact, it's not even a grain; it's a fruit of the *Fagopyrum* genus, a distant cousin of garden-variety rhubarb.

Its seed is the plant's strong point. The buckwheat seed has a three-cornered shell that contains a pale kernel known as a "groat." In one form or another, groats have been around since the 10th century B.C.

The first buckwheat groat blossomed in central Asia. Legends still abound in Manchuria of giants who roamed the earth, leaving mountains and valleys wherever their footprints fell, and who were nourished by seeds of night-flowering trees. Buckwheat was for centuries erroneously called "beech-wheat" in China because the seed was much like the nut of a flowering beech tree.

Europeans didn't taste buckwheat until the Middle Ages. It was a souvenir of Tartar raids on northern Europeans in the 1400s. The Dutch gave buckwheat its name in 1549 when they officially dubbed it *boek weit* (book wheat) to honor the Scriptures whose auspices, they claimed, brought it to flower on their shores. It's a simile not too far-fetched. Resistant to adversity, buckwheat thrives on poor soil and an inhospitable climate, and has been known to survive drought, frost, and even a flood from time to time.

It is only in recent history, since the rise of the health-food movement, that buckwheat farming has proven to be financially viable. Cultivated now from Maine to the Midwest, buckwheat is one of the hardiest fruits available.

Nutritionally, buckwheat is a powerhouse. It contains a high proportion of all eight essential amino acids, which the body doesn't make itself but are still essential for keeping the body functioning. In that way, buckwheat is closer to being a complete protein than any other plant source.

Whole white buckwheat is naturally dried and has a delicate flavor that makes it a good stand-in for rice or pasta. *Kasha* is the name given to roasted hulled buckwheat kernels. Kasha is toasted in an oven and tossed by hand until the kernels develop a deep tan color, nut-like flavor, and a slightly scorched smell.

Be aware that buckwheat is sometimes combined with wheat. Read labels carefully before purchasing buckwheat products.

Millet (WF/GF): Millet is said by some to be more ancient than any grain that grows. Where it was first cultivated is disputed, but native legends tell of a wild strain known as Job's Tears that grows in the Philippines and sprouted "at the dawn of time." We know it was also cultivated in ancient China, and was declared one of the country's five sacred crops. It was also cultivated in India and Africa, where it grew virtually all over the continent.

Millet is still well respected in Africa, India, and China, where it is considered a staple. Here in the United States, it is raised almost exclusively for hay, fodder, and birdseed. One might consider that to be a waste, when evaluating its high vitamin and mineral content. Rich in phosphorus, iron, calcium, riboflavin, and niacin, a cup of cooked millet has nearly as much protein as wheat. It is also high in lysine— higher than rice, corn, or oats.

Millet is officially a member of the *Gramineae* (grass) family and as such is related to montina.

Montina (Indian Rice Grass) (WF/GF): Indian rice grass was a dietary staple of Native American cultures in the Southwest and north through Montana and into Canada more than 7,000 years ago, even before maize (corn) was cultivated. Similar to maize, montina was a good substitute during years when maize crops failed or game was in short supply. It has a hearty flavor, and is loaded with fiber and protein.

Montina is currently grown as a reclamation species for range-land, roadside, and mining recovery projects. It is drought tolerant, although it can't be harvested with traditional harvesting equipment.

Quinoa ("KEEN-wah") (WF/GF): The National Academy of Science described quinoa as "the most nearly perfect source of protein from the vegetable kingdom."[1] Although new to North Americans, it has been cultivated in the South American Andes since at least 3000 B.C. Ancient Incas called this annual plant "the mother grain," because it was self-perpetuating and ever-bearing. They honored it as a sacred food product, since a steady diet appeared to ensure a full, long life; and the Inca ruler himself planted the first row of quinoa each season with a gold spade.

Like amaranth, quinoa is packed with lysine and other amino acids that make a protein complete. Quinoa is also high in phosphorus, calcium, iron, vitamin E, and assorted B vitamins. Technically a fruit of the *Chenopodium* herb family, quinoa is usually pale yellow in color, but also comes in pink, orange, red, purple, and black.

Quinoa's only fault is a bitter coating of saponins on its seeds. The coating comes off with thorough rinsing prior to cooking, and some companies have developed ways to remove the coating prior to delivering quinoa to stores.

The name, which is frequently mispronounced today, is ironically derived from a mispronunciation. According to Peruvian lore, it was the year 1532 when Francisco Pizarro and his army wandered into the Inca stronghold at Cuzco. Pizarro tasted a bowl of cooked quinoa, studied the plant's tall stalks and brilliant blossoms, and declared, *"Quimera!"* ("Fantastic!") The word was misheard—and misquoted—forever after.

Sorghum (milo) (WF/GF): Sorghum is another of the oldest known grains, and has been a major source of nutrition in Africa and India for years. Now grown in the United States, grain sorghum is generating excitement as a gluten-free insoluble fiber.

Because sorghum's protein and starch are more slowly digested than that of other cereals, it may be beneficial to diabetics and healthy for anyone. Sorghum fans boast of its bland flavor and light color, which don't alter the taste or look of foods when used in place of wheat flour. Many cooks suggest combining sorghum with soybean flour.

Soy and soybeans (WF/GF): Like the ancient foods mentioned at the beginning of this section, soy has been around for centuries. In China, soybeans have been grown since the 11th century B.C., and are still one of the country's most important crops. Soybeans weren't cultivated in the United States until the early 1800s, yet today are one of this country's highest yielding producers.

Soybeans are a legume, belonging to the pea family. Comprised of nearly 50 percent protein, 25 percent oil, and 25 percent carbohydrate, they have earned a reputation as being extremely nutritious. They're also an excellent source of essential fatty acids, which are not produced by the body, but are essential to its functioning nonetheless.

Teff (WF/GF): Considered a basic part of the Ethiopian diet, teff is relatively new to Americans. It made its way to the United States from Ethiopia by way of Wayne Carlson, a Peace Corps worker who spent a few years working in Ethiopia in the early 1970s. Carlson became accustomed to the flour and missed it when he returned home, so he began raising teff in southwestern Idaho near the Oregon border.

Five times richer in calcium, iron, and potassium than any other grain, teff also contains substantial amounts of protein and soluble and insoluble fiber. Considered a nutritional powerhouse, it has a sweet, nutty flavor. Teff grows in many different varieties and colors, but in the United States only the ivory, brown, and reddish-tan varieties can be found. The reddish teff is reserved for purveyors of Ethiopian restaurants, who are delighted to have an American source for their beloved grain.

Sprouted Grains

Some people believe that "sprouted grains" are gluten-free. Not true. The sprouting process sparks a chemical reaction that begins to break down gluten, so some people who are slightly sensitive to gluten may find that they can tolerate sprouted grains. But some of the peptides that are reactive for celiacs are still present, so sprouted grains are not safe for people with celiac disease or severe gluten intolerance.

Oats Notes

Today hailed as practically a miracle food, oats have had quite a cross to bear in terms of having a bad reputation. Once considered a food for the poor, oats flourished in lackluster soil where wheat and barley couldn't live, and were given to the poor in beggars' bowls.

Oats were even shunned by the medieval middle class, lest the stamp of poverty be cast(e) (that's a pun) upon them. But if strength is a virtue, oats began to rise above in the fifth century A.D., when Attila the Hun allegedly fed his barbarian troops only soups of oats, which apparently turned them as fierce as tigers.

And it's no wonder. Loaded with seven B vitamins, vitamin E, and nine minerals including calcium and iron, oats are also relatively high in protein and easily digested. Their composition of highly soluble fiber substantially helps to lower cholesterol levels in the blood, and oats are even hailed by the American Cancer Institute as having this power.

One reason oats are so healthy is because nothing but their inedible hull is removed. The bran and germ are retained in the edible kernel, or groat (which has nothing in common with buckwheat groats). In spite of their healthful benefits, oats are underappreciated as a food for humans; 85 percent of oat crops in the United States are still used as livestock feed.

Oats come in several different varieties, including the following:

- *Scotch or Irish oats (also called Steel-Cut):* These organic, unrefined oats are dried, rough-sliced, and processed with virtually no heat, so they retain most of their original B vitamins. They are a little bit chewy, so they usually require longer cooking times.

- *Rolled oats (old-fashioned):* Rolled oats are made by slicing raw oats into a confetti-like mixture that is steamed and then rolled into flakes and dried. They are thick and chewy.

- *Quick oats:* These are basically the same as commercial rolled oats in the way they're processed, but sliced finer and rolled into thin flakes over a heat source, which precooks them a bit. Producing them this way saves time in the kitchen.

- *Instant oats:* This is a faster, express variety of the preprocessed type. Only boiling water is needed to reconstitute them.

The oat found its way here in 1602 via a British sea captain who was retiring in the American colonies. He settled off the coast of Massachusetts on one of the Elizabeth Islands, and farmed for the rest of his life, planting fields of oats that survived the brutally cold Atlantic winters and kept well in his silo for the rest of the year. Colonists followed his example and planted oats, too, and the rest, as they say, is history.

R$_X$: Oats

For some reason, oats have long been used as a homeopathic treatment for a variety of maladies. Today, even American pediatricians (not often the champions of homeopathic treatments) often prescribe an oatmeal (Aveeno) bath for chicken pox and other itchy skin conditions such as eczema.

Other parts of the world are much more creative. The Russians believe equal parts of hot oatmeal and hot dry mustard will keep away pneumonia. The Scottish make a lotion of oats and rosewater for rough hands and knobby knees. In the Swiss Alps, oats and cream are pounded to a paste and spread on the body to keep away snow burns. The Japanese believe that cold oatmeal forced into the nostrils will stop a nosebleed (it probably will). In Rio de Janeiro, the women make a facial mask of oatmeal cooked in wine to cleanse the pores. Germans, whose proficiency in beer brewing sends them searching for the ultimate hangover remedy, believe that a healthy meal of oatmeal and fried onions will do the trick. And the French chew oats straight from the fields to sweeten their breath after eating garlic.

Feeling Your Oats

Few topics have been more hotly debated in the gluten-free community than the subject of whether or not oats should be allowed on the gluten-free diet (well, okay, there's vinegar, but we've already discussed that).

For years, oats were thought to contain gluten, but upon closer examination, it was discovered that they do not contain the peptides that harm celiacs and people with gluten intolerance. In the last chapter, you learned that the prolamin portion (gliadin) of gluten's protein molecule harms people with this sensitivity. Oats have a small prolamin (avenin) that does not elicit the same immune response as gliadin. End of controversy, right? Not by a long shot.

Studies on whether or not oats cause damage to celiacs have been conducted, with cautious yet relatively consistent results. In March 2000, Finnish researchers reported that oats elicited no immunological response in people with celiac disease.[2] They watched for both antibody response and intestinal damage, and found no indications of either when celiacs ingested oats. They did note, however, that "more clinical studies are needed to ensure the safety of oats when consumed permanently in a coeliac diet as well as to determine the effect of larger amounts of oats."

The Finnish study was corroborated by a study conducted by Ed Hoffenberg, M.D., and colleagues at the University of Colorado School of Medicine in Denver.[3] Hoffenberg looked at children who were newly diagnosed with celiac disease, and concluded that short-term consumption of commercially available oat cereal is safe for children with celiac disease who are new to the gluten-free diet. This team also emphasized, however, that the long-term effects of celiac children who eat oats still needs to be determined.

Personally, I find it interesting that they found the oatmeal to contain gluten, yet still concluded there were no deleterious effects on celiacs (keep in mind this was short-term consumption).

The Denver study also tested several samples of oats to see if they contained gluten. The results indicated trace amounts in most samples tested:

Irish oatmeal	0.006 percent
Quaker oatmeal	0.006 percent
Safeway oatmeal	0.005 percent
Jane Lee oatmeal	0.026 percent
Soy flour	0.001 percent
Brown rice flour	0.000 percent
Cornmeal	0.000 percent
Rice flour	0.000 percent

If, as we said earlier, oats don't technically contain gluten, where did these trace amounts come from? Since oats in the United States are often harvested and milled with wheat, they are at risk of contamination during several steps of production, starting with where they're grown. Crop rotation means that oats are usually grown in the same fields that grew wheat, barley, or rye in previous years. Anyone who has had a garden knows that "volunteers" from a previous crop often appear the following year amidst the current crop. Most mills have machines that sort the grains after harvest, though, and they separate the volunteers out.

The next point of possible contamination is in the grain-processing facilities, where several different types of grains are usually handled at once. Residues of one grain are often left in the equipment as the next batch passes through; some mills have equipment that can separate out even small amounts of contamination, while others do not.

One of the best discussions on the contamination issue that I've seen can be found on **www.celiac.com**, where Scott Adams analyzes information provided to him by Can-Oat Milling, one of the largest oat mills in North America. The mill's data indicates that they find between 2.1 and 4.1 kernels of barley or wheat in every 4,000 flakes of oats (0.0525 percent and 0.1025 percent, respectively). Legally, that level can go to a maximum of 10 kernels per 4,000 flakes (0.25 percent).

If you're on a wheat-free or gluten-free diet, the question of "to oat or not to oat" is a personal one, and a decision to be made only after you feel you're fully informed on both sides of the argument.

Contamination issues aside, now that you know what you can and can't eat, you're ready to put your money where your mouth is and go food shopping. The next chapter will teach you to save time and money at the grocery store, and will offer tips for getting your kitchen and pantry in order—to ensure that the foods you eat will optimize, not compromise, your health.

Chapter 10

Ready, Set, Shop!
Preparing Your Kitchen and
Stocking Your Shelves

"Better to light a candle than curse the darkness."
— Chinese proverb

If you're whining for wheat, or were a glutton for gluten, you're probably pining for pasta right about now. Hang in there. Before you can eat, you need to learn how to shop for your new lifestyle. That means knowing how to confirm that the products you buy are safe for you, and finding the best deals on specialty foods. You'll also need to organize your pantry and kitchen so you don't inadvertently contaminate everything you eat. You've worked this hard to feel better; now take the time to ensure that what you eat is truly wheat- or gluten-free.

Reading Labels

> General rule of thumb: The chance that a product
> is wheat- or gluten-free is inversely proportional
> to the number of ingredients it has.

Before you embark upon your first wheat-free/gluten-free shopping trip, it's important to know how to decode product labels. Reading ingredient labels on food products can be informative, enlightening, question-provoking, confusing, frustrating, time-saving, time-consuming—all in one. Furthermore, sometimes it's downright scary to see what's in the foods you eat. But for people who are serious about eliminating wheat or gluten from their diets, label reading is not an option, it's a skill to be honed and used all too often.

Reading labels may seem intimidating at first, especially since most processed foods contain all sorts of multisyllablic ingredients that you've probably never heard of, containing far more "y's" than the average word. (Most of those, by the way, are chemicals, and you'll be relieved to find many of them on the safe list.) Never fear; you'll get used to them, and before you know it, you'll be picking up a product, absently flipping it to the ingredients label, and scanning it for forbidden ingredients—all while you make mental note of how much you can save with your double coupons.

The key to efficient label reading is knowing what you're looking for. If you think you're looking for terms such as *wheat-free* or *gluten-free,* you're sadly mistaken (that's cute, though, in a naïve sort of way). No, unfortunately, foods are rarely marked that clearly. Your objective is to find out whether any of the ingredients contain wheat or gluten.

The safe and forbidden ingredients list in an earlier chapter is a good guide for reading labels. I recommend that you print a copy (or get a recent version directly from **www.celiac.com**), and take it with you when you shop. Then, when you encounter ingredients you've never heard of, you can look them up and, if necessary, call the manufacturer.

Calling Manufacturers

Before you start calling manufacturers, be sure to carefully read the label. If there's an obviously unsafe ingredient, don't waste your time or theirs. But if you've read the label and you have any questions, it's a good idea to call the manufacturer to confirm that there are no hidden sources of wheat or gluten.

Ten years ago, when we called manufacturers and asked them if their products were gluten-free, they would either suspect us of making a crank call and hang up; leave us on hold for 35 minutes while they "checked" (a euphemism for when they put you on hold and hope you hang up); or respond with a confident, "Oh, no, honey, there's no sugar whatsoever!"

Fortunately, most product labels include a toll-free phone number. Even more fortunately, today's customer-service representatives actually know what we're talking about most of the time, and can offer a knowledgeable answer that instills confidence in its accuracy.

When you call a company to find out if its product is wheat- or gluten-free, you'll generally get one of four responses.

1. *"No, our product is not wheat-free/gluten-free."* Do not take this as meaning, "No, our product is not wheat-free/gluten-free." I realize that's what they said, but it may not be what they mean. Probe deeper by asking, for example, "Can you tell me what in your product has gluten in it? I read the label and didn't see anything questionable." One time when I asked this, the woman told me it was whey that contained gluten. Penalty flag! Whey doesn't contain gluten! This is when you need to realize you're talking to someone who doesn't understand the concept, and you should ask to be transferred to a quality control supervisor.

Sometimes the "No, our product is not gluten-free" response is accurate, and either an ingredient wasn't clearly called out on the label (unfortunately, this is still legal), or you were calling about a questionable ingredient only to find out it's a good thing you called.

2. *"We can't verify its status."* Translation: "It's wheat-free/gluten-free, but we're covering our rear ends because we don't want someone to get sick and sue us after they eat our product."

Of course, this response could actually mean what it says—that they can't verify the status. Usually they'll tell you it's because they get their additives from other sources, and even though the supplier says it's gluten-free, Company A doesn't want to be responsible in case Company B used gluten. The risk factor in either case is probably low.

Every now and then, this response is given because the company has an "If we tell you what's in our product, we'll have to shoot you" mentality. Assure them that you're not trying to steal their secret-sauce formula, but that you have a serious medical condition that requires you to know if there are certain ingredients in the food you eat.

Sometimes you just can't get an answer, in which case you fall back to the golden rule: *When in doubt, leave it out.*

3. *"Yes, it is wheat-free/gluten-free."* You probably guessed that this doesn't necessarily mean, "Yes, it is wheat-free/gluten-free." You have to judge for yourself whether or not the person on the other end of the phone truly understand the concept. Sometimes they'll follow it up with, "There are no sources of wheat, rye, barley, or oats, and there are no questionable additives. Therefore, it's safe for someone with wheat allergies, gluten intolerance, or celiac disease." Ah, you just want to *kiss* those people.

Other times, when pressed, they get squirmy. If you say, for instance, "Oh, okay, then I can assume the modified food starch is derived from a non-gluten source?" and they give you an audible "blank stare," you might want to dig a little deeper before trusting their answer.

4. *"Huh?"* Fortunately, this isn't a common response anymore, but it does happen. Politely try to explain what types of ingredients might be in the product you're calling about, and if it still doesn't "click," ask to speak to a quality-control supervisor or nutritional expert.

Of course it's helpful and sometimes necessary to be specific in some cases, saying, "I'm calling to see if this product is gluten-free, which means it doesn't contain wheat, rye, or barley." Not only is this clarification helpful, but you may have educated one more person about gluten.

Many times, there's a benefit to calling, even if the product you were calling about turns out *not* to be okay: Some manufacturers will offer to send you a list of their wheat-free/gluten-free products (sometimes they even toss in a few coupons). Always take them up on it, and save the lists for future reference. Finally, here are four key things to remember about calling manufacturers:

- *Tune in to the person on the other end of the phone:* Do they sound like they understand what you're talking about? Are they giving you conflicting information? Can you trust what they say?

- *Learn from the answers:* If the label contained an ingredient that you had never heard of and wasn't on the safe or forbidden list, and you talked with a knowledgeable customer-service representative who told you the product was gluten-free, take note. That means the *ingredient* is gluten-free, too. Add it to your copy of the safe and forbidden list, and remember it for future label-reading experiences.

- *Appreciate their efforts:* Excuse me for a moment while I put on my Miss Manners hat, but it's important to be polite, professional, and appreciative when you call manufacturers. Not only will you get much better service, but we *need* them! We need them to know the gravity of our questions, and how important it is to be 100 percent sure that the answers they give us are accurate. We need them to understand that they can't guess at their answers, and that we very much appreciate it when they understand what we ask.

- *Call manufacturers frequently:* Not only is this a good habit for you, since ingredients change frequently, but it sends companies the message that if their labeling was clarified, we wouldn't bother them so often. It also tells them that millions of people avoid wheat or gluten, and maybe they'll think twice before using an ingredient that has a wheat source when they could use one that is wheat- and gluten-free.

While you're calling manufacturers, you might want to call some of the companies that make over-the-counter medications (see Resource Directory). When it's 3 A.M. and your four-year-old has an ear infection and a fever of 103, it's not the time to be wondering if the medications you have in the house are wheat- or gluten-free.

The Internet Is Your Friend

> Give a man a fish, and you'll feed him for a day.
> Teach a man to use the Internet, and he
> won't bother you for days.

The Internet plays a prominent role in the lives of people on a wheat- or gluten-free diet. From an educational standpoint, it provides up-to-date access to medical information, the latest research, new and proven products, and even other people's opinions of those products.

Shopping for specialty food products on the Web is efficient, and you can't beat the selection, not to mention the thrill of being able to do it in your jammies. Shopping online isn't exactly cheap, but in most cases, it's no more expensive than buying those same products from a health-food store, and it's a heck of a lot more convenient.

The Internet offers several "Listserv" groups (e-mail mailing lists you can subscribe to, which have a special-interest focus), chat sites, and Web rings for specialty audiences such as people with allergies or celiac disease. By joining these lists and sites, you can discover products you may not have known about, and find out where to buy them. There are also discussions on the conditions themselves, and lifestyle challenges and situations. Some of these lists and sites are listed in the Resource Directory at the end of this book.

A brief word of caution: Don't believe everything you read on the Internet. Anyone can build a Website, and there are absolutely no restrictions on what is posted to it. Most Listservs are well monitored by list owners, but they can't filter out opinion, so much of what you read is just that, and should be taken with a grain of gluten-free salt (yes, *all* salt is gluten-free). There are several excellent Websites; some trusted sites include the following:

General information	**www.celiac.com**
Celiac Disease Foundation	**www.celiac.org**
Celiac Sprue Association	**www.csaceliacs.org**
Gluten Intolerance Group	**www.gluten.net**

Raising Our Celiac Kids	**www.celiackids.com**
Celiac listserv	**celiac@maelstrom.stjohns.edu**
Food allergies;	
support and education	**www.allergysupport.org**

"Shop Till You Drop" Takes on a Whole New Meaning

Face it. Your days of dashing into the grocery store, flipping through your coupon organizer as you quickly calculate whether the double coupon or generic-no-coupon is a better deal, planning your menu as you proceed through the aisles, and blindly grabbing card-member-only-specials off the shelves—all in the 20 minutes before you have to pick the kids up from school—are long gone.

Well, okay, they're not really "long gone," they're just not going to be typical of your shopping experience—at least until you find brands of products you like, develop menu plans that work for your family, and learn where to shop for what.

The newly initiated may literally spend hours reading labels during the first few shopping excursions. Don't despair; it will soon become habit to pick up an item and—someday this part will require absolutely no conscious effort on your part—flip it to the ingredients label where you'll peruse it for safe, forbidden, and questionable ingredients.

"When my daughter was first diagnosed with wheat allergies and I realized that wheat is hidden in everything, I thought I'd never find foods that she could eat. When I did find something she'd eat (and she liked, which was tougher yet), I'd save the label in a notebook and bring it with me to the grocery store. Keeping a binder of labels from foods that are safe was a lifesaver for me as we first got started on the wheat-free diet."
— Deb S.

Major Grocery Stores Are Still Your Best Bet

Surprised? Don't be. Most of your shopping can and should be done at a major grocery store. Many people assume that health-food stores or specialty shops are best for buying wheat-free/gluten-free products because *those* stores carry brands that are labeled as such. That may have been true at one time, but these days, those "healthy" brands are often available in the health-food aisles of most major grocery stores.

By the way, don't think you have to buy "healthy." If you're a carob-instead-of-chocolate type person anyway, that's fine—you can choose to shop at health-food stores, and there's nothing wrong with that, if you can swallow the price tags. But don't think that because of this diet you *have* to shop in those places.

Besides being more convenient and economical (do we need more reasons than that?), there is what I believe to be an important psychological reason for shopping at "regular" grocery stores. This diet can seem somewhat isolating at times, at least if you allow it to. (Hopefully by the time you're finished with this book, it won't be the least bit isolating.) Being able to shop at a "regular" store and buy "regular" brands that everyone else buys is important psychologically. If you have kids, it's ten times as important, because everyone knows that conforming is important to kids (yes, they do dye their hair orange in an attempt to be unique, but only because all their friends are doing it!). If they can eat the same brand of chips or chocolate as their friends, it will help make them feel more "normal," which to kids ranks right up there with breathing, in terms of importance.

Major brands are manufactured by large companies that provide clear and specific labeling (improving by the day), and that usually put their toll-free number on the packaging. Which brings me to an important shopping rule: Bring your cell phone with you. That way, when you're trying to decide whether or not to buy the frozen potato skins that have modified food starch, you can pick up the phone and call, asking the source of their starch.

Important Shopping Rule: Bring your cell phone with you.

All of the major grocery chains have Websites (the addresses are usually very intuitive, such as **www.[nameofstore].com**), and many of those sites list their wheat-free/gluten-free products. If your favorite grocery store has such a listing, print it out and take it with you when you shop.

Most grocery stores are open to input from customers about products they'd like to see carried. Talk to your store manager about carrying some of your favorite specialty mixes or breads. You might be pleasantly surprised by the response you get.

Generics

Sometimes people assume that generics are off-limits on this diet. Nope. Most of the time, generics are as clearly labeled as major brands, and sometimes they even have a toll-free number you can call to be sure. Usually, though, they're labeled as being "distributed by" a grocery chain or other large middleman company, and with just a little digging, you can find someone to talk to who knows about the ingredients.

Sometimes nutritional experts from large grocery stores can tell you more about their "store brands." I was once told by a large grocery chain that *all* of their modified food starch was derived from corn. That piece of information was a huge help, because oftentimes the only questionable ingredient on a label is modified food starch.

Expand Your Ethnic Eating Horizons

Some cultures' indigenous foods are, for the most part, gluten-free. Thai food, for instance, is mostly allowable on this diet, with the exception of some questionable sauces (including soy) and some noodles. Primarily, though, they use 100 percent rice noodles, and fish sauce instead of soy sauce. Most Vietnamese soy sauce is gluten-free, although you still need to check labels carefully (and most labels are written in English in addition to the native language).

One of the most thrilling shopping experiences I've ever experienced was at a Vietnamese grocery store, where aisles were loaded with rice noodles in every size, shape, and variety; soy sauce and other marinades that use a wheat-free/gluten-free soy sauce base; cookies made with rice paper; desserts made from rice or corn; and all at prices a fraction of what I'd pay just a few miles away at the American grocery stores (although what they do with those huge live toads, I do *not* want to know).

Japanese food is also relatively low in gluten, and some Japanese soy sauces do not contain wheat (but others do, so be careful). People in some parts of Italy eat polenta (corn) instead of pasta, so many Italian recipes and restaurants feature this food, which is safe for wheat-free/gluten-free diets. Much Mexican food is safe, as is a lot of Indian food.

Product Listings and Guides

With a little bit of effort, you can create your own product listing of safe foods. The advantage to creating the list yourself is that you include the foods you like and that are readily available to you, as opposed to foods someone else has checked into, or those that stores in your area of the country don't carry.

When you call a manufacturer and determine that a product is wheat-free/gluten-free, add it to your product listing. It's a good idea to include the toll-free number you called, as well as the date, and if they send you an entire listing of their wheat-free/gluten-free products, add those to your list, too. The national support groups and listserv will appreciate it if you notify them as well.

You can find product guides with listings already compiled online at various Websites, and you can purchase printed handbooks of product listings through the support organizations. You can even program large databases into your Palm Pilot or other handheld computers, as well as bar-code scanning software linked to databases of gluten-free products (see the Resource Directory).

Shopping Tips

While shopping may seem more cumbersome and challenging at first, there are some things you can do to make it easier and more efficient:

- Bring your cell phone into the store.

- Don't go if you're rushed.

- Make a list; plan menus before you get to the store.

- Keep a binder of labels from foods that you like and that are safe; bring it with you when you shop.

- Bring a product guide or list you've created when you shop.

- Don't trust "trusted brands"; ingredients change.

- When you get home, use a permanent marker to mark foods "WF" or "GF" (wheat-free or gluten-free).

Ask for advice before spending too much money on specialty foods. Consult your local support group, or other people who have tried the products first, to see if they have opinions on which products are best. Remember, the early bird may get the worm, but the second mouse gets the cheese.

Shopping Online, by Phone, and in Specialty Stores

There are some foods that you probably can't get at your local grocery store, at least not yet. Wheat-free/gluten-free prepared breads, cookies, pizzas, bagels, and pretzels; pizza crusts; and mixes for pancakes, cookies, cakes, muffins, and other baked goods usually aren't available in major grocery stores.

These foods are best bought online, by phone, or at a health-food store, and frankly, these days they're so good that they're well worth the extra expense. If your local health-food store doesn't carry the mixes you order online or by phone, ask them to consider carrying them. Most are very cognizant these days of the importance of a wheat-free or gluten-free diet for many people, and will gladly stock your favorites, saving you shipping expenses.

The Resource Directory lists contact information for dozens of companies that provide wheat-free/gluten-free products by phone, online, and by mail.

Stock Up

When you find brands of safe foods you enjoy, stock up. Not only will this help you avoid the frustration if product ingredients change, rendering the food no-longer-okay, but it saves you time and money searching for good foods. If you're ordering foods online or by phone, you may also get quantity discounts and cheaper shipping costs by buying more.

Money-Saving Tips

There's no doubt that specialty foods, including those that are wheat-free/gluten-free, are more expensive than "regular" foods. A small loaf of gluten-free bread, for instance, can cost more than four dollars, whereas a loaf of bread in a grocery store starts at around a dollar. Before you take a second mortgage on your home to finance your special diet, consider these money-saving ideas:

- Shop at major grocery stores instead of specialty or natural foods stores.
- Buy generics.
- Get advice on which products are better than others so you don't spend a lot of money on products that no one likes.
- Stock up, especially if buying online or by phone.
- Make your own bread.
- Use mixes; you may toss a lot of bad experiments if you don't.
- If you *do* cook from scratch, buy flours in bulk (from a safe source; beware of bulk bins).

- If you buy flours in bulk, look into co-op opportunities in your area.

- Don't always buy specialty items; a lot of commercially available items are gluten-free, even if the label doesn't say so.

Don't worry; shopping for wheat-free/gluten-free products will get easier. Soon you'll have favorite snack items, routine menus, and brands you know are safe—or at least were the last time you checked. And just think of the time you'll save not having to go down the cookie and cracker aisle!

Your Pantry: It's Tidy Time

It may not be time for spring cleaning, but now that you've brought home your wheat-free/gluten-free groceries, it *is* time to organize the pantry. To someone on a restricted diet, a pantry full of food can look like a pantry off-limits, even if it's actually well stocked with a variety of safe alternatives.

Of course, if you live alone and never have guests, your pantry may not be an issue. You're probably not out buying Wonder Bread, anyway. But if you have a "blended" family, with one or some on a restricted diet and others not, or if you plan to entertain others and provide them with foods that you can't eat, you should organize your pantry so it has a "safe" side and a side for everyone else.

Not only will this make it easy to grab a quick snack, but it will eliminate confusion if other people less familiar with the diet offer to help prepare your meals, and it will reduce the chances of contamination. Be sure to allow plenty of room, because you'll probably find that the safe side is fuller than the side that's off-limits.

Mark-a-Lot: Go Crazy with Permanent Markers

Permanent markers can have an important—albeit less-than-aesthetic—role in the home of someone on a restricted diet. They're especially helpful if you have kids, since clearly marking food, storage areas, and kitchen tools will eliminate any questions and reduce the risk for accidents. Don't be shy, even if your spouse *does* cringe—live it up and go crazy with the permanent markers.

You might want to start in the pantry you just organized. Clearly label the safe side, so there's never any question about what's safe and what's not. Marking food is a great way to label it for others who might be in your kitchen, or to remember yourself. If you call a manufacturer about a product and find that it's gluten-free, mark it up! If you already know that a product is gluten-free, but others in your home prepare meals and they need to know, too, mark it up!

Permanent markers are important for labeling cooking tools in the kitchen, too. The best way to keep your wheat-free/gluten-free tools separate from other tools in the kitchen is to mark them with a permanent marker.

The Kitchen

If your entire family is following the wheat-free/gluten-free diet, I'm going to assume your kitchen is safe, since there wouldn't likely be any wheat or gluten in it. But most families are blended, with some members on the diet and others who are not. If that's the case in your home, it's vitally important that you take precautions in the kitchen to avoid contaminating the wheat-free/gluten-free foods.

The most important thing to know about sharing a kitchen with gluten is that cleanliness is fundamental. Crumbs are enemy number one. Too often I've seen people work really hard to prepare a beautiful gluten-free meal, only to set the sandwich down in a pile of "regular" crumbs. All that effort for naught.

It's no longer about you against the ants, because they're "so last week," to quote my young daughter. Crumbs are a thing of the past in the safe kitchen, as are used utensils and less-than-clean pots and pans. Cleanliness isn't an option anymore; it's essential to improving and maintaining your health.

Spreadables and the Gob Drop

No, it's not the latest pop music group. "Spreadables" are the things in your kitchen that you spread by knife, usually onto bread or other wheat/gluten food products such as crackers, pita bread, and tortillas. Spreadables include margarine, jellies and jams, mustard, mayonnaise, and other products in containers that you dip into before spreading. The problem with spreadables is that most people are double-dippers. Have you ever looked into your margarine container? For most people, it's a container full of toast crumbs mixed with a little bit of margarine.

Most people are in the habit of dipping a knife into a container, taking a bit of a spreadable, spreading it on the "spreadee," and taking another gob or two, repeating the process throughout. The problem, obviously, is that each time you spread the knife onto "regular" bread (or cracker, tortilla, etc.), crumbs get a free ride right back into the container, contaminating the entire tub or jar. As they say, one bad apple spoils the bunch.

The first thing you need to do is toss all the spreadables you have in your fridge and buy new ones, clearly marking them "WF" or "GF" (wheat-free or gluten-free) with your new friend, the permanent marker. Some people choose to buy squeeze bottles instead of tubs, thereby eliminating the problem of knife contamination (even cream cheese comes in a squeeze bottle now). Others choose to buy duplicate spreadables: one that's dedicated as being safe, and one that can be used by people not on a restricted diet (speaking of restricted diets, keep in mind that many spreadables contain lactose).

Still others choose to do what I call the "gob drop." It's a simple procedure, really. Just insert the knife, get a gob of the spreadable, and drop it onto the bread. If you need more, be sure to take it *before* spreading the first gob, or you'll defeat the purpose. A variation on the gob drop involves two knives: one is the scooper, the other the spreader. Either way is fine, as long as the spreader doesn't go back into the spreadable.

If your entire household is wheat-free/gluten-free, then it's not an issue. Crumbs found in the spreadables won't contaminate anything. But this isn't a good idea if you have a blended household in which some people eat wheat-free or gluten-free and others don't. You'll always wonder whether those crumbs are "good" or "bad," and you can guess the rule on this one: When in doubt, toss it out. After sacrificing a few jars of newly opened mayo at more than a dollar a pop because you're uncertain which type of crumbs are in there, you'll realize it's easier to just learn the gob drop.

Just say no to double-dipping!

Tips for Safely Sharing a Kitchen

Crumbs are enemy number one: It's important enough to say over and over again. Keep a clean sponge handy, because you'll be wiping up more than ever. You know the neat-freaks on those television shows who drive you nuts? Felix Unger of *The Odd Couple* may pop into your mind, or Monica on *Friends,* if you're of a younger generation; either way, take notes, because that's you now.

Toasters/toaster ovens: I recommend using a toaster oven (as opposed to a toaster), because it's more versatile. Since not everyone is on this diet, you'll sometimes find yourself cooking small quantities of food (for example, just a few taquitos), and the oven/broiler feature comes in handy. Whether you use a toaster or a toaster oven, it's a good idea to have a separate one for your wheat-free/gluten-free foods. Toasters and toaster ovens are absolute crumb havens, and no matter how clean you are and how diligent you promise to be, there's no way you can clean all the crumbs out. Mark one of the toaster ovens with a permanent marker so there's never any confusion or accidents. If you choose not to invest in a separate toaster or toaster oven, carefully wipe the toasting grill before cooking your gluten-free goodies.

Wheat-free/gluten-free first: Get in the habit of making the "special" foods first. For instance, if you're making a gluten-free grilled cheese sandwich and a "regular" one, make the gluten-free one first; that way, you'll need only one pan. If you make the "regular" one first, you'll either have to thoroughly wash the pan in between, or get another one dirty. Remember to make enough the first time, too. Just when you finish contaminating the pan with the "regular" sandwich, your gluten-free eater will ask for seconds.

Aluminum foil is your friend: Prepare to use more aluminum foil than you're used to. It's safest to cook on aluminum foil and throw it away when you can. Foil is also good for separating the different types of food you're cooking, and it's easy to clearly identify different foods by writing on aluminum foil with your friend the permanent marker.

Pots, pans, utensils, and tools: You don't need separate pots and pans, especially if yours have a good nonstick finish that washes clean easily. You should, however, have separate colanders and pasta servers, because pasta leaves a residue that can build up and prove hard to remove, even with a thorough washing (it does, however, come off nonstick pots and pans). Remember to clearly mark the gluten-free colanders and servers with—you guessed it—your permanent marker.

Use bright labels to mark leftovers: Brightly colored labels (available in office supply stores) are great to stick on containers of leftovers to clearly mark which ones are wheat-free/gluten-free.

Don't forget the gob drop: This is an extremely important practice, since double-dipping can contaminate an entire container in one fell swoop.

Vacuum sealers: Products that vacuum-seal foods are not just fun to use, they'll also save you time and money. Homemade foods don't have preservatives, so they don't last as long as store-bought foods. Vacuum sealers extend the life of the food, and better prepare it for freezing. They also make it easy to individually package foods for extra convenience and a lower risk of contamination.

Freezing is your friend, too: Because some of these foods take more time, energy, and money to prepare, you may find yourself coveting them, and angrily shooing away people who aren't on the diet but want to dig in. Rather than hoarding and saving, you may want to make more in the first place, when you already have all the ingredients out. You can freeze the leftovers, wrap them individually, and use them when you need them.

Wash your hands frequently: This is, obviously, a good rule for the kitchen anyway, but with the whole contamination issue it's no longer just a matter of good hygiene. It doesn't do much good to spend hours baking gluten-free cookies if you handle them with hands that are covered with gluten.

Too Many Guests in Your Kitchen

If you thought too many cooks in the kitchen was a problem, wait till you have guests. Just picture it: Your entire family, including the two-year-old, has perfected the gob drop, and all of your cans are clearly marked "WF" or "GF" so there's no confusion about which foods are allowed and which aren't. The anxiety levels are decreasing all around as everyone is finally settling in to the new lifestyle, when you get a call that Aunt Glenda—you know, the one who isn't there five minutes before she's straightening pictures on the wall and refolding the bathroom towels, and must have orange juice with breakfast but does not drink orange juice with a frozen-can lineage—is coming for a visit.

It's not that Aunt Glenda doesn't help. She does. Therein lies the problem.

If your visitors are one-time or occasional guests, they probably won't do too much harm. Keep an eye on them, and give them "safe" jobs to keep them busy and let them feel like they're helping. If they're frequent visitors, though, you'll need to provide some tutoring.

Most vulnerable are your spreadables. Try to teach your guests the gob drop. If they truly seem to understand its importance, you can probably trust them to use your spreadables safely. If they're prone to intentionally ignoring your requests or are truly unable to understand the importance, buy separate spreadables and clearly mark them with the permanent marker so there's no question about which is which. Squeezable margarine or butter are great when guests come to visit.

Finally, to the Food!

Now that you've learned how to read labels, call manufacturers, shop safely and efficiently, and keep your kitchen free from wheat or gluten contamination, it's time to get cooking. Planning your menus will not only save you time and money in the long run, it will also help you realize that the foods available to you aren't as limited as you may at first think.

Chapter 11

Menu Planning and Cooking: The Wheat-Free/ Gluten-Free Chef

*"Our lives are not in the lap of the gods,
but in the lap of our cooks."*
— Lin Yutang

An entire book about diet, and it's more than halfway through before we finally talk about *eating?* What's up with that? Well, believe it or not, we're not quite there yet. First, we need to take a look at menu planning, and the key word is *planning,* because your life will be much easier if you go into this with some sort of preparation. Planning doesn't mean having your local pizza delivery joint on speed dial anymore.

When planning your meals, try not to think in terms of eliminating wheat or gluten, but rather think in terms of making substitutions. Don't be afraid to stick with menu plans that you would have used before embarking upon this lifestyle, because in this chapter, you'll learn several alternatives for ingredients that are no longer on your diet. Most important, don't feel as though you have to do without your favorite meals. With a little creativity and some tips from this book, you'll be eating your favorites again before you know it.

Start by planning a few days' menus at once. The sample menus and snack ideas in this chapter will give you some good ideas to get you going, but remember this simple acronym as you embark on your new adventure: KISS (Keep It Simple, Sally). Even if your name isn't Sally, it's important to keep it simple, especially in the beginning, so you don't feel frustrated and defeated by this diet. Don't bite off more (gluten-free bread) than you can chew. Start slowly, and work up to more complicated dishes.

All the tips you'll find in this chapter, as well as the menu suggestions, are fairly simple, require no special tricks or tools, and are fast and easy. They're completely made up in my own little head, so they're as unofficial as recipes get. Take them for what they're worth—starting points.

Let me also warn you that Julia Child I'm not. I absolutely love to cook and experiment in the kitchen, but complex recipes that require tricky procedures and ingredients that can be purchased only in France aren't up my alley. If a recipe has more than ten ingredients or calls for a sifter, I don't make it. I also don't measure, so I usually refer to an amount as a gob, dopple, tad, and so on. In the recipes I offer, I'll try to approximate in measurements that "real" cooks use, but if your gob turns into a dopple, it probably won't make a difference. And finally, I'm not a very patient person. I, like the rest of you, have a busy life, and am not inclined to be drawn to recipes that take two hours of preparation for two minutes of gobbling.

If you, on the other hand, are interested in more complex or precise recipes, the next chapter features some by Connie Sarros, author of several excellent wheat-free/gluten-free cookbooks. There are also a number of outstanding wheat- and gluten-free cookbooks available, many of which are listed in the Resource Directory at the end of this book.

Note: Throughout this chapter, any reference to recommended substitutions or ingredients refers to wheat-free/gluten-free ingredients (whichever is appropriate for your diet). If, for instance, I recommend deep-frying bread cubes to make croutons, I'm referring to gluten-free bread.

The Main Ingredient: Creativity

You'll find a whole array of ingredients to experiment with in wheat-free/gluten-free cooking: various types of bean flours, xanthan gum, buckwheat, quinoa, amaranth . . . but the most important ingredient you'll use from here on out is your creativity. I always enjoy it when someone complains that they miss their favorite food. I accept that as a challenge to come up with a way to make that food fast, tasty, and gluten-free.

If you have a favorite recipe that's not allowed on your diet, don't give up in despair and deprivation; think of ways to make it okay. The following are some creative substitution ideas to get you started.

- *Breading and coatings:* If a recipe calls for breading, bread crumbs, flour coating, or a similar preparation, you have several options. Consider using a wheat- or gluten-free mix you have lying around—bread mixes or even muffin mixes and others work well for coatings on chicken nuggets and other fried goodies. Cornmeal or corn flour (masa) with some seasonings works well, as do crushed potato chips (try barbecued chips for a flavorful alternative).

- *Soy sauce:* If a recipe calls for soy sauce, use a gluten-free variety or Bragg's Liquid Aminos (found in health-food stores).

- *Thickeners:* For sweet things, try dry pudding mix. Arrowroot flour and tapioca starch are both excellent substitutions for flour and other thickeners as well. Cornstarch is a great thickener; also consider using one of the baked-goods mixes you have lying around. Bread or baking mix works well for just about anything, but don't be afraid to use a muffin or cake mix. The sweet flavor can be a pleasant surprise.

- *Flour:* If your recipe (for example, gravy) calls for flour, consider using cornstarch or any of the gluten-free flours or mixes you have in your pantry.

- *Binders:* I personally wouldn't use a recipe if it called for binders, but if you do, consider using gelatin, xanthan gum, or guar gum.

- *Pie crust:* Use crushed cookies, a sugary gluten-free cereal (there are several), or something even more bland. Crush the cereal, add some butter or margarine, and mush it into the pie tin. Bake it at (guessing) 325 degrees or so for (guessing) 15 minutes or until it's finished. (I always love that line in recipe books—like I'm supposed to *know* when it's finished!)

- *Filler:* I'm not sure if this is the correct culinary term or not, but it refers to when you make, for instance, meat-loaf and need fillers to, well, fill it up. Usually bread is called for, so try using either gluten-free bread or bread crumbs, crackers, flour or mixes, or other starchy food you have in the pantry. Again, even an unsweetened cereal would work.

- *Bread crumbs:* This is a no-brainer. Anyone who has eaten gluten-free bread knows that there are plenty of crumbs in the bag (on the plate, on your shirt . . .) to use as extras for cooking. Crumbling the bread is easy: just look at it. You might want to toast or broil the crumbs to make them crunchy.

- *Croutons:* "Regular" recipes for croutons call for stale bread. I don't recommend that approach for gluten-free croutons, since you'll end up with crumbled crouton bits instead. Use fresh sliced bread, cutting it into cubes. Deep fry, then roll in Parmesan cheese and spices.

- *Granola:* Make your own, using cereal (for example, Nutty Rice), seeds, nuts, and dried fruit (soak in warm water for ten minutes to soften). Toast nuts and seeds; mix together; add honey, vanilla, a tiny bit of oil, and any other spices or seasonings you want. Bake at 300 degrees for an hour, stirring every 15 minutes. Add fruit, let cool, then refrigerate or vacuum seal and freeze.

- *Trail mix:* Most trail mixes are safe (but beware—dates are often dusted with oat flour). If you want to make your own, use peanuts, raisins, dried fruit, and lots of M&Ms (be careful—recently, a new, blue "crispy" variety of M&Ms was introduced that contains malt and is not gluten-free).

- *Oatmeal/hot breakfast:* Try grits (corn). They can be eaten like oatmeal as a hot cereal with any topping you choose (butter, cinnamon, sugar), or they can be fried. Hot cereals are also available from the producers of gluten-free flour.

- *Flour tortillas:* Use corn tortillas or rice wraps found in Asian markets (often used in Thai cooking).

- *Bun (burger or hot dog, for instance):* Use lettuce instead of a bun, or use gluten-free bread or corn tortillas.

- *"Secret sauce" (like the kind on burgers):* The secret's out: Use mayonnaise and ketchup, like the restaurants do. Also try melted cheese, nacho sauce (check the label), or salsa.

- *Teriyaki:* A couple of gluten-free brands are available, but it's easy to make your own, too. Use a gluten-free soy sauce (or Bragg's), and add equal parts of sugar and red wine to taste.

Variety Isn't Just the Spice of Life; It's Nutritionally Important, Too

As you become more comfortable with safe substitutions, keep in mind that part of being creative involves trying new foods. It's easy to get into a rut once you find a few safe foods you like, resulting in a limited and ultimately boring and unsatisfying diet. Nutritionally, it's important to eat a variety of foods; you get a more complete spectrum of nutrients that way.

Nutrition is an important part of our lives. If it wasn't, there wouldn't be much point in this book, would there? As healthy as the wheat-free/gluten-free diet is, it can result in some nutritional deficiencies if you're not careful.

Nancy Patin Falini, a registered dietitian and expert on the subject of wheat-free/gluten-free diets and celiac disease, has contributed a comprehensive section on nutritional requirements specific to the wheat-free/gluten-free diet. It includes information for pregnant women and seniors, as well for anyone restricting wheat or gluten. You'll find it in Tech Talk in the back of this book.

Meanwhile, don't be afraid to experiment with the many new flours available, including bean flours, and some of the more "exotic" flours like amaranth. They're nutritious, and they add great flavor. Buy new magazines or cookbooks, watch cooking programs on TV, practice with safe substitutions, and before you know it, you'll be livin' la vida loca with all sorts of new taste treats!

Put Away Your Pride:
Rely on Mixes and Prepared Foods, at Least at First

It doesn't matter whether you're Emeril Lagasse, Wolfgang Puck, or Julia Child. If this diet is new to you, it's a good idea to take advantage of the great-tasting mixes and prepared wheat-free/gluten-free products that are now available.

When my son was young, we didn't have any of these terrific-tasting products. I'm not Martha Stewart, but I wanted so badly to bake cookies with my son that I bought the several different flours, xanthan gum, and other ingredients (to the tune of about $50), donned an apron, and started to mix. What emerged was, well, sort of close to a cookie-type food, and I was excited that for the first time in more than a year, I could watch my three-year-old son eat a cookie. His buddy A.J. was visiting, so with my best Mrs. Cleaver impersonation, I presented milk and cookies to the boys and took one for myself. I was horrified and heartbroken when A.J., who had the heart of an angel but the tact of a three-year-old, spit his cookie no less than ten feet across the kitchen. I would have cried, but I was still trying to swallow the dry wad that had once impersonated a cookie.

Don't go there! Yes, there are some terrific cookbooks, and I encourage you to be courageous and creative in your cooking efforts, but this chapter is about getting started, which means the diet is still new to you. You have enough to think about without having a three-year-old spit a cookie (worth about $6.50, I figured) across the kitchen.

More important, you have options. The mixes today for brownies, cookies, cakes, breads, and other baked goods are excellent. They're so good, in fact, that my daughter (who doesn't have to be gluten-free) prefers some of them to "regular" cookies. (I'm torn: Let her eat the gluten-free cookies that she prefers, with the added benefit of proving to my son that they really *are* great and we're not just saying that because he can't eat "the real deal," or forcing her to eat store-bought cookies that aren't, literally, worth their weight in gold. Hmmm . . .)

Many of the pre-made foods are delicious, too. Pizzas, pizza crusts, bagels, doughnuts, cookies, even frozen chicken nuggets and just about anything else you thought you'd have to do without, can be purchased with the click of a mouse or the tap of a few numbers on the phone.

Bread: Past, Present, and Future

Did I mention how great the cookies are? Okay, I'll admit it—gluten-free breads still have a way to go before people who don't *have* to choose them over "regular" bread do so, but they've come a long way, baby, and many of them are really quite good.

Again, I highly recommend the mixes and prepared breads that you can buy from the Internet, phone, or specialty stores. Many of the mixes even work well in a breadmaker, which provides the added advantage of filling your house with that wonderful fresh-baked bread smell (maybe they charge extra for that, which is why it's so expensive!).

Breadmakers

Breadmakers are a must, in my opinion, especially if you're using mixes. (If you're willing to mix your own concoction of four types of flours, xanthan gum, and 14 other ingredients to make bread, you probably don't care that you have to knead it, let it rise, and put it in a loaf pan to bake it.) Be sure to buy one that has a strong motor, because gluten-free dough tends to be heavier than "regular" dough.

It's a good idea to buy a bread slicer to go with your breadmaker, and I'm not referring to a serrated knife. The slicer you need is one that you put the loaf of bread into, and it has slots so you can cut slices evenly. Most slicers come with electric knives, but if not, a long bread knife works fine. If you're preparing bread for kids, this is absolutely essential, since we parents know that how food looks is at least as important as how it tastes.

Toasting gluten-free bread does it wonders (that was supposed to be a pun, sort of). Even if you're preparing a sandwich in the morning for a sack lunch, toast the bread first, then prepare the sandwich. Heated sandwiches, such as grilled cheese and tuna melts, work well with gluten-free breads, too. Even for these, toast the bread first to help it from crumbling apart.

Because your homemade breads (and most prepared specialty breads you buy) don't have preservatives, they won't last as long as "regular" bread. Once it's cooked, slice the loaf, let it cool, and freeze it. If you find that your slices stick together, put wax paper between them before freezing. Since you usually toast the bread before you eat it anyway, it won't matter that it's frozen.

The future of gluten-free breads promises to be terrific. Food producers have managed to come up with absolutely delicious baked goods, and are working to improve the quality and bring prices down.

Alternatives to Cow's Milk: Udderly Delicious and Nutritious

When my family first embarked upon the wonderful world of gluten-free living, I was well aware that I was going to have to think outside the box. Surely there *must be* foods out there other than Pop-Tarts, pasta, pizza, crackers, and bread. Sure enough, we discovered flavored rice cakes, pasta made from grains we had never heard of and couldn't pronounce properly for years, and a myriad of foods we never knew existed (like Mochi!).

Tucked away in the refrigerator section of our favorite health-food store was something I had never encountered until I began thinking outside the gluten-free box: rice milk. At that point we were trying to eliminate lactose as well as gluten, so it caught my eye—but I couldn't help but wonder, if milk comes from cows, and goat's milk comes from goats, where on earth does rice milk come from?

After painstaking research, I will share with you what I have learned. Rice stalks, even in their natural form, do not have udders. Rice milk is made by soaking rice in boiling water, grinding the "muddy" mixture, then filtering the rice particles out. Sweeteners (often malt, so check those ingredients) are usually added, as are other types of flavorings.

By the way, if you're looking for milk alternatives, you may want to look at soy milk. In 1999, the U.S. Food and Drug Administration stipulated that products containing at least 6.25 grams of soy protein per serving could be promoted as reducing heart disease. The soybean also has been credited with easing hot flashes of menopause, reducing the risk of osteoporosis, and helping to control and inhibit the growth of cancer cells. Soy milk tends to be lower in carbohydrates and higher in protein and most vitamins and minerals than rice milk. It is, however, lower in folic acid.

Soy milk has been used in place of animal milk throughout much of Asia for centuries. Most soy milk is made from hulled soybeans; some milks include the hull, while others contain soy protein ingredients. Typically, the higher the protein, the "beanier" the flavor.

Milk substitutes are also made from almonds and other plant sources. Sometimes they're fortified with calcium and other nutrients, resulting in a more nutritious alternative.

Most important for anyone avoiding gluten, be aware that many of these milk alternatives are sweetened with malted barley or processed with barley enzymes. As always, be diligent about checking labels.

Junk Food: Go for It!

Most diet books extol the virtues of cabbage and pine nuts, trying to convince you to steer clear of anything remotely resembling a caramel-chocolate gooey mess. If you're more the tofu type than the sweets sort, please skip this section and accept my most sincere appreciation for your commitment to an even healthier diet than the one I've written about. Already I'm mired in guilt for allowing myself (and worse yet, my family) the indulgence of chips and chocolate, and it will only make me feel worse to know that those of you who think raisins are a dessert item are reading in horror as I laud the many junk-food products that are safe on the wheat-free/gluten-free diet.

Don't get me wrong; I'm not advocating a diet of candy bars and ice cream just because they're gluten-free. I am, however, a believer in the motto "everything in moderation," including junk food. I know it's not good for you; I know it adds pounds and inches; and in fact, I even know it's politically incorrect to take the stand I take. Why do you think they call it "junk"?

If I may digress for a moment, I'd like to offer my two cents on the virtues of junk food. I hope by now you realize that this diet isn't as limiting as it may at first appear. It is, nonetheless, a *restricted* diet, and a strictly restricted one at that. Because you already have to cut so many other things out of your diet, why not allow yourself the indulgence of a candy bar or bag of chips from time to time? Psychologically, it could be a huge boost if you're feeling at all deprived.

The other great thing about junk foods is that they're name-brand products you can eat. In an earlier chapter, I touched on the psychological benefit of eating the same brands that everyone else eats, and the idea that there's a lot to be said for eating "regular" foods. By virtue of your diet, you *are* different from other people, and that's okay. But it doesn't hurt to know that you can eat "regular" foods from time to time, too.

Those of you who feel deprived on the diet can think again as I enlighten you to the wonderful world of junk food. I can't mention specific products, because ingredients change, and if anyone ever got sick, I suppose somehow someone could figure I'm liable for what they put in their mouth. I do, however, suggest you check the candy aisle for products with names *similar* to Margarine-Toes, R&Rs, Planet-Eruptions, Skattles, Jelly-Stomachs, and others. A good start might be to call the major candy manufacturers listed in the Resource Directory and ask them to send you their list of gluten-free products. You'll probably be pleasantly shocked by the number of products on their lists.

Chocolate and sugar, the main ingredients in most candies, are inherently gluten-free. Watch for additives such as malt or malt flavoring; "rice crisps" (usually these contain malt); and of course, flour or other obvious no-nos. Some people claim that candy bars are rolled in flour to prevent the packaging from sticking, but as you learned earlier in this book, if that occurs, "flour" or even "wheat" would have to be included on the ingredients label.

Chips are another terrific surprise, since the list of allowed chips is much longer than the list of those that are not allowed. Most of the chip makers in North America are large companies that have voluntarily begun more specific labeling, so usually if the label looks okay, the chips are safe. At least one huge manufacturer of chip products makes dozens of varieties of gluten-free chips, but says they can't verify the gluten-free status. Refer to the chapter in this book on calling manufacturers; just because the company says they can't verify the gluten-free status of their chips doesn't mean they're not okay (and please forgive the triple negative).

Not to be forgotten in the less-than-esteemed category of junk foods are frozen foods—you know, the ones that you grab in a pinch, rationalizing that they're nutritious because they contain meat or cheese (and candy bars don't). You'll find all sorts of greasy-when-you-warm-them, gluten-free goodies in the frozen-food aisle.

Sample Menus

The suggestions that follow are simply meant to be used as a starting point—remember to get creative, and modify these ideas as necessary to meet other dietary needs or your personal preferences. I feel compelled to reiterate that all items referred to will assume you're using wheat-free/gluten-free products. If I suggest yogurt, for example, I assume you've checked to make sure it's gluten-free; if I suggest a grilled cheese sandwich, you don't need to e-mail me to inform me that bread has gluten. I'm suggesting that you make a grilled cheese sandwich on *gluten-free* bread. You get the point.

Breakfast

- Yogurt: toppings such as fruit, cereal, and other "enhancers" add to the experience

- Eggs, any style

- Egg-in-a-basket: Cut a hole out of the bread, and butter both sides (since gluten-free bread tends to crumble, you might want to use spray-on butter, or put the butter in the pan or on the griddle); fry bread, and crack an egg into the cutout; grill both sides

- Fruit, any variety: My family loves it cut into pieces, and tossed with strawberry yogurt and a tiny squeeze of lime juice

- Upside-down-fruit and yogurt: Dig a scoop of fruit out of a kiwi (for instance), and fill it with yogurt

- Fruit smoothie: Crush fresh or frozen fruit in a blender with milk, protein powder, and ice; sweeten with honey if necessary

- Instant breakfast smoothie: In a blender, combine a package of instant breakfast powder, protein powder, milk, and ice

- Toast (with jelly, cream cheese, margarine, cinnamon-sugar, cottage cheese)

- French toast

- Sausage

- Bacon
- Pancakes: Some of the mixes are truly amazing, and most syrups are gluten-free
- Waffles: Use the mixes or buy them frozen; just heat in a toaster oven
- Cottage cheese
- Muffins: Try sneaking fruit or shredded zucchini into them; the kids might not notice
- Cold cereal: Watch for malt flavoring in most big-name commercial cereals; several good gluten-free cereals are sold at health-food stores
- Hot cereal or grits
- Hash browns

Lunch or Dinner (Entrées)

- Steak, chicken, or other meat (watch the seasonings)
- Marinades: Many commercial brands are gluten-free; make your own by using sesame oil, Bragg's or wheat-free soy sauce, garlic, and lemon juice
- Lasagna
- Pizza
- Pasta
- Shredded beef
- Pot roast
- Quiche: Use pie crust mix or no crust at all
- Caesar salad with chicken
- Chicken nuggets: Cut chicken breast into strips; roll in crushed potato chips or a mix you have lying around; deep fry or bake

- Stuffed hot pocket-like sandwiches: Use bread dough and roll flat; fill with your favorite filling; pinch closed, and bake
- Stir-fry
- Quesadilla: Quesadillas (pronounced "kay-suh-DEE-uhs") are corn tortillas with cheese melted on them
- "Wrap": Like a quesadilla, but instead of cheese, use sauteed veggies
- Chili
- Sandwiches: It's fun to make a peanut butter-and-jelly sandwich on waffles
- Mexican food (tamales, tacos, taquitos, enchiladas—watch the sauce)
- Hot dogs: For a bun, try wrapping a corn tortilla around the hot dog and putting it in the microwave; the juices from the hot dog will moisten the tortilla
- Tuna melt
- Meatloaf
- Taco salad
- Macaroni and cheese
- Seafood
- Shish kebab

Helpful hint: Many of these suggestions call for corn tortillas. If yours tend to crumble or tear, try wrapping them in a damp paper towel and heating in the microwave for 20 seconds.

Side Dishes and Snacks

- Veggies (fresh or cooked)
- Potatoes (mashed, scalloped, fried, baked, French fries):

Feel free to slip in some chopped veggies, but don't tell the kids

- Deviled eggs
- Tuna: The new snap-top lids are great for lunch boxes
- Rice (saffron, Spanish, wild, brown, or other variety)
- Quinoa "couscous": Regular couscous is made from wheat; quinoa comes in a style that is the same size and consistency as couscous, and can be prepared the same way
- Gravy: Add cornstarch (or arrowroot, sweet rice flour, or tapioca starch) to chicken stock; it works best if the cornstarch is dissolved in water first, and if the gravy is not on a high heat when you add the cornstarch
- Bread rolls rolled in Parmesan and spices
- Pigs-in-a-blanket: Wrap dough or cheese-bread around smoked sausages and bake
- Chips
- Potato skins: Fill them with your favorite filling
- Nachos
- Meatballs: You have to use a toothpick to eat them or it's no fun
- Cheese squares
- Cream cheese wrapped in ham slices
- Caviar on crackers
- "Chex" mix: You can buy wheat- and gluten-free cereals that look and taste just like Chex; use them in place of Chex
- Fruit rolls
- Rice cakes (with jelly, cream cheese, or peanut butter)
- High-protein health bars
- Nuts

- Hard-boiled eggs
- Baked beans
- Sloppy Joe's
- Soup
- Deep-fried or steamed egg rolls (using Asian rice wrap)
- Fruit (fresh, dried, canned)
- Popcorn
- Celery with peanut butter or cream cheese
- Fried cheese sticks: Roll string cheese in crushed potato chips and fry in butter
- "Poppers": Fill bread dough with cream cheese and chilis, pinch closed, and bake or deep fry

Desserts

- "Rice Krispies" treats: The commercial brand of Rice Krispies contains malt at the time of this printing, and is therefore not gluten-free; however, several brands of "look-alike" cereals substitute well for making these irresistible treats
- Cookies: Make from scratch or use mixes; the mixes today are, in my family's opinion, better than the "real deal"—add chocolate chips, M&Ms (not the new crispy ones), raisins, or other ingredients to "kick it up"
- Cakes
- Doughnut holes: Again, I cheat, because I don't even attempt to make doughnuts from scratch; instead, I use any sweet mix I have lying around (muffin, cake, cookie), roll the dough into little balls, deep fry, drain, and roll in powdered sugar or cinnamon-sugar mixture

- Brownies
- Muffins
- Ice cream, ice cream sundaes
- Chocolate milk
- Flan
- Cheesecake: Most "innards" of a cheesecake are gluten-free; use crushed cookies mixed with butter and pressed into the pie pan for the pie crust
- Meringues (easy to make)
- Pie: See cheesecake above for making crust
- S'mores: Use gluten-free crackers, chocolate, and marshmallows

My cooking method, which is heavy on creativity but light on conventionality, is definitely not for everyone. I love cookbooks, but the truth is, I buy them just for the pictures (hey, at least I admit it). If you're more the type who actually *uses* the lines on your measuring cups, you're in for a treat. The next chapter includes recipes by Connie Sarros, author of several wheat-free/gluten-free cookbooks. She's compiled a number of delicious recipes for this book, all of which are wheat-free/gluten-free, and some of which also meet the needs of those avoiding casein, sugar, and meat.

Chapter 12

Sumptuous Solutions for Special Diets: Recipes by Connie Sarros

"In creating, the only hard thing is to begin:
a grass blade's no easier to make than an oak."
— James Russell Lowell

Connie Sarros is the author of the *Wheat-Free, Gluten-Free Children's Cookbook;* the *Wheat-Free, Gluten-Free Reduced Calorie Cookbook;* and the *Wheat-Free, Gluten-Free Dessert Cookbook.* Her wheat-free/gluten-free recipes not only accommodate vegetarian, diabetic, and casein-free diets, they're also incredibly delicious and easy to make.

GF = Gluten-free
CF = Casein-free
D = Diabetic (sugar, salt, fat, and carbohydrate reduced)
V = Vegetarian

Gluten-Free Flour Mixture

Some of these recipes call for a gluten-free flour mixture. You can buy this type of mixture through specialty vendors, or make your own with the following recipe:

2½ cups rice flour
1 cup potato starch flour
1 cup tapioca flour
¼ cup cornstarch
¼ cup garbanzo bean flour
2 Tbsp. xanthan gum

Sift above ingredients together.

Night-Before French Toast   GF/D/V   Serves 3

Just about all kids love French toast. Your children can prepare this themselves the night before.

To make this recipe CF: Use soy milk in place of the low-fat milk, and granulated white sugar may be used in place of the brown-sugar substitute.

6 slices porous GF bread
2 whole eggs
3 egg whites
⅔ cup low-fat milk
1 tsp. GF vanilla
⅛ tsp. salt
½ tsp. cinnamon
2 tsp. brown sugar substitute
2 tsp. maple syrup
GF nonstick cooking spray

Spray an 8" x 11" baking pan with GF nonstick spray. Cut each slice of bread into four strips; put bread in a single layer in prepared pan. In a bowl, whisk together remaining ingredients; pour over bread. Cover and refrigerate overnight. In the morning, bake bread at 350 degrees for 25 minutes, turning once.

Calories: 182, Total Fat: 3 g; Saturated Fat: 0; Cholesterol: 43 mg; Sodium: 282.5 mg; Carbohydrates: 38 g; Fiber: 1 g; Sugar: 7 g; Protein: 11.5 g.

GRECIAN FLAT BREAD (PITA)   GF/CF/D/V   Makes 4 flat breads

Both sides of the bread should be nicely browned, but watch closely while it cooks so it doesn't burn.

1 cup GF flour mixture
¼ tsp. salt
⅔ cup water
⅛ tsp. oregano
⅛ tsp. basil
Dash garlic powder

Sift flour and salt into a bowl; stir in oregano, basil, and garlic. Make a well in the center and gradually pour in the water, mixing well with a fork to form a supple dough. Knead the dough for about 5 minutes, adding a little more flour mixture as needed. Set dough aside for 10 minutes. Divide dough into 4 equal portions. Roll out or pat each piece to form a large circle on a board lightly sprinkled with GF flour. Place a heavy skillet on high heat until pan is very hot, then lower heat to medium. Place a flat bread in the pan; cook until it starts to bubble, then turn it over. Carefully press down on the pita with a flat spatula and turn the pita over again. Remove from pan and continue to cook remaining 3 bread circles.

Calories: 100; Total Fat: 0; Saturated fat: 0; Cholesterol: 0; Sodium: 132 mg; Fiber: 1 g; Sugar: 1 g; Protein: 3 g.

BARBECUED SOUP   **GF/CF/D/V**   Serves 6

A delightful cross between traditional bean soup and meatless chili; your taste buds will be fully aware of the spices.

2 small onions, chopped
2 cloves garlic, minced
2 tsp. olive oil
¾ tsp. chili powder
¾ tsp. cumin
⅛ tsp. ground cloves
¼ tsp. pepper
¼ tsp. salt
1 can (14.5 oz.) salt-free diced tomatoes, chopped (with juice)
1 can (15.5 oz.) pinto beans, rinsed and drained
¼ cup roasted red peppers, chopped
4 cups GF low-salt beef broth
2 tsp. GF molasses
1½ tsp. GF cider vinegar

In a large saucepan, saute onions and garlic in oil until softened and beginning to brown. Stir in seasonings and simmer 1 minute. Stir in remaining ingredients; cover and simmer for 1 hour, stirring occasionally.

Calories: 80; Total fat: 2 g; Saturated fat: 1.2 g; Cholesterol: 0; Sodium: 959.6 mg; Carbohydrates: 14.3 g; Fiber: 3 g; Sugar: 2.8 g; Protein: 4 g

RICE PAPER ZUCCHINI ROLLS   **GF/D/V**   Makes 6 rolls

These rolls may be made ahead, covered, and refrigerated until baking time. They make an attractive appetizer.

1½ cups zucchini, shredded
¾ cup green onion, chopped
2 tsp. garlic, minced
1 tsp. olive oil
¼ cup GF white wine

¼ tsp. lemon juice
2 Tbsp. parsley, chopped
½ tsp. dill
¼ tsp. pepper
⅛ tsp. salt
3 Tbsp. GF low-salt feta cheese, crumbled
3 Tbsp. GF Parmesan cheese, grated
2 egg whites
6 rice papers
GF nonstick cooking spray

Squeeze zucchini dry, then pack into measuring cup to measure. Saute zucchini, onion, and garlic in oil in a pan that has been sprayed with GF nonstick spray. When lightly browned, stir in wine, lemon juice, and seasonings. Spoon mixture into a bowl to cool. When cool, stir in cheeses and egg whites. Soak rice papers in water 3 minutes or until softened. Lay one rice paper on a cutting board; spray with GF nonstick spray. Fill with 1/6th of the filling mixture; roll, folding in sides to encase filling. Place seam-side down on a baking sheet that has been sprayed with GF nonstick spray. Spray tops of rolls. Bake at 375 degrees for 15 minutes or until rice paper is crispy.

Calories: 32; Total Fat: .8 g; Saturated fat: .5 g; Cholesterol: 2.9 mg; Sodium: 6 mg; Carbohydrates: 5 g; Fiber: 1 g; Sugar: 0 g; Protein: 1.6 g

SPINACH TARTLETS   GF/D/V   Serves 8

Rice paper is the perfect edible container for these attractive appetizers. Serve them warm. They may be assembled, covered, and frozen; thaw before baking.

1 cup GF plain nonfat yogurt
1 large clove garlic, minced
¼ tsp. cayenne pepper
½ lb. fresh collard greens, chopped (discard stems)
6 oz. frozen chopped spinach
¼ green onion, chopped

2 Tbsp. fresh mint, minced
1 tsp. olive oil
1 Tbsp. dill
¼ tsp. pepper
¼ tsp. salt
3 Tbsp. GF canned roasted red peppers
⅔ cup GF low-salt feta cheese
2 egg whites, slightly beaten
8 sheets rice paper
GF nonstick cooking spray

Yogurt sauce: In a small bowl, stir together yogurt, garlic, and cayenne pepper. Cover and refrigerate.

Tartlets: Place collard greens in a large pan and cover with water; bring to a boil. When greens are tender, add spinach and continue to cook until it's completely thawed. Drain greens and spinach, and squeeze dry. In a small skillet, saute green onion and mint in oil. Stir in greens, spinach, seasonings, and red peppers. Remove from heat. When spinach mixture is cooled, stir in cheese and egg whites. Soak rice papers in water for 3 minutes to soften. Spray 8 mini-muffin tins with GF nonstick spray. Spray 1 rice paper with GF nonstick spray; fold in half. Place rice paper in a tin, gently pushing paper to conform to tin shape. Using a pair of kitchen shears, cut off any paper overhang. Repeat procedure with remaining 7 papers. Spray papers with GF nonstick spray. Fill papers with spinach mixture. Bake at 350 degrees for 15 minutes or until filling begins to puff up. Serve warm, topped with a dollop of yogurt sauce.

Calories: 72; Total fat: 3 g; Saturated fat: 2 g; Cholesterol: 13 mg; Sodium: 279 mg; Carbohydrates: 5 g; Fiber: 1.2 g; Sugar: 2 g; Protein: 5 g

Mexican Potato Salad   GF/CF/D/V   Serves 6 as a side dish

Cayenne, cumin, and red pepper flakes combine to create a hot, zesty taste sensation! This salad holds well for several days, covered, in the refrigerator.

3 large potatoes
4 Tbsp. olive oil
2 Tbsp. GF white wine vinegar
⅛ tsp. salt
⅛ tsp. pepper
Dash red pepper flakes
⅛ tsp. cayenne
¼ tsp. paprika
⅛ tsp. cumin
1 can (7 oz.) salt-free corn, drained
¼ cup celery, sliced
½ cup carrots, shredded
⅓ cup green pepper, chopped
¼ cup onion, chopped
1 tomato, cut in half, then cut in wedges

In a saucepan, cook potatoes in boiling water until tender. Drain, cool slightly, then peel and cube. In a small bowl, whisk together oil, vinegar, and spices; add to potatoes and toss well. Cover and refrigerate 2 hours. Fold in remaining ingredients, cover and chill 1 hour more.

Calories: 249.9; Total fat: 9.1 g; Saturated fat: 1.2 g; Cholesterol: 0; Sodium: 144.8 mg; Carbohydrates: 37.8 g; Fiber: 37.9 g; Sugar: 3.8 g; Protein: 4.5 g

ASIAN COLE SLAW GF/CF/D/V Serves 4 as a side dish
If you don't have rice vinegar, substitute apple cider vinegar.

½ cup rice vinegar
1 Tbsp. sesame oil
2 tsp. olive oil
½ tsp. salt
¼ tsp. pepper
1 head Savoy cabbage, thinly sliced and tough ribs discarded
8 oz. carrots, shredded
4 green onions, thinly sliced

½ cup parsley, chopped
1 Tbsp. poppy seeds

In a large bowl, whisk together vinegar, oils, salt, and pepper. Add remaining ingredients, tossing well to coat evenly. Cover and refrigerate several hours.

Calories: 133.4; Total fat: 118 g; Saturated fat: 1.5 g; Cholesterol: 0; Sodium: 347.5 mg; Carbohydrates: 17.9g ; Fiber: 9.5g; Sugar: 1.2g; Protein: 3.9g

Spinach Rice Tomatoes   GF/CF/D/V   Serves 6 as a side dish
Freeze the pulp from the tomatoes to use in soups or stews.

6 medium tomatoes
2 onions, chopped
¼ cup carrots, shredded
3 Tbsp. olive oil
1 Tbsp. parsley, chopped
1 Tbsp. dill
1 box (10 oz.) frozen chopped spinach, thawed
¼ cup rice
⅛ tsp. pepper
¼ tsp. salt
3 Tbsp. salt-free tomato sauce
¾ cup water
GF nonstick cooking spray

Cut a slice off the stem-end of each tomato; remove pulp. Cut a small "X" on the bottom of each tomato; place in an 8" x 10" baking pan. Pour 1/2" of water in the pan; cover and bake at 350 degrees for 15 minutes or until tomatoes are soft but still hold their shape. Remove tomatoes with a spatula; drain water from pan. Spray pan with GF nonstick spray, then return tomatoes to pan. Saute onions and carrots in oil slowly until golden brown, stirring frequently. Stir in remaining ingredients. Simmer, covered, 15 minutes or until moisture is absorbed. Remove from heat and cool 10 minutes. Fill tomato cavities with spinach mixture. Cover and bake 15 minutes.

Calories: 129.9; Total fat: 7.2 g; Saturated fat: .6 g; Cholesterol: 0; Sodium: 239 mg; Carbohydrates: 15 g; Fiber: 2.4 g; Sugar: 1 g; Protein: 2.7 g

BROILED VEGETABLES AND RICE **GF/CF/D/V** Serves 4 as a main entree

Other vegetables may be added, such as asparagus, broccoli, eggplant, or artichoke hearts.

2½ cups GF vegetable broth
1 cup rice
2 Tbsp. parsley, chopped
2 zucchini
1 yellow squash
2 portobello mushrooms
½ green pepper
½ red pepper
1 tomato
1 onion, sliced
3 Tbsp. olive oil
2 Tbsp. GF balsamic vinegar
2 tsp. GF low-salt soy sauce
¼ tsp. salt
¼ tsp. pepper
¼ tsp. garlic powder
½ tsp. dill
GF nonstick cooking spray

Bring chicken broth to a boil in a saucepan. Stir in rice and parsley; lower heat, cover, and cook 20 minutes or until moisture is absorbed. Cut vegetables into large julienne slices; spread out vegetables on a cookie sheet that has been sprayed with GF nonstick spray. In a small bowl, whisk together oil, vinegar, soy sauce, salt, pepper, garlic, and dill. Drizzle over vegetables. Broil vegetables 3 inches from heat for 4 minutes; turn vegetables and continue to broil until vegetables are browned but still slightly crisp. To serve, spoon vegetables over hot rice.

Calories: 237; Total fat: 47.5 g; Saturated fat: 1.4 g; Cholesterol: 0; Sodium: 687 mg; Carbohydrates: 33.3 g; Fiber: 1.7 g; Sugar: 1.6 g; Protein: 5.1 g

SPINACH LASAGNA   GF/V   Serves 6 as a main entree

Lasagna will stay warm for at least an hour if kept covered. This may be assembled ahead, then frozen; to serve, thaw in the refrigerator, covered with foil, 2 days before baking. When boiling GF lasagna noodles, do not overcook; GF pasta tends to cook much faster than its wheat counterpart.

To make this recipe D: Take half a serving as a side dish.

½ cup water
1 cube GF vegetable bouillon
1 onion, chopped
2 cloves garlic, minced
3 cups salt-free tomato sauce
¼ tsp. salt
½ tsp. basil
¼ tsp. oregano
¼ tsp. pepper
½ cup GF plain fat-free yogurt
1½ cups GF fat-free cottage cheese
6 oz. GF lasagna noodles
1 box (10 oz.) frozen chopped spinach, thawed
5 oz. GF low-fat mozzarella cheese
GF nonstick cooking spray

In a saucepan, crush bouillon in water. Add onion and garlic and saute. Add tomato sauce and seasonings; simmer 20 minutes. Mix yogurt and cottage cheese. Cook lasagna according to package directions; drain well. Squeeze spinach dry. Spread a little of the tomato sauce in a shallow 9-inch baking dish that has been sprayed with GF nonstick spray. Layer of noodles, then spinach, then cottage cheese mixture, then mozzarella. Repeat layers, beginning with tomato sauce. Form one last layer of noodles; cover with tomato sauce and remaining mozzarella cheese. Bake at 350 degrees for 45 minutes. Cover during last 15 minutes of cooking if top is getting too browned.

Calories: 225; Total fat: 3.5 g; Saturated fat: 1.3 g; Cholesterol: 1.6 mg; Sodium: 480 mg; Carbohydrates: 130 g; Fiber: 9 g; Sugar: 31 g; Protein: 88.6 g

DAIRY-FREE TACOS   GF/ CF/D/V   Makes 1 taco
When you're in a rush, this lunch can be assembled and baked in a few minutes and eaten on the run.

To make this recipe D/V: Substitute GF light cream cheese for the soy cheese, or try a slice of GF sharp cheddar cheese.

1 GF corn tortilla
2 Tbsp. GF refried beans
2 Tbsp. soy cream cheese
½ small tomato, sliced thin
Dash of pepper

Place tortilla on a sheet of wax paper. Spread with beans, then with cream cheese. Lay tomato slices on top; sprinkle with pepper. Roll up tortilla, then wrap wax paper around it. Microwave for 45 seconds until tortilla is warmed.

Calories: 247; Total fat: 13 g; Saturated fat: 5 g; Cholesterol: 20 mg; Sodium: 404.5 mg; Carbohydrates: 25.5 g; Fiber: 3.2 g; Sugar: 2 g; Protein: 7.2 g

BREADED PORK FINGERS   GF/CF/D   Serves 6
Let kids help in the kitchen. They love to dip their fingers in the margarine/lemon mixture, then shake the bag to distribute the coating mix. These "fingers" taste great when made with chicken tenders, too.

¼ cup GF flour mixture
¼ cup cornmeal
1 tsp. paprika
¼ tsp. salt
¼ tsp. pepper
½ tsp. dried parsley, crushed
¼ tsp. garlic powder
¼ tsp. oregano
1 Tbsp. GF milk-free margarine, melted
½ tsp. lemon juice
1½ lbs. boneless lean pork chops, cut into 1-inch strips
GF nonstick cooking spray

In a plastic bag, mix together first 8 ingredients. In a bowl, stir together margarine and lemon juice. Dip pork strips into margarine mixture, then place strips in plastic bag. Toss well to coat strips evenly with flour mixture. Spray a baking pan with GF nonstick spray. Set the strips in a single layer on the baking pan. Bake at 375 degrees for 10 minutes; turn strips over and continue to bake another 10 minutes or until meat is no longer pink in center.

Calories: 257.8; Total fat: 14 g; Saturated fat: 6 g; Cholesterol: 73 mg; Sodium: 164 mg; Carbohydrates: 7 g; Fiber: .5 g; Sugar: 0; Protein: 23.5 g

RASPBERRY CHICKEN   GF/CF/D   Serves 4
In place of the raspberry preserves, try using orange marmalade, apricot preserves, or pineapple preserves.

2 tsp. olive oil
½ cup onion, chopped
½ tsp. thyme
½ tsp. salt
4 skinless, boneless chicken breasts
¼ cup all-fruit raspberry preserves
2 Tbsp. GF balsamic vinegar
¼ cup water
¼ tsp. pepper

In a large nonstick skillet, heat oil 1 minute; add onion, and saute over medium heat until soft, about 5 minutes. Sprinkle chicken with thyme and 1/4 tsp. salt. Add chicken to pan and saute 6 minutes per side or until just cooked through. Remove chicken. Reduce heat; add remaining 1/4 tsp. salt, preserves, vinegar, water, and pepper. Cook, stirring constantly, until preserves melt. Return chicken to pan and baste with sauce. To serve, place chicken on serving dishes; spoon sauce over meat.

Calories: 242; Total fat: 5.7 g; Saturated fat: 1 g; Cholesterol: 96 mg; Sodium: 349 mg; Carbohydrates: 10.5 g; Fiber: 0; Sugar: 9 g; Protein: 35 g

CHICKEN WITH LENTILS   **GF/CF/D**   Serves 4
Lentils will not cook through if salt is added too early.

2 cups dried lentils
3 cups water
1 cup carrots, sliced thin
1 large onion, sliced
1 cup celery, sliced
2 bay leaves
3 Tbsp. parsley, chopped
¼ tsp. salt
¼ tsp. pepper
1½ Tbsp. GF apple cider vinegar
1 can (8 oz.) salt-free tomato sauce
1 tsp. olive oil
4 bone-in chicken breasts, skin removed
GF nonstick cooking spray

Combine first 7 ingredients in a saucepan; bring to a boil. Lower heat and simmer 45 minutes or until lentils are tender, adding more water if needed. Stir in salt, pepper, vinegar, and tomato sauce; simmer 5 minutes more. Spray a large skillet with GF nonstick spray. Add oil and saute chicken pieces over high heat until browned on both sides. Spoon lentil mixture over chicken, lower heat to medium, cover pan and simmer 25 minutes or until chicken is fork tender, adding more water if needed.

Calories: 354; Total fat: 6 g; Saturated fat: 1 g; Cholesterol: 96 mg; Sodium: 294 mg; Carbohydrates: 29.5 g; Fiber: 9.5 g; Sugar: 7.7 g; Protein: 45.5 g

GRECIAN STEWED BAKED FISH   GF/CF/D   Serves 4
Even people who never touch fish will love *psari plaki*. Prepare it using the freshest fish possible.

4 pieces flounder, cod, bass, scrod, or haddock, 5 oz. each
Juice of ½ lemon
¼ tsp. salt
¼ tsp. pepper
1 Tbsp. olive oil
2 onions, chopped
½ tsp. garlic, minced
¼ cup shredded carrots
¼ cup chopped celery
1 box frozen chopped spinach, thawed
1 can (8 oz.) salt-free tomato sauce
2 Tbsp. chopped parsley
½ cup GF white wine
¼ cup water

Put fish in a baking pan; sprinkle with lemon juice, salt, and pepper. In skillet, saute onions, garlic, carrots, and celery in olive oil. Drain spinach and squeeze out excess water; stir into vegetables in pan. Stir in remaining ingredients. Spoon vegetable mixture evenly over each piece of fish. Cover with foil and bake at 350 degrees for 45 minutes or until fish flakes easily.

Calories: 187; Total fat: 4.7 g; Saturated fat: .7 g; Cholesterol: 58 mg; Sodium: 750 mg; Carbohydrates: 12 g; Fiber: 3 g; Sugar: 6 g; Protein: 23 g

PORK WITH APRICOT STUFFING   GF/CF/D   Serves 8

To assure the roast is juicy and tender, do not overcook. Pitted prunes may be used in place of, or in addition to, the apricots.

To make this recipe CF: Substitute regular brown sugar for the sugar substitute.

¼ cup brown sugar substitute
2 cloves garlic, minced
1 tsp. ground ginger
⅛ tsp. salt
¼ tsp. pepper
⅛ tsp. cinnamon
Dash ground cloves
2 lb. lean pork tenderloin
4 dried apricots, cut in quarters
1 Tbsp. GF low-salt soy sauce
GF nonstick cooking spray

In a small bowl, combine first 7 ingredients to form a seasoning rub. Slice meat down center lengthwise and insert apricots, then tie roast together in several places with string. Brush soy sauce over surface of meat, then rub seasoning mixture onto top of meat. Insert meat thermometer near center of roast. Spray grill with GF nonstick spray, and preheat to medium setting. Place meat on grates. Cover and grill about 20 minutes, turning frequently. Slice meat. Serves 8. (If you don't have a grill, place meat in a roasting pan and broil about 20 minutes, turning meat once.)

Calories: 217; Total fat: 6.8 g; Saturated fat: 2 g; Cholesterol: 100 mg; Sodium: 161 g; Carbohydrates: 4 g; Fiber: .5 g; Sugar: 3 g; Protein: 33 g

SOUTH-OF-THE-BORDER PORK CHOPS   GF/CF/D   Serves 4

Cut all visible fat from chops before cooking. If available, buy very lean pork.

2 tsp. olive oil
1 large onion, sliced thin
1 green pepper, chopped
1 can (16 oz.) chopped tomatoes, drained
1 cup frozen corn, thawed
¼ tsp. marjoram
4 pork chops (4 oz. each)
GF nonstick cooking spray

Heat oil in a large skillet over medium heat. Add onion and green pepper; saute 5 minutes. Add tomatoes, corn, and marjoram; raise heat to high and cook 5 minutes more. Transfer tomato mixture to a 1½ quart casserole that has been sprayed with GF nonstick spray. Lay pork chops on a broiler pan and broil 4 inches from heat, about 3 minutes per side or until chops are browned and juices are sealed inside. Lay chops on top of the tomato mixture. Cover with foil and bake at 350 degrees for 40 minutes or until chops are cooked through and fork tender.

Calories: 383; Total fat: 20 g; Saturated fat: 6.5 g; Cholesterol: 91 mg; Sodium: 590 mg; Carbohydrates: 15.7 g; Fiber: 3 g; Sugar: 6 g; Protein: 31 g

CHERRY ROLL   GF/CF/D/V   Serves 8
Rice papers are readily available at oriental stores. The rolls may be assembled ahead, covered with plastic wrap, then refrigerated up to 2 days before baking.

8 Tbsp. all-fruit cherry preserves
1 tsp. GF cherry liqueur
8 sheets rice paper
GF nonstick cooking spray

In a small bowl, stir together preserves and liqueur. Soak rice papers in water for 3 minutes to soften; pat dry. Spray rice papers with GF nonstick spray. Divide filling among the rice papers. Fold sides into center, then roll rice paper into a cylinder. Lay rolls on a baking sheet that has been sprayed with GF nonstick spray. Spray tops of rolls with GF nonstick spray. Bake at 400 degrees for 15 minutes or until heated through. Serve warm.

Calories: 42; Total fat: 0; Saturated fat: 0; Cholesterol: 0; Sodium: 21 g; Carbohydrates: 11 g; Fiber: 0; Sugar: 12 g; Protein: 0

LINZER COOKIES **GF/CF/D/V** Yield: 30 cookies
These cookies are very fragile; when spreading jam, use a light touch to avoid breaking the cookie.

To make this recipe CF: Substitute 2/3 cup granulated sugar for the fructose.

1¼ cups GF milk-free margarine, softened
2½ Tbsp. fructose
1 tsp. GF vanilla
2 cups GF flour mixture
½ tsp. cinnamon
1¾ cups ground almonds
5 Tbsp. all-fruit raspberry jam
¼ cup semisweet chocolate chips

Cream margarine and fructose until light and fluffy; whip in vanilla. Sift flour and cinnamon over margarine mixture; add almonds, and mix until blended. With hands, form dough into a ball and wrap in wax paper; refrigerate for 1 hour. Sprinkle a small amount of GF flour mixture onto a sheet of wax paper and roll out half of the dough until 1/8" thick. Use a 2" round cookie cutter to cut circles from half of the dough (this should give you about 18 circles); place circles on an ungreased cookie sheet. Roll out remaining dough and cut 2" round circles. Use a 1" round cookie cutter to cut out the center of each circle; lay these "cookie rings" on a cookie sheet. Re-roll cutout centers to form additional cookie rings. Bake at 325 degrees for 10 minutes or until lightly browned. Cool cookies on a wire rack. With a light touch, spread jam on each of the whole circles; top each with a cookie ring. Melt the chocolate in the top a double boiler over barely simmering water. Put a small dollop of chocolate in the center of each cookie ring.

Per Cookie: Calories: 125; Total fat: 10 g; Saturated fat: 2 g; Cholesterol: 0; Sodium: 106 mg; Carbohydrates: 10.5 g; Fiber: 3 g; Sugar: 35 g; Protein: 2.3 g

APPLE BREAD PUDDING   GF/CF/D/V   Serves 8

This is a simple recipe that children may make themselves once Mom has cut the apples.

To make this recipe CF and V: You may prefer to use regular brown sugar in place of the sugar substitute.

To make this recipe D and V: You may prefer to use milk in place of the water for a richer dessert.

6 apples, peeled and cored
2 Tbsp. lemon juice
3 Tbsp. brown sugar substitute
½ tsp. cinnamon
2 Tbsp. maple syrup
¼ tsp. GF vanilla
4 slices GF bread
3 Tbsp. GF milk-free margarine
1 cup water
GF nonstick cooking spray

Cut apples into thin slices and place in a bowl. Add lemon juice and toss well to coat evenly. Mix in brown sugar substitute, cinnamon, maple syrup, and vanilla. Tear bread into very small pieces and toss with apple mixture. Spoon half of apples into a 9" pie plate that has been sprayed with GF nonstick spray. Top with small dabs of 1½ Tbsp. of the margarine. Repeat layers. Pour water slowly over the top. Spray a piece of foil with GF nonstick spray; place sprayed-side down on pie plate to cover. Bake at 350 degrees for 1¼ hours or until apples are tender.

Calories: 141; Total fat: 4 g; Saturated fat: 1 g; Cholesterol: 0; Sodium: 131 mg; Carbohydrates: 26 g; Fiber: 3 g; Sugar: 16 g; Protein: 1.4 g

❀ ❀ ❀

Up to this point, this book has given you some great starter ideas for cooking wheat-free/gluten-free foods. But what if you just don't feel like cooking, or want to enjoy the luxury of having someone else do all the work? Is it possible to eat safely in restaurants? Can you travel without worrying that your trip will be ruined because of the foods you might eat?

Not only is it *possible* to venture out of the house, but it's important to do so. In the next chapter, you'll find loads of strategies for eating at restaurants and when taking vacations, while still maintaining a healthy, wheat-free/gluten-free diet.

Chapter 13

Venturing Out of the House: Restaurant Realities and Travel Tips

"It is good to have an end to journey toward,
but it is the journey that matters in the end."
— Ursula K. LeGuin

E ven the most seasoned wheat-free/gluten-free eater (forgive yet another pun—"seasoned eater") may feel a little uncomfortable venturing out of the home. It's true that your risk of getting unsafe foods *does* increase when you leave home, but most people agree that the life experiences of travel, or even just the social aspects or convenience of eating at a restaurant, are well worth it. This chapter includes some rules for traveling and eating out that will minimize your risk.

Restaurant Realities

In reality, when you eat at restaurants, some chefs will "get it" and work to ensure a safe meal for you, and others won't. Going to restaurants isn't really about eating as much as it is the ambience, the company, and, well, okay—the convenience. Focus on those primary reasons for going to a restaurant, and make the food secondary, even if there's very little you can eat. If you've been following the rules of this book, you stuffed yourself before you left the house, so you're not hungry anyway.

Defensive Dining

It's been said that the best offense is a good defense, which probably applies to restaurant excursions as well as it does to the football field. I'm not encouraging you to be offensive; in fact, quite the opposite. It's not, after all, the waiter's or chef's responsibility to accommodate your diet. If they do, be prepared to leave a big tip, because their job descriptions definitely do not include understanding the intricacies of this diet. Nor do you have to fill them in on all the minutiae.

A brief education is all they should need, because you should already have narrowed down the choices on the menu that look as though they might be safe, or at least may be prepared in a way that would make them be safe. It's okay to ask that your food be prepared in a special manner; people do that all the time, without special diets to accommodate.

Most important, you need to be aware of specific foods and ingredients to avoid when eating out. Some things are more likely to be okay than others, and you should make it easier on yourself by choosing items that are more likely to be wheat-free/gluten-free.

Plan Ahead

Your days of eating at Italian restaurants with ease are probably behind you (although many Italian dishes are made with polenta, which is gluten-free). Pizza joints: not likely. Chinese: doubtful. Don't set yourself up for disappointment by selecting restaurants that will fill you with frustration by the very nature of their menu selection. Instead, choose restaurants with a large selection, or select a restaurant based on its ethnicity or culture because it's likely to offer more wheat-free/gluten-free foods. Thai foods, for instance, are often gluten-free, since they use fish sauce instead of soy sauce for a lot of their marinades and seasonings. Study your ethnic foods so you know the ingredients they contain and can make good choices when it comes to restaurant selections.

Knowing what to order is just as important as knowing where to go. Consider, for instance, an American-style restaurant such as Denny's or Sizzler. For breakfast, you're better off contemplating the eggs, hash browns, and bacon than you are the Waffle-Mania, even if it *is* only $3.95. For lunch or dinner, you can almost always find a restaurant that will offer you a burger (no bun), fries, and a salad (no croutons).

Be aware of things that are likely to be problematic. For instance, most sushi is okay, but some of the products, such as imitation crab- meat, usually contain wheat, while other sushi items can contain soy sauce, which usually also has wheat. Cajun cooking often uses beer to cook shrimp and other shellfish, and of course beer is off-limits on a gluten-free diet.

Make it easier on yourself by choosing foods that are more likely to be safe for you. What you end up with may not be your first choice, and you may find yourself longing for the days when you could order from a menu with your eyes closed. Don't whine about what you can't have, and focus on the things you can. Remember, eating out isn't just about the food. It's about the atmosphere, the company, and the fact that *you're* not cleaning up.

Talk to the Waiter and Ask the Right Questions

Sometimes talking to the waiter is an exercise in futility. If you realize this is the case, either order what you deem to be safest, order nothing at all, or leave.

A cooperative waiter or waitress, on the other hand, is your first line of defense in keeping bad food away. Make friends. Be kind. Tip well. After you've picked what you think could be a safe menu selec- tion or could be made into one, ask questions. Don't be shy; it's not rude or uncommon for people to ask questions, even when they're not accommodating a restrictive diet. Ask if the hamburger patty is

100 percent beef or if it has fillers; ask if the eggs are all-egg, or if they have fillers; check to make sure the fries aren't coated with breading or anything else that would make them off-limits. Check sauces and marinades; even if you mention that you can't eat wheat or gluten, people rarely realize, for instance, that soy sauce usually contains wheat.

Once you've made your menu selection, the waiter isn't dismissed. At this point it gets a little awkward because you've probably already asked a lot of questions, but there are a few more to ask, because how the food is prepared is important, too. You need to make sure that the hamburgers aren't grilled on the same rack as the buns, and that the croutons aren't just plucked out of your salad, but rather that they never were put in. You even need to ask about the oil the fries are cooked in, because if they're cooked with breaded foods, you really shouldn't eat them.

At this point, even the most patient of waiters is likely to be giving you a stiff smile with that "Is there anything *else* you'd like to know?" expression. Offer to talk to the chef, if it would make things easier. Chefs, although not often educated in the fine art of accommodating restricted diets, are usually interested in them nonetheless, and are usually quite fascinated when you talk to them about the wheat-free/gluten-free diet. Each time you talk to a chef, you're educating him or her and making it easier for the next wheat-free/gluten-free patron who comes along.

Restaurant Cards

If you find the aforementioned discussion exasperating, you might want to look into making or buying restaurant cards. These cards convey to the chef something similar to the following:

> *Due to a severe intolerance (wheat allergy/celiac disease/gluten intolerance), I can't eat gluten, which is in wheat (flour), rye, barley (malt), and possibly oat products. It can also be hidden in additives, seasonings, sauces, and condiments. Please make sure my meal does not contain any of the ingredients listed above, as well as additives where these*

ingredients could be hidden (for example, "seasonings" that aren't listed on the label).

It's also important that my food doesn't touch other gluten-containing foods during the preparation process. Please don't cook my food in the same oil or use the same utensils you used for foods with gluten in them.

Thank you!

Feel free to use the above as a guide, and tailor it to your liking. Some people who are sensitive to buckwheat, for instance, might want to add buckwheat to their cards. The same is true for those with any other intolerances. Restaurant cards are easy to print on a computer, and to leave with the chef for future use. Preprinted cards, many of which are beautifully designed and produced, and even come in a variety of languages, are also available from a variety of resources listed in the Resource Directory at the back of this book.

Do Your Homework

Many national restaurant chains have lists of their wheat-free/gluten-free products available by phone or on their Websites. Collect lists from your favorite restaurants and fast-food chains, and keep them in a folder for future reference. You may even want to consider putting them in a three-ring binder that you keep in the car.

Once you've done all the work to find restaurants that work for you, by all means don't worry about getting in a rut. There's nothing wrong with "tried and true" when your only other option is "guessed and now I'm sick." Don't get too complacent, though, because just like products at the grocery store, menu items at restaurants sometimes change ingredients. Check frequently, and remember that even if you think it's safe, if something makes you sick, don't eat it!

Buffets Are a Good Bet

Maybe it's a numbers game, but for whatever reason, buffets are usually a good bet when you're eating out. Their extensive selections usually include fresh fruits, vegetables, and other safe assortments. Obviously not everything will be okay, but chances are usually good that you can find something safe to eat. (You may be paying $16 for a plate of fruit, but at least you can eat!)

BYOF (Bring Your Own Food)

It probably wouldn't be too cool for a group of eight to walk into a lovely Italian restaurant, with everyone carrying their entire meal in a brown paper bag, simply to enjoy the ambience. But if you go to a restaurant and bring a small amount of food with you—even if it's the main course—it's certainly not rude. Some (but not many) restaurants have regulations about preparing food, and are allowed to serve only food that they've prepared and provided. Most, however, have no problem if you bring in your own pizza and ask them to heat it for you.

If you do bring your own food, make sure you it's wrapped in aluminum foil to avoid contamination during the heating process. Pizza ovens, for instance, sometimes have fans that can blow the flour from other pizzas around the oven, contaminating yours. If you bring bread and ask them to toast it for you, they're likely to put it in the slot of a toaster, contaminating it with "regular" crumbs and ruining your pristine bread. In that case, you might want to explain that it can't be put in a toaster, but if they have a toaster oven or broiler (that isn't blowing flour around), that would be wonderful. If you're asking them to microwave something, of course, they'll just remove the aluminum foil. The most important thing to remember if you're bringing your own food is to leave a big tip.

Sprechen Sie Gluten?

When eating at restaurants of different cultures and ethnicities, it's a good idea to know the language, especially if the restaurant is staffed by people who speak a language other than your own. Learn the important words to best communicate your special needs. For instance, in Spanish the word for *flour* is *harina*, but that can refer to corn flour or wheat flour, so you need to know that the word for *wheat* is *trigo*, and *corn* is *maize*. Some restaurant cards come in a variety of languages. Additionally, some Websites offer translation capabilities (see **http://babelfish.altavista.com/tr**).

Tipping

I'm aware of the redundancy in my continual references to tipping and the importance of being extra generous at tip time, but I believe it bears repeating. When it comes to asking people to accommodate the gluten-free diet, it seems imperative that we express our gratitude to those who generously oblige our requests. As awareness of this diet increases over the next few years, it will be more common for restaurateurs to understand these restrictions and accommodate them. Anything we can do as a community to enhance their understanding and acceptance will benefit us all in the long run.

Planes, Trains, and Automobiles: Wheat-Free/Gluten-Free Travel

There's no point in finally getting your health back if you're sitting at home pining away for excitement just because you're afraid to venture too far away. You have to live life to its fullest—you should be livin' la vida loca! There's no reason whatsoever to limit or, worse yet, give up travel because of this diet. Traveling wheat-free/gluten-free might be a little intimidating at first, but really, it just takes a little more planning, and an extra suitcase or two.

Most of the rules already discussed in this book apply to travel, too, including doing your homework, being prepared, and bringing your own food.

Pre-Travel Checklist

Before you leave, research your destination: Check with a support group in the area you're visiting to see if they have a list of restaurants or suggestions for stores to visit. Also search the listserv archives for frequent posts about gluten-free-friendly restaurants. You might want to go to the Internet and look up your destination city to see if they have a health-food store. If so, call the store and ask what gluten-free products they carry; if you have a favorite product, ask that they order it before your trip so they have it in stock when you arrive.

Be aware of legal considerations when crossing borders: Some countries have laws about what foods can be imported. Make sure you know what the laws are, and don't try to bring foods with you that might be confiscated.

Know the language (at least key words): Learn at least a few key words of the language spoken in the country you'll be visiting. Make sure you can say *wheat, flour,* and other key words. Bring restaurant cards written in the language(s) of the country you're visiting, or use translation software (that is, **http://babelfish.altavista.com/tr**).

Ask for rooms with a kitchenette, or stay in a condo: Even a small kitchenette with a microwave, refrigerator, and sink will make your life a little easier.

Ship food to yourself: If you're traveling a long distance or are going to be gone for a long period of time, consider shipping some of your favorite products to your ultimate destination so they're waiting for you when you arrive.

Carry a "kitchen in a suitcase": If you're accustomed to making your breads, cookies, and other baked goods from the mixes that you order online or find in specialty stores, bring them with you; it may be difficult to find them at your ultimate destination. Bring your specialty tools or appliances, too, like your bread slicer, if you plan on cooking while you're away.

Grab your gadgets: Manufacturers offer some ultra-convenient travel gadgets these days, even for the traveling eater. Most sporting goods stores carry a small refrigerator (there are several brands) that plugs into the cigarette lighter of your car, making it easier to bring yogurt and other perishables on long drives. And we all know how toasters can present a problem since "regular" toast seems to spray its crumbs everywhere, contaminating them for gluten-free eaters. A travel toaster available on the Internet (**www.fsmarket-place.company.uk/traveltoasters**) eliminates the worry; just take your own and you're set.

BYOF: Even gluten-free bread travels well if you slice it and pack it in a hard plastic storage container. Hard-to-find cereals, pretzels, and favorite treats, as well as cookies that you've baked in advance and frozen, make great snacks for en route or when you arrive. Don't forget to pack food for the travel itself, as well as for once you've arrived at your destination.

There are grocery stores everywhere you go: When you arrive at your ultimate destination, stop in at the local grocery store and stock up on some of the basics. Don't forget to buy aluminum foil and resealable lock bags, which work well to store leftovers from restaurants or food you brought with you.

Remember your restaurant rules: Use the tips earlier in this chapter for eating out at restaurants, since you'll probably be eating out more than you do when you're at home. If you're traveling to Europe, you might be pleasantly surprised to find that McDonald's offers two types of hamburger buns: gluten-free and "regular."

Getting There

When planning how and what you're going to eat on your trip, you have to first decide where you're going and how you're going to get there. How much and what you bring depends on whether you're taking planes, trains, or automobiles.

Driving: Driving allows you the most flexibility, and is easiest when you're trying to accommodate a restricted diet. If you're driving in the United States, there will most certainly be national fast-food chains all along the way. Even if you don't want to rely on greasy burgers and fries as a staple for your entire drive, you know you have a backup just in case. National restaurant chains (even those that are not of the fast-food, greasy-burger variety) have branches in all major cities; find out which restaurants are along your driving route (you can check **www.mapquest.com** or a similar Website), and contact them for their list of wheat-free/gluten-free products (this is where your three-ring binder with restaurant lists that you leave in the car comes in handy). Even if the restaurants you find don't have such a list or you didn't check in advance, you can rely upon the skills developed earlier in this chapter on eating at restaurants to get you through.

Most important, BYOF. You would probably bring snack food to munch on while you drive anyway, so just make sure you're loaded with snacks that are easy to eat in the car, travel well, and of course, meet your dietary restrictions (and don't forget the paper towels or wet wipes).

Flying, cruising, and riding the rails: There's less flexibility in how and where you can eat when you're at the mercy of a commercial airliner, ship, or train, but you still have a number of options. Many commercial airlines offer a selection of specialty meals, including gluten-free. Be careful, though, and read labels if the food has them, because sometimes our gluten-free meals have come with fluffy, doughy bagels (that obviously aren't gluten-free). If mistakes are made, don't be mad. They tried, and at least they considered a gluten-free meal as an option. Be glad they made the attempt, and consider writing a polite, gratuitous letter to the food supplier offering information on what's gluten-free and what isn't.

These days, airlines restrict the number of carry-on bags, so you'll have to be more efficient in packing snacks and meals for the flight. Snack items that you might include in a sack lunch usually make good take-along foods for the airplane.

Cruise ships always have executive chefs. They're accustomed to accommodating restricted diets, some of which can have dangerous consequences if mistakes are made, so they take the subject very seriously. By contacting the administrative offices of the cruise line several weeks in advance, you can arrange for the chef to provide you gluten-free meals throughout your cruise.

Trains are tougher, since most of the foods found in cafe cars are usually along the lines of packaged sandwiches, croissants, pastries, and other oh-so-not-nutritious goodies. I highly recommend bringing food on the train, and not just because of your restricted diet, if you know what I mean.

Disneyland, Disney World, and Other Theme Parks

Disney theme parks aren't just the happiest places on earth, they're among the most accommodating for people with restrictive diets. When planning a trip to any theme park, call a couple of weeks in advance and ask to talk to the executive chef. Tell the chef what day you'll be there, and specifically what your restrictions are (Disney parks are well versed on the gluten-free diet). Indicate the type of food you'd like to eat, and if you've been there before, you may even specify the restaurant of your choice. The chef will ensure that you have a safe, enjoyable meal.

Once You're There

For some reason, people who worry about traveling sometimes forget that other cities have grocery stores, too. In fact, just about any city I've ever been to has a store of some sort or another. It's the most convenient thing!

When you first arrive at your destination, check out the local grocery stores and see if you can sniff out a health-food store or two. They may carry products you've never seen before, which is always an added bonus. If you call a few weeks before you arrive, you can even request that they order some of your favorite products and have them in stock when you get there.

If you'll have kitchen facilities and plan to do a lot of your own cooking, you'll find that being away from home isn't much different from being there, especially if you pack your kitchen in a suitcase and come equipped with some of your favorite foods.

> *Bob & Ruth's Gluten-Free Dining and Travel Club was started by Bob and Ruth Levy in 1998, and promotes an assertive, optimistic approach to traveling and eating out. The club arranges gluten-free getaways, provides "gluten-free friendly menus," holds workshops throughout the country, and has a quarterly newsletter. See the Resource Directory for contact information.*

After reading this far, you've learned a lot about what you can and can't eat, where to shop, how to cook, and even how to eat at restaurants and travel safely. Most of all, you've learned that your diet never needs to stand in the way of your activities and adventures. You're ready to live the lifestyle.

But are you ready to *love* the lifestyle? As much as I'd like to tell you it's a breeze in every way, wheat-free isn't always worry-free. In the next part of this book, you'll learn to deal with the many emotions behind the diet, so that you can live—and love—the lifestyle.

Part III

Wheat-Free Isn't *Always* Worry-Free: Dealing with the Emotions Behind the Diet

The first part of this book dealt with the many medical, nutritional, and possibly even genetic reasons you may have had for giving up wheat or gluten. The second part taught you what you can and can't eat, and explored some of the practicalities of living a wheat-free/gluten-free lifestyle. But what about the emotional implications of living with a restricted diet? As you embark upon your new lifestyle, or even if you've been living wheat-free/gluten-free for years, you may experience difficult situations and unpleasant emotions as a result of your diet.

If you're feeling afraid, angry, deprived, lonely, and even if you're grieving for the foods you'll never eat again, you're not alone. Everyone experiences a myriad of emotions, mostly—frankly—unpleasant ones. This part of the book will focus on those emotional ups and downs, and will offer inspiration for dealing with your emotions in an optimistic yet realistic manner. It will also help you with challenging issues such as dealing with family and friends who don't understand the diet, and raising happy, healthy, gluten-free kids.

Chapter 14

Emotional Devotionals: Mastering the Ups and Downs of the Diet

"Life consists not in holding good cards,
but in playing those you hold well."
— Josh Billings

You've decided to give up wheat or gluten, and are well on your way to learning what you can and can't eat. In fact, some of you may be old pros, having been wheat-free or gluten-free for years now. You're all set, right? You hold all the cards in the game of achieving better health and happiness, right? Not so fast. The most important hand you'll play in this particular game concerns your attitudes and emotions.

You may think that because you're not the touchy-feely type, you don't have any emotional issues to deal with. You think you're Stable Stephanie? A real rock, are you, Roger? That's okay—just mark these pages for later perusal (or feel free to sneak into a closet with this book and a flashlight, if you're having trouble admitting you're human).

Even the strongest men and women aren't prepared for the onslaught of emotions they sometimes feel when forced to initiate this diet. If it's your child who must eliminate gluten, take those emotions and triple them—then realize you're not alone in this, and memorize and chant my mantra: *Deal with it; don't dwell on it.*

Emotions are a funny thing. One minute you feel like you have the tiger by the tail, handling life's ups and downs in a way worthy of praise from talk-radio host Dr. Laura Schlessinger; the next, you're pummeled by feelings you didn't even know you had. The other funny thing about emotions is that even if you can control them, it's very hard to change them. (I actually have some tips on changing them, but we'll get to that in a later chapter.) One thing you *can* do is understand them.

The Downs

Starting with "the downs" instead of "the ups" may seem backwards, maybe even a little pessimistic, and certainly out of character for someone whose nickname is "PollyDanna," but really, we're just going in chronological order here, because realizing you can no longer eat many of your favorite foods might make you a little grouchy at first. In fact, you might feel a *lot* grouchy, and you'll most likely experience a whole bunch of other unpleasant and uncomfortable emotions.

It's important to realize that these feelings are perfectly normal, they will pass, and learning to live a wheat-free or gluten-free lifestyle *does* get easier with time. Some of the most meaningful and difficult lessons we have to learn in life involve dealing with negative emotions.

Remember, when you're spending energy dealing with negativity, that energy is *not* being spent on the positive things in your life. Try to put your energy into productive, positive efforts.

Sheer Shock

> "I found out yesterday that my son has severe wheat and corn allergies. I've been through a lot of trauma in my life, and usually I handle difficult situations pretty well. But I'm embarrassed to say that this has turned me into a basket case, and I just don't know where to start. I'm so overcome with emotion that I can't even think of what questions to ask."
> —Tamara R.

If this diet is a must for you because you've been diagnosed with allergies, celiac disease, or gluten intolerance and have been told you have to exclude all wheat or gluten from your diet for the rest of your life, chances are you experienced or are still experiencing a mild (or not so mild) state of shock. Just being told that your condition has a name can sound so ominous, not to mention that at first glance it appears as if all of your favorite foods and beverages are now off limits. Then there are other considerations: psychological implications of feeling deprived; resentment and lack of understanding on the part of family members; the fact that you have a *lifelong* condition; and associated conditions that may have developed or still could develop as a result of years of eating gluten.

On one hand, it all seems so sudden. There you are in the doctor's office, talking about bowel movements or lack thereof, and next thing you know you're branded with a condition that will change the way you think about food for the rest of your life. Yet, on the other hand, it's not sudden at all, because chances are you've been feeling terrible for years, and finally someone has given you the key to feeling better.

It's not at all uncommon to feel stunned. The good news—let's see, there has to be a bright side to the shock phase—ah, yes—the good news is that while some of these other sensations may come back time and time again, by definition, you'll only experience shock once. Now . . . take a deep breath (or hundreds), and try to relax, because there are still lots of *other* feelings you can look forward to in your pursuit of acceptance and comfort.

Pure Panic

The difference between shock and panic is sort of like the difference between frozen fingers and thawing ones. While they're frozen, they're so cold that they're almost numb; when they start to thaw, watch out! That's when the pain sets in. When you first find out that you have allergies, intolerance, or celiac disease, you're likely to be in shock, and somewhat in a fog, trying to take it all in but not understanding the implications and what it all means.

As reality sets in, so does the panic. You know the feeling . . . it's that heart-pounding, blood-thumping, stomach-churning sensation that fills you with dread as you realize you aren't prepared to handle the situation at hand. Remember the saying in an earlier chapter: "When the only tool in your toolbox is a hammer, every problem begins to look like a nail"? Well, when the only food you can eat is gluten-free, every menu item begins to look like a croissant.

It's typical to wonder if you'll ever be able to eat again, and to panic, thinking there isn't a single food on this planet that you can safely consume. Grab a bag of gluten-free chips (there are lots) and relax. The list of things you *can* eat is a heckuva lot longer than the list of things you can't. But know that your initial feelings of panic are normal, and that you will quickly adapt to your new lifestyle.

Analysis Paralysis: When You Just Can't Get off the Mark

For some people, analysis paralysis is an everyday occurrence. If you're analytically inclined, you may find yourself getting caught up in trying to understand the minutiae of the whys, hows, what ifs, and what nows. It's hard to get things done when you're so deeply delving into the details.

In panic situations, even the analytically challenged can find themselves suffering from analysis paralysis. Panic itself creates a flurry of questions and hypothetical situations, causing chaos in the brain, and sometimes all those details can clog the plumbing.

If panic has you feeling like a deer caught in the headlights, try to relax and clear your mind, then deal with the issues one at a time.

Dignified Denial

It is with all due respect, Doctor, that I have decided not to accept your diagnosis, and would like to resume eating Twinkies at my earliest convenience. Tempting thought, isn't it? Unfortunately, it doesn't work that way. Surprisingly, though, many people *do* go through one type of denial or another.

The first type of denial is usually immediate. It sets in right when the doctor declares that you have an allergy, intolerance, or celiac disease. *Me? Naw . . . couldn't be. No one I know has that.* Or maybe you have a child who was diagnosed with celiac disease, and the pain of accepting the diagnosis is just too much to bear. Parents will often seek a second or third opinion, hoping that by asking someone else, they'll get a different diagnosis (much in the same way a child will ask Daddy after Mommy says no). Others simply refuse to believe the diagnosis, especially if they had only mild symptoms or none whatsoever.

The next type of denial occurs a few days or weeks into the diet, when the reality of doing this *"for the rest of my life"* sets in. One angel (the good one, of course) sits on one shoulder whispering, "You know you need to stay gluten-free—keep it up—you can do it! Mmm, yummy cheese on this gluten-free toast." The other shoulder is home to the Devil-in-Denial: "No *way* are you going to another happy hour and order wine and celery sticks while all the other guys are drinkin' beer and deep-fried stuff. You don't have no stinkin' intolerance. Come on—just one beer. It won't hurtcha . . . ."

The most dangerous type of denial occurs several months into the diet, when all of a sudden you realize you feel so good that you don't even remember the last time you felt bad. That's when people often think, *I knew I just needed a little bit of time to get over that bug I had! I feel great. I'll bet I never even had anything wrong with me.* That's when it's tempting to run, not walk, to the nearest bakery.

Resist the temptation. Yes, you feel great, but it's *because* you're not eating wheat or gluten, not in spite of it. The danger in testing the waters is that you may not have any reaction when you do, and then you're likely to jump to the obvious (by which I mean "desired") conclusion that you never needed to eliminate wheat or gluten in the first place.

If you still wonder whether or not you have a medical reason for cutting wheat or gluten from your diet, here are a few things you can do to help solidify things in your mind:

- Get properly tested.

- Get a second (or third) opinion.

- Talk to other people who have been diagnosed with the same condition about your symptoms and your feelings of denial (chances are they'll grin and say, "Yep, I felt that way at one point, too").

- Write it down: List your symptoms, the symptoms of the condition, and how you feel if you've been following the diet. Sometimes seeing it in writing is the just the proof you need.

Denial, by the way, is one of the most compelling arguments in support of proper testing and diagnosis. If you've been confirmed with a diagnosis, you may be tempted to fall into a state of denial, but it's going to seem pretty silly, even to you.

Remember, if it looks like a duck, walks like a duck, and quacks like a duck, it's most likely a duck, even if you wish it was a pigeon.

Abject Anger

"At first, I did okay when I found out I had wheat allergies. Sure, I missed some of my favorite foods, but I learned to handle it pretty well. Now, though, I find myself getting mad when other people are able to eat things I can't have. Is it normal to be angry at them? Sometimes I'm even mad at God for giving me allergies. I know this isn't good, but I don't know how to deal with it. I'm just angry all the time."
— David T.

So the shock has worn off, the panic has subsided, and although you had almost convinced yourself the entire diagnosis was a figment of your imagination, you shook the denial and accepted reality. What now? At this point, you may just feel fightin' mad. Mad at your parents or whoever passed the "defective gene" your way; mad at God for allowing you to suffer this way; mad at your family for not even *trying* to understand; mad because cereal companies just *have* to put malt flavoring in nearly every cereal ever made; or mad at yourself for having imperfections, experiencing emotions that make you uncomfortable, or not being able to control them.

You're just plain peeved, and that's okay. Anger is a healthy emotion, and learning to control it is one of the most valuable lessons you'll learn in life. It's okay to be mad, but as you should do with the other unpleasant emotions, *deal* with it; don't *dwell* on it. To dwell on the anger won't get you anywhere, other than angrier.

How you deal with anger is a personal and subjective decision. It certainly wouldn't be out of line to feel the need for professional counseling or psychological help. It's okay to need help, and it's okay to reach out. But don't *lash* out, especially at the people closest to you.

One of the most frustrating things about this diet is that family members don't always take the time to understand it (a subsequent chapter will explore in depth how to deal with this issue). It's understandable to be angry when a spouse, parent, or best friend doesn't seem to care enough to learn even the most basic requirements of the diet you must follow. Be careful to deal with this issue in a constructive manner, or it will consume you with hostility toward people you care very much about.

Grim Grief

If you're feeling sad, lonely, and melancholy, don't be alarmed. It's common and natural to feel a sense of despair, loss, or grief when diagnosed with a condition that has such a major impact on your lifestyle. What you're experiencing, in a way, is a sense of mourning. In fact, those other emotions you may have felt—panic, anger, and denial—are all typical of mourning and grieving periods, which is natural, because you *have* experienced a loss. Maybe it's the loss of who you were and what you were able to eat. Or perhaps, if it's your child who must become wheat-free or gluten-free, you feel a loss for the future you always dreamed he or she would have. Whatever the focus of your sadness, it's okay to feel this; it's part of the adjustment you're experiencing in adopting a new lifestyle.

One of the best ways to cope with grief is to reach out and help others. It's hard to feel sad when you're making others happy, and doing so shifts your focus away from yourself and onto other people and projects. Other coping strategies include writing down the many things you have to be grateful for, and trying to focus on things other than food.

If you find yourself feeling desperate, unable to cope, or considering destructive or harmful actions, get psychological or psychiatric help immediately. Sadness is completely reasonable, but if it becomes destructive, professional intervention may be necessary.

Don't get stuck. Sometimes it's easy to get trapped in this phase, especially because it seems at times that everything revolves around food. Work your way out of the grief, and you'll be well on your way to "the ups."

Mourning Your Loss of Convenience

Our society has become so dependent upon convenience that our food practically eats itself. Food products these days come pre-washed, precooked, and so prepared that it sometimes seems as though the only thing it can't do is predigest itself. Of course, it all comes in easy-to-open, self-closing packaging. All that's left for us is to chew.

All that convenience seems to vaporize when you're forced to contemplate the wheat-free/gluten-free diet. The days of absently plucking products off the grocery store shelves are gone. Choosing items from a menu makes you long for the days when price was your only concern. Spotting a pizza delivery vehicle can incite a case of road rage.

While it's true that the wonderful world of convenience foods is no longer your oyster, you can learn to choose convenient foods that *are* wheat-free/gluten-free. Tips from Part II of this book, a couple of phone calls, a little bit of homework on your part, and you'll be zipping and ripping packaging, and flying through fast-food joints just like the old days.

Secretive Self-Pity Gives Way to Gradual Guilt

> "*My daughter was diagnosed with celiac disease when she was ten. We were so relieved; she had been sick for six years, and we couldn't figure out what was wrong with her. Finally, we got the diagnosis, and she's been gluten-free now for almost a year. Of course we're happy that she's so healthy now, but I'm having a tough time dealing with the feelings of my own self-pity. This diet is hard—not for my husband, and not even really for my daughter, but I'm the one that cooks and plans the menus. Now I'm feeling guilty about feeling so sorry for myself.*"
> — Simone W.

Whether you're cutting calories, weaning from wheat, or bootin' gluten, being on a diet stinks. It seems like everyone you see is stuffing their face with things you can't eat, and it's easy to feel sorry for yourself. To make matters worse, feeling sorry for yourself can make you feel guilty because you think you're being narcissistic.

If you're the parent of a child excluding wheat or gluten, you may feel an extra burden. Now, with this dietary consideration, you as a parent have a tougher job than the other parents you know. This is especially guilt-generating, since you know it's your *child* who has the restricted diet. Often this same child has been sick for months, if not years, with a condition he or she will never outgrow, and you're feeling sorry for yourself because you can't whip up a quick box of macaroni and cheese anymore. It's easy to drown in guilt and self-pity.

Sometimes the guilt is related to nagging questions such as: "Will I pass this on to my kids?" or "Why did I have to give this to my child?" We can't argue with genetics, and many of the conditions discussed in this book are genetically inherited. But so is eye color, and you don't feel guilty about that, do you? You might be tempted to see your condition as a flaw or a defect, but is it really? Is it really such a bad thing to be forced to eat a healthier diet than the general population? You might want to think twice before feeling guilty about passing this on to your kids. Surely as a parent you have a lot more solid reasons for feeling guilty. Save the guilt for something you've earned!

In reality, this *is* a tough diet, and it's okay to feel sorry for yourself. Brace yourself, because self-pity and guilt are emotions that seem to come back to haunt you years after you've given up wheat or gluten, even once you've adapted to the diet. Know that it's okay to feel this way, but don't wallow in it; pull yourself out of it and move on, because there's nothing to be gained by spending your energy on self-pity.

Dabbling in Depression

If you're embarking upon this diet for medical reasons, chances are you were sick for quite some time before realizing that a wheat- or gluten-free diet could be your key to better health. Sickness in and of itself can cause depression, especially when the condition is misunderstood and one that most people have never heard of.

Many people who have allergies, intolerances, or celiac disease are accused of "making it up," or suffering from a psychosomatic illness ("It's all in your head"). These accusations in and of themselves can be so hurtful and can cause so much frustration that the person goes into a state of depression. Additionally, depression is a symptom of celiac disease, and while the celiac is eating gluten, depression is just as real and just as much a symptom as diarrhea or any other physiological manifestation of the disease.

Depression is a very real problem. For some who have little tolerance for mood swings or no understanding of the physiology behind emotions, it can seem as though a depressed person just chooses to focus on the negative, or intentionally wallows in their own misery. Sometimes, this is the case; other times, it's not.

Depression caused by feeling ill can result in a vicious cycle: physical symptoms lead to suffering and depression, depression makes the physical symptoms worse, and physical symptoms are amplified. When those physical symptoms are gastrointestinal in nature, the feelings of embarrassment and isolation can be extreme. The "cure," a wheat-free or gluten-free diet, can be socially isolating as well, since it can be difficult at first to socialize and maintain the strict diet.

Extreme depression, or depression caused by a chemical imbalance of neurotransmitters in the brain, requires psychiatric treatment involving antidepressants and ongoing counseling.

Depression that results from being diagnosed with a condition requiring you to dramatically change your diet is *perfectly normal*. Some ways to cope with this type of depression include the following:

- *Exercise*: Exercise generates endorphins (opiates produced by your brain), which make you feel good. Exercise also helps you get rid of stress hormones that can build up in your body.

- *Avoid alcohol*: Alcohol is a depressant, and while it seems to have a relaxing effect, it can in fact make you further depressed. It also interrupts important sleep patterns that are essential to feeling your best.

- *Eat well*: For most people reading this book, that means sticking to a wheat-free or gluten-free diet. It also means avoiding empty carbohydrates and sugar, which wreak havoc on your blood sugar levels and affect your moods.

- *Force yourself to relax:* Few of us spend enough time making sure our own needs are met. If you suffer from depression, taking time to do something special for yourself is crucial, even if it's just for a short time each day.

- *Reach out and help others:* It's hard to be depressed when you make other people happy. Volunteer at a local community center, or offer to help a newly diagnosed celiac with the diet. The satisfaction you get from seeing how happy you've made someone else will do wonders for *you*.

> *A good rule of thumb for any negative emotion:*
> *Deal with it; don't dwell on it.*

The Ups: Acceptance and Adjustment

One of Newton's laws says something like, "If a ball drops down, it will bounce back up." Well, maybe it wasn't Newton, and maybe that's not a real law of physics, but emotionally speaking, we all tend to bounce back, even after the toughest of experiences. If it seems like "the downs" section of this chapter is longer than "the ups," that's because it is. Once you've reached "the ups," you won't need emotional support from me or this book. I've yet to see any books on the bestseller list called *How to Cope with Extreme Happiness*. Acceptance and adjustment are your rewards for the effort you've put into learning to live and love your new lifestyle.

When you achieve this milestone, you know you're going to be okay. You can handle this. You no longer feel anger, denial, despair, and grief. You're moving on, adjusting to the diet and lifestyle, and learning to deal with it rather than dwell on it.

You may even reach a point when you wonder why it seemed so difficult at first. Maybe you're talking to someone who is new to the diet, someone still questioning every ingredient known to man, and you wonder if you're being a little lax, because it's just so easy for you. This is when you *really* know you've made it. Revel in your peace of mind, and realize you've acclimated to a new (and healthy) way of life. You may want to use this acceptance phase as a catalyst for making the effort to reach out and help others who are still having a tough time with the diet.

A word of warning—some of those thorny emotions you felt at first may come back and nip at your heels from time to time, especially the self-pity and guilt. Deal with those feelings as they come up, but always remember to deal with them and not dwell on them, because nothing positive or constructive can come from wallowing in negativity.

The lessons in the next chapter will teach and encourage you to better handle the unique situations you'll face because of this diet— but from a larger perspective. I hope you'll find that these "attitude adjusters" have a positive effect on your life beyond the diet.

Chapter 15

Deal with It, Don't Dwell on It: Lessons in Life(style)

"An inexhaustible good nature is one of the most precious
gifts of heaven, spreading itself like oil over the troubled sea
of thought, and keeping the mind smooth and equable
in the roughest of weather."
— Washington Irving

Life is all about attitude. The very essence of who you are is partially determined by how you deal with adversity and hardship, as well as how you deal with blessings and good fortune. Your attitudes aren't at the mercy of your circumstances—they're fully within your control.

I said your attitudes aren't at the mercy of your circumstances, but I didn't say they're completely unrelated. When we found out that our toddler son would have to be gluten-free for the rest of his life, we were more than just a tinge on the grumpy side. We realized, though, that we could despair about the foods he'd have to give up, or we could rejoice in the newfound health and strength that we were beginning to observe in our once-sickly child.

You, too, have been given one of the greatest gifts of all: a key to better health for the future. The wheat-free or gluten-free diet itself will strengthen and nourish your body, giving you renewed health and vitality that you most likely couldn't have even imagined at one point. But you may not be prepared for some of the effects that this diet may have on your relationships, and other adjustments you may need to make to your lifestyle. How do you handle friends who don't understand the diet? What about family members who won't even try? How can you adopt a lifestyle that seems to deprive you of all your favorite foods?

Some unique and interesting dynamics appear when you adopt a new and restrictive diet, whether by choice or from medical necessity. Dealing with them may present a challenge, requiring patience, understanding, and usually a few tweaks of your attitude. This chapter will help you learn to be happier and more content by offering attitude adjusters that will help fine-tune your outlook on your restricted diet, and on life in general.

Embrace Adversity and Accept Injustice

> *"Smooth seas do not make skillful sailors."*
> — African proverb

If you've been told you have to cut wheat or gluten from your diet, you likely want to shout, "Why me (or my child)?" or "It's not fair!" At the least, I'm sure you'd agree, you're dealing with a difficult situation: adversity.

You've heard the trite expression, "[Blank] builds character," where "blank" is filled in with any unpleasantry. It's true. Character doesn't usually come from a calm, smooth life; it's built by difficult situations. With no twists, turns, or bumps in the road, it's easy to be a good driver. But what happens when a child runs out in front of you, or a sharp turn sneaks up on you, or you get a flat tire? Handling life's little surprises puts you to the test and builds tolerance, humility, and competence.

How you handle adversity and injustice says a lot more about you than how you handle Easy Street. You have to look for and find the *good* in adverse situations; if you don't, the adversity wins. No, it's not fair that you have a medical condition that requires you to eliminate some of your favorite foods, and you may resent your friend for being able to order from a menu without having to interrogate the chef. And yes, the diet is tough. But you can choose to consider it an opportunity to become stronger as a person, more educated as a consumer, and more tolerant of *other* people's restrictions and limitations.

Fake It 'til You Make It: *You* Can *Change Your Emotions*

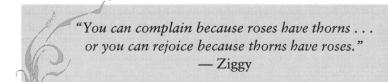

> "*You can complain because roses have thorns . . .*
> *or you can rejoice because thorns have roses.*"
> — Ziggy

When it comes to showing emotions, people generally fall into either the "I-wear-them-on-my-sleeve-and-can't-figure-out-how-everyone-knows-what-I'm-thinking" category, or they're more of an "I'm-ready-to-blow-a-fuse-but-look-like-I-just-woke-up-from-a-nap" type. People by nature also generally fall into one end or the other of the optimism-pessimism spectrum, with some finding good and beauty in even the bad and ugly, and others finding optimism downright depressing.

Whatever your inherent personality type or emotional persona, feeling a little more optimistic about your diet and new lifestyle couldn't hurt. And even if you're one of those who can't hide or control your emotions, you *can* change them.

The key to changing how you feel is to fake it. I know, it goes against the politically correct conventional "be true to yourself" type of thinking, and most people espouse the importance of honesty, especially when it comes to interpersonal relationships and communication. Don't get me wrong; I'm not recommending you *lie* to people, nor am I a fan of fake people. I'm simply recommending that you use your brain's unique power to see things in a more optimistic light.

Fake people are distasteful because they try to portray themselves to the outside world as something they're not. Unlike fake people, faked *optimism* isn't distasteful because the only person you're trying to impress is you. You're faking an emotion temporarily to generate an optimistic outlook from within.

Try envisioning this diet as a challenge, rather than a curse. Make a list in your head (or write it on paper if you think it will have a more powerful impact) of all the reasons this diet will be a *good* thing in your life. Maybe it will force you to focus on healthier foods and lifestyle. Maybe you'll spend more time thinking about meals and family time and less time thinking about work. Maybe it will bring you and your family members closer together. Maybe someone in the family who doesn't have symptoms will be tested for allergy, intolerance, or celiac disease and find that they have it—and will now be at less risk of developing associated conditions.

Make your list and pretend, if you have to, that adopting this diet has really been a wonderful thing in your life (to many of us, it really *has* been). Get excited about it—tell others about how this has been a good thing in your life, and spread the word as though you just won the lottery. Guaranteed, you'll begin to feel more optimistic, and before you know it, you won't be faking it.

> *"Watch your thoughts; they become words.*
> *Watch your words; they become actions.*
> *Watch your actions; they become habits.*
> *Watch your habits; they become character.*
> *Watch your character; it becomes your destiny."*
> — Frank Outlaw

Don't Be Easily Annoyed or Offended

> *"I have a nine-year-old daughter who was
> diagnosed with celiac disease three years ago.
> She's on a soccer team, and all of the parents
> share the responsibilities of bringing snacks to each
> game. I told all the parents about her diet before the
> season started, yet nine times out of ten, the family
> responsible for snack forgets and brings something
> my daughter can't eat. Why are they so insensitive?
> Don't they realize how bad it makes my daughter
> feel when she can't eat the snack that all
> the other kids are having?"*
> — Karen V.

Because you're reading this book, chances are you or a loved one has embarked upon a new, different, and somewhat restricted diet and lifestyle. By virtue of that fact alone, you've probably already gained a newfound respect for food, an understanding of what it means to be deprived of foods you love, and a heightened sensitivity to those who must abstain from anything.

The rest of the world, meanwhile, has gone on, unenlightened to the difficulties of living in a world where it seems the most common substance on the planet is gluten. They're not trying to be insensitive, nor are they intentionally excluding you when they offer food or beverages that are off limits. In most cases, they're distracted with their own lives, and have simply forgotten or don't understand the dietary limitations as you've explained them.

You *will* be in situations where people forget that you're on a restricted diet and offer you foods you can't eat; you *will* find yourself feeling somewhat ostracized from time to time; you *will* most likely get your feelings hurt because you expect others to be more sensitive.

Yes, it can be frustrating, annoying, somewhat offensive, and most definitely aggravating, especially when the person doing the forgetting is someone who should know better. In most cases, however, the person isn't doing it to be malicious, and doesn't realize the impact that their forgetting about your diet has on you.

It's not up to others to accommodate your diet. If you're going to be in a situation involving food (don't they all?), fill up before you leave the house, and bring yourself something to eat. If your child is the one with the restricted diet, make sure the snacks or treats you bring are even *better* than what the other kids will be eating, or at least just as good. Be the snack mom every week if you have to, and then you won't be offended when others don't remember. If they *do* remember, kiss the ground they walk on, because it's not their responsibility, and they have gone above and beyond the call of duty in being conscientious about your dietary restrictions.

Don't be easily annoyed or offended, and don't feel entitled to special treatment because you have special needs. Realize that other people have busy lives, and that your diet isn't first and foremost on their minds, even if you think it should be. When you're feeling annoyed and offended, you're wallowing in negativity that can destroy relationships and put stress on your body and soul. You're also wasting precious energy on negativity, when that same energy could be directed toward more positive and productive things in your life.

Forget Deprivation: Focus on What You Can Eat

Most people who have to go wheat-free or gluten-free complain in the beginning of feeling deprived. And really, who wouldn't feel that way? After all, for appetizers, you're stuck with things like prawns dipped in cocktail sauce, shish kebabs, or the ol' standby of chips and guacamole. Dinner may be some measly meal like flank steak marinated in tangy orange sauce, salmon with dill, or vegetarian enchiladas. Salads can't *even* come complete with croutons (although crumbled tortilla chips work well as a substitute), and dessert is limited to scant selections such as hot fudge sundaes or tapioca pudding. Yes, it's a sad existence, indeed. *Not!*

If you've felt deprived, please don't be offended by my sarcasm. It's perfectly natural to feel as though your selections are limited (they are), and to pine away for fresh-baked bread and take-out pizza. It's easy to peruse a menu in a restaurant and feel as though the only thing you can eat is the side serving of cottage cheese ("Oops—you're lactose-intolerant, too? I'll see if the chef can drum up some carrots and broccoli for you"), or to stare blankly at a full snack cupboard and see only the saltines.

If it's your child who can't eat wheat or gluten, you may find yourself thinking that she's feeling deprived. She *must* be, you figure, since she can't eat "regular" crackers, cookies, breads, and the other things you grew up on and that are such a huge part of our American diets.

Actually, today's gluten-free breads, cookies, crackers, cakes, and muffins are as good as or better in many cases than "the real deal." But philosophically speaking, as parents it's often *our* disappointment for our kids that's so hard to handle. We guess that they're feeling deprived, because we might feel that way if we were in their place, and any parent knows that the heartache we feel when our kids hurt is exponentially painful to us as parents.

The truth is, depending upon how old they are, your wheat-free/gluten-free kids will probably grow up giving it little more than a thought here or there. Their way of life is to eat foods that don't have wheat or gluten—that's all they know (or will know soon). You could raise them to believe that it's your family's tradition to eat earthworms each day at two o'clock, and that's what they would do (they may have trouble getting dates later in life, but that's another book in itself).

Kids who grow up with diets that are different because they're from a different culture or ethnicity just accept the fact that they eat different foods than their friends do. Treat this situation the same way you would if your family was of a different culture or ethnicity. Be proud, not ashamed, and feel like a model, not a martyr.

Focus on the foods you *can* eat. You don't hear vegetarians walking around complaining that they'd really like to sink their teeth into a good, greasy pork chop, do you? No. They revel in the healthy diet they have and the wonderful meals they can make using a variety of fresh fruits and vegetables. At some point, the wheat-free/gluten-free diet will likewise become your way of life, and without thinking about it or realizing it, your lifestyle will simply no longer include wheat or gluten.

It's important to realize that the list of things you *can* eat is a heck of a lot longer than the list of things you can't. A diet based on fresh fruits and vegetables, meats, dairy (if you're not lactose-intolerant), and a myriad of specially made gluten-free goodies is hardly a diet of deprivation.

Refrain from "Unpleasantry One-Upmanship"

> "I was talking with my best friend the other day, and she was complaining about how tough her schedule is because she has to chaperone her kids to all their events. Frankly, just because of this diet alone, my schedule is WAY worse, having to find specialty foods, prepare special meals, AND chauffeur the kids everywhere. I guess I'm still feeling resentful, but I can't stand to hear other people whine because this diet makes MY life really hard compared to theirs."
> — Cindy C.

You've probably found yourself in one of these conversations before: "Oh, I have such a headache." "You think *you* have a headache? My head was pounding so hard last night I thought I was going to faint." "Oh yeah? Well, I *did* faint one time when . . ."

I call this little game "unpleasantry one-upmanship." If you're on a wheat-free or gluten-free diet, you hold all the cards in this game. You can use words such as *chronic, lifelong, disease, intolerance, illness,* or *allergy,* and then there's the trump card: *diarrhea.* You worry about ensuring that the foods you eat are safe, while your friend's biggest concern at mealtime is making sure she pokes a hole in the plastic covering before microwaving the boxed meal she pulled out of the freezer. You want to scream, "Oh, you had to actually *make* a meal for your family instead of ordering Chinese?! Oh, my heart *bleeds* for you." Yes, you most definitely hold all the cards in the game of unpleasantry one-upmanship.

Don't play them. Just don't go there. For one thing, people who play this game usually don't care much about the person they're playing it with. They don't care about your diet; they don't care about your headache. They care only about whining about their circumstances, and while they want you to listen to their sad tale, they really don't care to hear yours.

An even more important reason to opt out of the unpleasantry one-upmanship game is that by being a player, you're focusing on your difficulties, and that's a negative force in your life that you don't need. So what if your life is more complicated than your friends'? So what if they don't understand, sympathize, or care at all? Your life is your business, and your focus should be on having a positive attitude and a productive influence on people. Next time someone deals you in on the game, tell them you're sitting this hand out.

Don't Become "Consumed" with Food (Get It?)

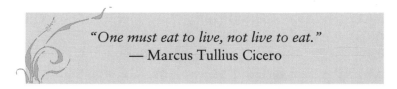

> *"One must eat to live, not live to eat."*
> — Marcus Tullius Cicero

Do you live to eat, or eat to live? Anyone who has ever been on a diet for any reason knows how hard it is to avoid foods, especially when they're suddenly off-limits. Nothing will make you think more about and wish you had a great big, juicy apple than to be on an apple-free diet. It's basic Child Psychology 101. Want your kid to eat a burger? Tell him he can't have a burger; he has to order the chicken. Guess what he'll want to order . . . yep, the burger.

The same psychology applies to grownups. What we can't have, we usually want. It's easy to become consumed with food (is that such a clever pun, or what?), but food fetishes can eat you up inside (okay, I'll stop). In reality, food fetishes can be the basis for some severe eating disorders, and should be taken seriously.

It seems at times that *everything* revolves around food. It's just about impossible to attend social events or any type of gathering without having people place a huge emphasis on the subject. This can be a nightmare if you're on a restricted diet, especially when you must adhere strictly to the diet for medical reasons.

Remember to *keep food in perspective*. Yes, it seems like we're always eating, and yes, everywhere we go, people are serving foods you may not be able to eat. But life is not *all* about food, and dealing with these situations does get easier. Bring your own treats, or talk to the host and ask what's being served. There are many ways to deal with eating away from home, and by the time you finish reading this book, you'll have a veritable menu of ideas at your disposal.

For now, it's important to keep things in perspective, and remember that your diet is just a small part of your life. Before you had a restricted diet, what were the important things in your life? Your family? Your job? Hobbies? Friends and activities? Those should still be at the top of your list. If this diet is new to you, it may seem as though your diet is all you think about. But as you become more comfortable with eating out, talking to people about the diet, and substituting safe for forbidden foods, you will go back to prioritizing your life in the right order.

> *Take control of this diet.*
> *If you don't control your feelings*
> *about this diet, the diet will control you.*

Face the Facts: You Are Different, and That's Okay

People on this diet nearly always feel a little awkward at first because they feel so different from the rest of the world. Our society has brainwashed us to believe that we're supposed to conform, and if we don't, especially because of something as out of our control as a diet that has been forced upon us, we feel uncomfortable.

When the food we eat looks and tastes different, we get a little squirmy. We wonder, *Do people notice? Of course they notice; my sandwich is crumbling as we speak.* We'd like to offer to share a meal, but will they like the "strange" food we're eating? It's easy to begin worrying that we're standing under a spotlight with everyone staring because we're different.

If it's our children on the diet, our concern about how they may feel multiplies exponentially. We talk about how we want our children to be unique and distinctive, to express themselves and their individuality. But we also want our children to be like the other kids, because we know from our own experience that to be perceived as being different feels uncomfortable.

You *are* different (or your child is different). And that's okay. The food you eat might be a little limited at times, and the bread you eat might, well, crumble when you look at it. So you can't eat wheat or gluten, which *does* make you different—but no different from the Middle Eastern family who only eats Persian food, or the highly allergic person who will die if he eats peanuts. For that matter, you're no more different because of your diet than you are because of your hair color. In other words, we're *all* different—and that's okay.

When you accept that fact, you will realize that you never were under the spotlight. Chances are, fewer people even notice than you think.

Surround Yourself with Positive Influences

> *"Always do right. This will gratify some people, and astonish the rest."*
> — Mark Twain

Purge yourself of the negative. It requires a conscious effort on your part, and you'll probably have to do it more frequently than you realize, but just as you take your trash out every week and have it hauled away, purge yourself of the negative influences in your life on a regular basis.

If you have friends or family members who consistently bring you down, spend less time with them. If you find that your job is dissatisfying or excessively keeping you away from the family, find a different one. People say, "But I worked so hard to get to this point, how can I give it all up?" You always have options. A new job might not be as prestigious or as lucrative, and you may even have to start a new learning curve. But will it give you more time with the family? Will it reduce the amount of stress in your life? The choice is yours. It may not be *easier,* but then again, easy isn't always best.

Sometimes the purging has to occur from within. If you find yourself constantly thinking negative thoughts, muddling in the difficulties of life, or being especially judgmental, you may need an internal attitude adjustment. That's not to say you're a negative person, but we all find ourselves off-center from time to time, and it requires a conscious effort on our part to refocus and ask ourselves if we're being who we really want to be, living our lives as we want to live them.

I'm not suggesting that you renounce your family, reject your friends, and quit your job . . . unless, of course, those things are required for you to truly be happier. The easy route isn't usually the best route, nor will it always bring you to where you want to be in life. Just don't use the excuse that you're "stuck" in a bad situation. Keep the end in mind, pursue your dreams and goals, and remember that you are in full control of your actions and your destiny.

Don't Be Stupefied by "Restricted Diet Stigma"

"After my son was diagnosed with celiac disease, I tried talking with my in-laws about the condition. My mother-in-law thought I was being overly dramatic, and accused me of making the entire thing up. My father-in-law, who spends more than his fair share in the bathroom with 'classic symptoms' of celiac disease (and who, by the way, is an M.D.), refuses to listen when I try to explain the condition to him. Not only will they not take the time to understand my son's condition, but they refuse to be treated, as do three other members of the family, all of whom have 'classic' symptoms. What gives? I'm just trying to help them, and to talk to them about my son's condition."
— Diane K.

Someday there will probably be a medical term along the lines of RDSS (restricted diet stigma syndrome) to describe the strange phenomenon that occurs among the family and friends of people on a restricted diet. It's the strangest thing—no one wants to talk about it. It's not because these allergies or intolerances deal with gastrointestinal distress, and are therefore too personal in nature. No . . . politicians will go on national TV and talk about their need for Viagra; national news anchors will openly discuss their battles with colon cancer; famous actors will talk about their hair loss or prostate problems; and celebrities will glom onto and promote awareness of medical conditions they don't even have. But find a celebrity who will talk about their celiac disease or gluten intolerance? No way! (At least not until Rich Gannon and his family came along—our thanks and appreciation to them for their generous contributions of time, energy, and finances dedicated to raising awareness of celiac disease.)

What is it about celiac disease, gluten intolerance, wheat allergies, or the wheat-free/gluten-free diet that makes people treat you like a pariah? Friends sometimes stop inviting you for dinner; relatives can have every classic symptom, yet refuse to be tested; doctors can be told that everyone in the family has been biopsy-confirmed, yet still not see a need to pursue testing; and people who feel better on a gluten-free diet will often say, "I feel better when I don't eat gluten, but I don't have celiac disease" (and haven't been tested). What is it with that?!

At first I thought it was celiac disease itself that made people squirm, and figured maybe it was because the word *disease* has such an ominous tone. But in talking with people who are wheat-free because of allergies, it became apparent that the stigma extends beyond celiac disease, and reaches into the far more inclusive world of restricted diets.

People, it seems, would rather take a pill every day for the rest of their lives than to hear that they have to change their eating habits. Doctors are trained, as Dr. Pietzak pointed out earlier in this book, that if they hear hooves, they should look for horses, not zebras—and these conditions are zebras.

Be aware of the fact that there *is*, for now, some type of stigma associated with this diet, and that people may not always understand, accept, or even want to know about your dietary restrictions and reasons for them. Don't buy into this defiance and denunciation, and don't be offended by it. As awareness of the benefits of a wheat-free/gluten-free diet increases, people will be far more accepting of the medical reasons that necessitate it.

Cliff Notes for Attitude Adjustment

We've covered a lot of ground in this chapter. Here's a brief summary of some of the most important attitude adjusters:

- *You create your own experiences:* If something isn't working for you, change it.
- *Clear your plate:* Something may have to give; get rid of things that are getting in the way of having what you want.
- *Deal with it; don't dwell on it.*
- *Take care of your body:* If wheat or gluten isn't good for your body, don't eat it. Get plenty of exercise, eat nutritious foods, and avoid excessive alcohol, drugs, and cigarettes.
- *Purge your life of the negative:* It may not be easy to give up extra income, friends or family who create negativity in your life, or other emotional burdens, but it's important to take inventory of the influences in your life and purge your life of the negative to make room for more positive, productive energy.
- *Spend extra time on things that offer you emotional or spiritual support.*
- *Make someone else's day.*
- *Lean on your friends, support groups, and other people who are positive and encouraging.*

That last point brings us to the topic of the next chapter: What if your friends, friends, family, and other people *aren't* positive and encouraging? What if they just don't seem to care about your dietary restrictions or health considerations? Should you try to educate them? And if so, how? You'll find the answers to these and many more questions in the next chapter.

Chapter 16

Family, Friends, and Strangers: Talking to Others about the Diet

"To talk to someone who does not listen is
enough to tense the devil."
— Pearl Bailey

No matter what your reason for your dietary restriction, one of the hardest things about this diet is talking to people about why you must be wheat- or gluten-free, and trying to explain the diet itself. Responses range from complete understanding (sorry, this is extremely rare), to people who *think* they understand but don't ("Oh, this is just like when I gave up liver for Lent!"), to those who don't care an iota about your diet, to the other 95 percent of the population who really *want* to understand, but just don't get it.

There is an art to talking to people about your condition and the diet, but first there are a few basic ground rules you should know and follow.

Attitudes Are Contagious

When you're talking with other people about your diet, especially close family members who will be "in this" with you for the rest of your life and who may also someday learn they must go wheat-free or gluten-free, remember that attitudes are contagious. If you give the impression that this diagnosis has ruined your life, and that the diet is worse than astronaut food, others will feel that way, too.

First, these things aren't true, even if it seems that way at first. Second, you don't want your spouse or kids to feel this way, especially if they're the ones on the diet. Be careful what you say. Even when they appear to be tuned out, kids and spouses hear what you're saying. Feelings can be hurt, and lasting impressions can be made. Portray a positive attitude about the diet if you can; you may even find it rubs off on yourself.

Educate, Don't Berate

It's important to educate those around you, especially the people you spend a lot of time with. But you don't need to send out a press release upon your diagnosis, nor do you need to walk into a room and loudly declare that you can't eat wheat or gluten.

Usually the best way to inform people about any medical condition or complicated diet is to give them credible, published material that they can read at their convenience when they're most receptive to the information. This book, several Websites, and other resources listed in the Resource Directory will be a good start. If you have a child on the wheat-free or gluten-free diet, refer to my first book, *Kids with Celiac Disease: A Family Guide to Raising Happy, Healthy, Gluten-Free Children*. Many people find it helpful to loan or give the book to teachers, grandparents, and caretakers because the more people understand this diet, the less afraid they are to discuss it, accept it, and learn more.

Be aware, though, that some people really don't want to know about your condition or your diet, even if you think they should. They're not interested, they don't feel a need to know, or maybe they don't want to hear about it because they know they have all the classic symptoms and should be tested, but are in denial. Telling these people too much about your condition or the diet only pushes them away and makes them less receptive than ever. Don't beat your head against a wall. They don't get it, don't want to get it, and aren't going to get it, no matter how hard you try.

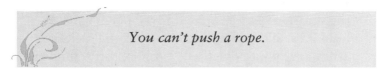

You can't push a rope.

Everyone's a Doctor

Before you begin talking to people about your medical condition, you should know that nearly everyone, regardless of education (or lack thereof), is a doctor. Especially when it comes to gastrointestinal distress, a subject that nearly everyone on the planet is at least vaguely familiar with.

Once you get past the squeamish introduction, you're likely to be cut off by people who want to tell *you* what you have. "It's lactose intolerance," your best friend assures you. "No, I think you have all the warning signs of colon cancer," argues Doctor Dad. "You just need acupuncture in your butt," advises your eight-year-old wannabe doctor son who just learned the word (*acupuncture*, not butt).

You may have trouble getting everyone to stop with the advice and listen, but try to get through your dissertation. Then you can look forward to one of several responses (percentages are based on personal experience, not scientific findings):

- *Complete understanding (0.1%):* These people will listen intently as you discuss villi, bowel movements, gluten, and modified food starch, barely moving a muscle as they hang on your every word, taking careful notes so as not to poison you at your next get-together. These saints have also been known to hang flyers in their kitchens, listing safe and forbidden foods in case you drop by for an unexpected visit. Worship the ground these people walk on, because they're few and far between.

- *Pseudo-understanding (they think they get it but they don't) (0.9%):* These people are easily identifiable, because they nod much too quickly when you explain the situation to them. Staccato-type nodding of the head is usually accompanied by rapid-fire successive affirmative phrases such as, "Uh-huh, sure, mm-hmm, yep, gotcha, sure, yep, of course, mm-hmm." Don't burst their bubble; these people are *used* to knowing everything, and usually can't be told otherwise. I recommend that you bring your own food to get-togethers with these people.

- *Absolute and unveiled lack of interest and concern (4.0%):* Gotta hand it to 'em, these folks are honest. Don't try to push a rope.

- *Desire is there, but they just don't get it (95.0%):* These people mean well, but either don't have the ability or don't want to take the time to understand. Don't be annoyed, offended, or otherwise put off. Their attitude can't change the fact that you feel a lot better now that you've eliminated wheat or gluten, and *that's* what really counts. Don't disown them (especially because most of your friends and family will fall into this category), and don't berate them, either. Your diet isn't their concern, even if you think they should care more than they appear to.

When Those Closest to You Just Don't Get It

Obviously, dealing with this last (and vast) category is difficult. Already you're saddled with the extra responsibilities and challenges inherent to the diet, and it may not sit well with you that some of the people closest to you are those who put forth the least effort to understand. We expect family and friends to support us, show concern, offer assistance, and make things that are important to us important to them, yet often it is exactly those people who disappoint us the most.

In this situation, we have the additional challenge of dealing with the fact that we're around them frequently, and food is often a part of social situations. Trusting them to provide foods that are safe, or worse yet, dealing with the anger and resentment when they don't even bother, can test the most solid of relationships.

If they just don't get it because they're simply not capable, forgive them and move on. Some people are set in their ways, and others are intellectually incapable of grasping the intricacies of the diet. Be aware and be prepared with your own foods when getting together.

When loved ones are capable but just don't want to bother taking the time to learn about the diet and your condition, you may experience feelings of hostility and resentment. It's okay to be mad, but don't wallow in the anger; it serves no purpose, and will provide you no benefit, because they're not going to change, and you can't force them to want to care.

It's important to avoid falling into the role of the victim. You may have some serious medical conditions, and you could be getting some sort of reinforcement from feeling victimized, both by the condition and the people around you. It gets you nowhere, except into a rut of negativity.

People who just don't get it aren't going to suddenly show interest in you, your condition, and the diet. Just as they don't *have* to cater to your diet, you don't need to cater to their insensitivity and thoughtlessness. Forgive them for their lack of sensitivity, their narcissism, and their indifference (but unless you want to start a family feud, do it in your heart rather than out loud), and move on. They may be sensitive, generous, caring people in many ways—or maybe they're not. In either case, you can't force them to care or learn about your condition or diet, and as frustrating as it can be, your only choice is to accept that fact. Don't allow yourself to get mired in the negativity that their apathy can create, and don't lower yourself to their level, either, by caring less about their situations.

The Less-Than-Supportive Spouse

The previous paragraphs describe how hurtful it can be when people you love don't show the support you expect from family or close friends when something as big as this impacts your life. But when that loved one is your wife or husband, the hurt magnifies exponentially. Your spouse, after all, is supposed to love you for better or for worse, to have and to hold, till death do you part, till gluten you do without. Your spouse is supposed to be your rock when you need stability, your lifeline when you feel you're drifting aimlessly, and the giver of unconditional love and understanding.

Sadly, many stories of marital turmoil follow a diagnosis that requires a wheat-free or gluten-free diet. Usually, when a spouse (as opposed to other friend or relative) appears apathetic or uncaring, it's not that they're indifferent or hardhearted at all—actually, quite the contrary. In most cases, it's that they care *so* much that they don't know how to react, or maybe they're afraid they'll look stupid or foolish if they don't completely comprehend the diet. Rather than risk their embarrassment or accidentally "poisoning" you because they don't fully understand your new restrictions, they back away, leaving you feeling deserted and abandoned.

At the risk of sounding sexist and stereotyping genders, I have to point out that it's usually (but most definitely not always) the husbands, rather than the wives, who pull away and retreat to their caves when confronted with this situation. Wives, or women in general, are more inclined to talk things out, so they're more likely to want to discuss the situation, admit they're confused about the diet, and make an attempt to understand. Furthermore, because they're usually (again, stereotypical but often true) the cooks in the family, it's important that they do so; they need to make sure they prepare safe foods for everyone involved.

Men, however, may feel intimidated about the diet partially because they don't do a lot of cooking, or they aren't accustomed to reading labels or being involved in the food selection process. Intimidation and embarrassment, topped with a touch of guilt and self-consciousness, are likely to send a man running for the nearest cave (conveniently appointed with TV, remote, and comfy couch), where he can safely and confidently armchair quarterback the game of the week.

To make matters worse, wives sometimes unknowingly blame their husbands, make them feel stupid because they don't get it, or make them feel guilty because they're not being "sensitive" to a serious medical condition. Soon the situation has escalated from fear and frustration into criticism and resentment, and both sides retreat to opposite corners with a chasm in between.

Of course, sometimes the roles are reversed. I've been told many stories of wives who appear disinterested and husbands who feel abandoned.

Whatever your gender, if you're the one in the relationship who feels forsaken in this matter, remember that most spouses want to be sensitive and supportive, but don't know how. Chances are, they've withdrawn because they don't understand the diet and aren't sure how to communicate that to you without looking stupid. Your job is to help them understand without being patronizing, judgmental, or in the least bit condescending.

In fact, one of the best ways to help people learn the diet is to teach them without their knowing they've being taught. If you offer "instruction," it implies a superiority that may put them on the defensive and push them into a cave. Instead, encourage their involvement in meal planning, ask them to read labels at the grocery store, and initiate discussions in which you point out gluten-free foods. They'll be making mental notes, and will most likely become more involved as they get more confident in their mastery of the diet.

If you're the one who is hiding in the cave, and your spouse is the one on the diet, by reading this book you've already taken a huge step in the right direction, and should be applauded for your efforts. It might be tough to ask for help in understanding the diet, but don't be shy, and definitely don't feel as though you're going to look stupid for asking. It's not an easy diet to understand (or there wouldn't be a need for books like this). Give yourself a break, and ask for a little assistance. Learning about this diet is an ongoing process, and one that can bring you together rather than rip you apart.

✼ ✼ ✼

Relatives in Denial

> "When our daughter Desiree was diagnosed
> with celiac disease, we started to realize that
> several people on my husband's side of the family
> had symptoms of celiac disease. We suggested
> they be tested, since we know it's a genetic condition
> and it's certainly possible that they could have it too,
> but they refuse. Some were tested, and their results
> came back 'iffy,' so they chose to accept that as a nega-
> tive result. Others have even tried the gluten-free diet
> and feel better, but insist they don't have celiac disease.
> They just refuse to take it seriously, but we know it can
> have serious associated conditions. It's frustrating."
> — Shawna L.

Nearly everyone who has been diagnosed with celiac disease has relatives who have classic symptoms, yet refuse to be properly tested. Besides the "I don't want to know I have *that*" syndrome, parents and grandparents sometimes feel the guilt of having passed along a "defective" gene, and therefore choose to assume the position of, "It didn't come from me, because I don't have it."

For some reason this is intensely frustrating to those who *are* diagnosed. For one thing, we want to help these people feel better, and we suspect the gluten-free diet may help. For another, we worry about associated conditions that can develop, and want to help prevent them from developing if we can. And finally, from a probability standpoint, chances are pretty good that a first- or second-degree relative of someone who has been proven to have celiac disease, could have it—even if they have no symptoms what-soever.

But you can't push a rope. No matter how hard you try, you can't *make* these people be tested. You can gently encourage them, and you can remind them of the many associated conditions that can develop if they continue to eat gluten, but you can't steal blood from them while they're sleeping, nor can you shove an endoscope down their throats and take a biopsy of their small intestines. We're once again reminded that we need to learn to accept the things we cannot change.

Strangers: On a Need-to-Know Basis

Some people need to know a lot about your dietary restrictions, while others don't need to know anything about it. Strangers or acquaintances whom you see infrequently are on a need-to-know basis, and how much you tell them about your diet will depend upon their need-to-know rating. You may want to base your decision on the criteria below. Some suggestions for appropriate responses are also given.

Need-to-Know Rating Criteria

High: Will these people prepare food for me? If so, it's important for them to understand which foods and ingredients are safe and which are forbidden. If you can narrow it down for them, do so. For instance, don't go to a restaurant and ask them what they have that's wheat- or gluten-free and expect to get a good answer. Instead, peruse the menu, and figure out what looks as though it is safe, or could be made wheat- or gluten-free. Then you can get into the intricacies of cooking procedures, contamination issues, and ingredients.

Sometimes it's easiest to explain your condition in terms of an allergy, even if your condition is celiac disease (which is not an allergy). People understand, for instance, that peanut allergies are severe, and even a little peanut can cause a serious reaction. Sometimes it's necessary to explain that you have a "severe toxic reaction" to wheat or gluten before people will take your condition seriously. Otherwise, they may think it's okay just to pluck the croutons off the salad after the fact.

Medium: Are they asking out of curiosity or nosiness? Most people who ask about your diet do so out of genuine curiosity rather than abject obnoxiousness. Maybe they have dietary restrictions of their own, and wonder if yours are the same as theirs. Maybe they're nutritionists, or maybe they're just genuinely curious. In any case, don't be offended, but don't feel as though you have to give a dissertation on the advantages of a wheat- or gluten-free diet, either. Offer as much information as you're comfortable giving, and as much as it looks like they're truly interested in hearing.

A good response is usually generic at first, adding information as the listeners seem to want it. "I have a condition that makes me unable to tolerate gluten, so I eat a gluten-free diet" is usually a good start. If they want to know more, they'll ask.

Low: Do they warrant a response? When the 16-year-old kid wearing a paper cap and taking your order at the drive-up window asks with a strong Valley Girl accent, "Like, what's wrong with the bun, dude? How come you ordered, like, all your burgers without, like, the bun?" your best response is to bite your tongue. No response is needed, unless you can muster a good, "Like, what-EVER, dude, I like 'em that way."

> *A good response for strangers or people with a low need-to-know rating is that you're on one of the currently popular low-carb diets.*

Speaking of gnarly teenagers and young people in general, if your child is the one on a wheat-free/gluten-free diet, you may have come up against a whole host of questions, emotions, and situations that haven't been addressed yet. Lest you think I've forgotten about you, the next chapter addresses the needs and concerns of both parents and the children who live with wheat allergies, gluten sensitivity, and celiac disease. You'll also find the answers to many other questions that you still may have, including whether this diet is nutritious; whether the whole family should be wheat- or gluten-free; how to handle the temptation to cheat; and much, much more.

Chapter 17

Kid Conundrums and Answers to the Rest of Your Questions

*"There is nothing so easy to learn
as experience and nothing so hard to apply."*
— Josh Billings

So far, this book has taught you how to select safe foods, how to prepare them, how to venture out of the house, and how to deal with the emotional ups and downs of a wheat-free/gluten-free diet. I hope you found at least a few nuggets of generally good advice for maintaining a positive attitude and an optimistic outlook on life. But you probably still have questions about how to lead your new life: *What if my kids are the ones on a wheat-free/gluten-free diet? Should the whole family be wheat-free/gluten-free? What if I'm tempted to cheat? How do I handle special occasions? Should I decline to take communion since the wafer has wheat?* This chapter includes the answers to these and other questions you may not even have thought of.

Where Can I Get More Help If My Child Is the One Who Needs this Diet?

Everyone thinks they know what it's like to be a parent—after all, most people have parents, and we all pretty much understand the job description and associated responsibilities before applying for the position. What I don't think any person can ever adequately anticipate is the intensity of emotions that a parent (bio or otherwise) experiences, beginning the instant they make contact with their child. Sure, we all know we're going to adore our children, and we eagerly await every new behavior as their little personalities emerge and transform. But as the months and years pass, the intensity of our feelings for them increases exponentially, and even the word *love,* used as a noun or a verb, doesn't do those feelings justice.

Undoubtedly that's why it's so difficult for us when we discover that our child has a dietary restriction that will change his or her life forever. We don't want their lives to be harder or more complicated; we would literally lay down our lives to protect them from the pain we're afraid they'll experience in having to deal with this life-altering condition. We're flooded with heartache, grief, anger, guilt, and the many other emotions discussed in the beginning of this book, but those feelings are multiplied by infinity, because it's not *our* pain, suffering, or loss, but our child's. I'm sure I speak for every parent who has a child with *any* health problem when I say that, if we could, we would assume the condition ourselves if it would only restore our child's health and happiness.

Aha! Therein lies the beauty of this condition. We *can* restore our children's health, and we can help them to be happy, optimistic, and well adjusted, regardless of their dietary restrictions. I'm not in any way diminishing the feelings of disappointment, fear, or panic that you may experience. In fact, I believe that raising kids with a dietary restriction as tough as this one is much harder than dealing with it as an adult, and I should know, because I'm "Mom" to a celiac kid.

At the beginning of this book, I described the nightmare we experienced in finally arriving at a diagnosis for our son. It took nine months, four pediatricians, a pediatric gastroenterologist, tears galore, and a lot of tenacity to finally figure out that Tyler had celiac disease. Diagnosed at the age of 18 months after growing progressively more lethargic and malnourished, he was what we know today as a "classic" celiac child, with the distended abdomen and chronic diarrhea. With greater awareness of the condition, children (and adults) with classic symptoms should be diagnosed more rapidly in the future. Sadly, children who don't have classic symptoms, but rather suffer from atypical symptoms such as constipation, seizures, neuropathy, or behavioral problems, may not be diagnosed until later in life, if ever.

If you're the parent of a child newly diagnosed with allergies, intolerances, or celiac disease, it may seem devastating now, and believe me, I understand. Know that it gets easier, and that someday your child will be healthier, happier, and the difficulties you're experiencing now may actually present themselves as opportunities to be thankful for.

More than a decade later, we feel blessed by Tyler's condition. (Yes, he does, too!). For one thing, we know now that his condition isn't, as we were told when he was diagnosed, a rare one. In fact, it's the most common genetic condition that we know of, yet most people aren't fortunate enough to be diagnosed, so they suffer the symptoms, as well as the risk of associated conditions. From a more philosophical perspective, our entire family feels privileged to be in a position to help others with this condition.

But enough about us. You're still feeling a little lost and could use some help, right? All of the tips in this book pertain to your child as well as to adults, but what you *really* want to know are things like these:

- My child has a tummy ache—how do I know if it's because of gluten?

- How do I handle sending them to school?

- Can I leave them with baby-sitters?

- How do I deal with birthday and team parties?

- What can I do about peer pressure?

- Can you give me some lunch and car-friendly snack ideas?

- How do I safely send them to camp?

- How should I talk to teachers and friends about their condition?

- What are the legal issues and rights of my child?

I know you have these questions and others, because I've been there myself. I've also talked with thousands of parents who have been there, too, because I founded and run R.O.C.K. (Raising Our Celiac Kids), a national support group for families of kids with celiac disease or kids on a wheat-free/gluten-free diet for any reason. Their needs, issues, concerns, and challenges are much different than those issues facing adults on the diet.

You'll find everything you need to know about raising happy, healthy, wheat-free/gluten-free kids in a book called *Kids with Celiac Disease: A Family Guide to Raising Happy, Healthy, Gluten-Free Children,* by yours truly. The book also deals with the "terrific teens," an age group like no other. It warns parents of teens' tendency to manipulate by using their condition as a sympathy card, and delves into some of the unique issues that teens on a restricted diet deal with at a time in their lives when conforming is as important as being unique.

If you have a child on a wheat-free or gluten-free diet, you're covered. Between *Kids with Celiac Disease,* with its focus on wheat-free/gluten-free kids, and this book, with its broader focus on all aspects of the wheat-free/gluten-free lifestyle, you're well equipped to help your child of any age develop an optimistic yet realistic approach to dealing with dietary restrictions and ensure a happy, healthy, wheat-free/gluten-free future.

On that note, I'd like to share with you a beautiful poem you can read aloud to young children to help them understand their restricted diet and the importance of sticking to it.

The Trouble That Jack Had
by Jane and Diane Pintavalle

This is the trouble that Jack had.
These are the grains that caused the trouble that Jack had.
These are the fields that grow the grain,
The grains that we learned caused the pain and the swollen
    belly that Jack had.

This is the doctor, kind and wise, who looked in Jack's ears
    and then in his eyes;
      then noticed his belly, too big and too round.
He tested Jack further and here's what he found . . .
In Jack's intestine some villi weren't working.
They lay down flat, their job they were shirking.
"This is not good," the doctor said.
"But there is a solution," and he scratched his head.

"Gluten-free is the way to go!
It helps children like Jack, I know it is so.
These are some things you'll be able to eat . . .
    strawberries, bananas, pork chops, and peas,
    potatoes and rice and popcorn and cheese.
There are too many to mention and all are delicious.
Some are crispy or crunchy and all are nutritious."

This is the challenge that Jack has.
Gluten intolerance or celiac sprue,
Whatever you call it, here's what to do.
Mom and Dad must read every label
And check all the food that they put on the table.
Jack packs his own treats for parties and school
And thinks gluten-free brownies are "better than cool."

This is the boy who lives gluten-free.
He is active and happy and strong as can be.
He is growing and learning and having fun.
He rides a two-wheeler and, boy, can he run!

The trouble that Jack had has gone away.
His belly is better. No more pain today.
To change what he's eating, we decided to try it
And now Jack sticks to his gluten-free diet.

Is This Diet Nutritious?

Absolutely. In general, the wheat-free/gluten-free diet consists of fresh fruits, vegetables, dairy, and meat. When eliminating wheat or gluten, you're primarily reducing your intake of carbohydrates, and it's easy to make those up in other forms, such as fruit or gluten-free baked goods. As with any diet that involves restrictions, it's important to avoid getting stuck in a rut. Variety is more than just the spice of life; it's the key to achieving balance in your diet.

For detailed, specific information on the nutritional implications of the wheat-free/gluten-free diet, see Tech Talk. You'll find a section written by a registered dietician who specializes in wheat-free/gluten-free diets.

Can I Eat Out?

Your first tendency may be to retreat into your home and avoid social occasions that involve food. After all, you just spent all that time reorganizing the pantry and marking everything in the kitchen with a permanent marker. You don't want all that hard work and graffiti to go to waste now, do you? It's natural to be afraid of going out, to want to pass up dinner out on the town, or to think about politely refusing an invitation to a friend's house because you don't want to inconvenience the host with your dietary accommodations.

Really, most hosts don't mind. Get out—have some fun! Don't avoid restaurants, happy hour, travel, and other of life's pleasures because of your diet; it's not *that* restrictive, and it's certainly possible to do all the things you did before, without eating wheat or gluten.

Yes, you are at risk of getting gluten every time you venture outside the safety of your own (clean, permanently marked-up) kitchen, and yes, you need to be 100 percent gluten-free if possible. So, how do you do both? Obviously, you don't.

You *are* going to get gluten from time to time. Accidents happen, and there's no such thing as 100 percent gluten-free until people become perfect and we're all walking on water. Unfortunately, you'll probably suffer some consequences when those accidents do happen, but they won't kill you, and if you're not a chronic mistake-maker, you won't suffer long-term effects. I'm not advocating that you cheat, nor am I saying that a little bit of gluten is okay, nor am I encouraging you to be lax and consider it okay to subject yourself to risky situations on an ongoing basis, but simply to accept the fact that there's no such thing as perfection; you can only do the best you can do.

By going out, you increase the risk of accidents. The judgment call is yours to make, but it seems to me that the risk of *possible* ingestion is worth a night on the town, a weekend getaway, or a family vacation. All those and more are completely manageable when you practice what you've learned and use good judgment.

Bursting Out of the Bubble

One of the most vibrant examples of how a person decided not to live her life in a bubble is Jackie Mallorca. As a professional food writer and copywriter for food magazines, Jackie's life—or at least her career—really does revolve around food. Not only does she write about it, but she's a food developer, taster, and tester, too.

When she was told she had celiac disease more than a decade ago, she was shocked. She could have changed careers, and, in fact, as a writer, her career had all sorts of doors that she could have opened. The one she chose was to stay on track with her food writing, developing, and testing. If obliged to test a recipe containing gluten, she tastes as a wine-taster would, trying a small bite but not swallowing it, and rinsing well afterward (she's a professional; please don't try this at home).

Author of *The Wheat-Free Kitchen: A Celebration of Good Food*, she has become an expert on—and writer about—gluten-free foods. She's not just "making do," though; she's reveling in the opportunities available to her now. A fan of interesting flours such as amaranth, buckwheat, quinoa, and tapioca, Jackie is definitely able to have her cake (gluten-free, of course) and eat it, too.

Always Be Prepared

Your diet, as emphasized throughout this book, is your responsibility. Just as you shouldn't expect others to accommodate it, you can't expect to find wheat-free/gluten-free foods available everywhere you go. It's important to always be prepared.

Don't leave the house hungry unless you know you're headed to safe-food territory. Always fill up before you leave, especially if you'll be gone for an extended period of time. Also, get in the habit of carrying food with you, hiding stashes in your purse, car, office, or anywhere else you can squirrel it away. Hunger seems to magnify feelings of deprivation; don't wait until you're hungry to start tracking down safe foods, because it will seem more than ever as though the only foods on this planet are foods you can't eat.

Disaster Kits—Be Ready for Anything

People don't plan for accidents or disasters. If you've prepared an earthquake or disaster kit, remember to include the things that are essential to your special diet. Many canned goods and convenience packages are gluten-free; it may just take a little extra thought on your part to compile a safe emergency kit.

Should the Entire Family Be Wheat-Free/Gluten-Free?

This is one of those questions that has no correct or incorrect answer, so I'll share with you my personal views on the pros and cons of both sides.

Pros: It's easier when the whole family is wheat-free/gluten-free, because you're making only one version of every meal, as opposed to two or three. There is less risk of contaminating safe foods because there aren't any "unsafe" foods in the house. Preparation is easier, and there's no need for the gob drop or any other tricky maneuvers.

And finally, from a psychological standpoint, you avoid having some people feel ostracized because their food is different and made separately foods from the rest of the family's food.

Cons: First, it's more expensive and sometimes more labor-intensive for everyone to eat specialty foods. Feeding the whole family homemade gluten-free bread at nearly $5 a loaf, when three out of four family members *could* be eating a less expensive commercial brand, can impact the family's time and finances. Try not to be a "saver," though. Sometimes, after spending $3 each for sugar ice cream cones, I'll find myself guarding them like a hawk. I've now accumulated several boxes of untouched, coveted-but-stale gluten-free cones.

The second and more important con, especially if children are involved, is that forcing the entire family to be wheat-free/gluten-free because of one person's dietary restrictions can put a strain on relationships. Resentment is almost inevitable at some level if some family members are forced to give up their favorite foods for another member of the family. Sometimes this works in both directions. In my family, for instance, my daughter would resent being forced to be on a 100 percent gluten-free diet (even though we're pretty close to that anyway) because that's how her brother eats. Interestingly, though, it works the other way, too. Tyler doesn't *want* his sister to be deprived of a bagel, nor does he resent her for being able to eat one (especially because the gluten-free bagels we buy over the Internet are so good these days!).

The last con is probably the most compelling, and is the primary reason I haven't forced my entire family to be wheat-free/gluten-free: It's not reality. Again, this is more important when a child in the family has the restricted diet, because the real world is filled with wheat and gluten, and most people on this planet eat it—lots of it. Children on a wheat-free or gluten-free diet need to learn how to handle the fact that, for the rest of their lives, they'll be surrounded by people eating things that they can't eat. If that makes them feel bad, sad, or mad, that's okay. What better place to learn to deal with those unpleasant emotions than in the loving environment of their own home? They may be more tempted to cheat because the food is in their home and others are eating it; again, there may be no better place to deal with temptation and learn to resist it than in the loving environment of their own home.

The compromise: In no way am I advocating someone waving a Krispy Kreme donut in your face singing, "Nah-nee-nah-nee-nah-nee . . . you can't eat this" in an effort to build character. With the excellent specialty products available today, it's easier than ever to compromise by keeping your home *relatively* wheat-free/gluten-free. Try to buy salad dressings, condiments, spices, and other foods and ingredients that are safe for the entire family when you can. For foods like pasta, bread, and pizza, you can make two varieties, one of which is wheat-free/gluten-free and prepared carefully to avoid contamination.

Cost aside, I don't see any reason to bake "regular" cookies and baked goods anymore. The wheat-free/gluten-free mixes are so incredible that my kids and their friends prefer them to "the real deal." They're easy enough for kids to make, and it's a psychological upper for my gluten-free son when his sister and friends can't get enough of "his kind" of cookies.

You'll probably find that because it's easier to make one meal than two, you'll gravitate toward wheat-free/gluten-free menus. With good planning, and a kitchen well-stocked with safe condiments and ingredients, it's likely that your entire family will inadvertently become at least relatively wheat-free/gluten-free without realizing it, and without the resentment that might have developed if the issue had been forced.

If you *do* end up relatively gluten-free as a family, or if you eliminate gluten completely, remember that anyone who is going to be tested for celiac disease (and if there is a diagnosed celiac in the family, all relatives should be) must be eating gluten for at least several weeks prior to taking the tests.

How Can I Handle the Temptation to Cheat?

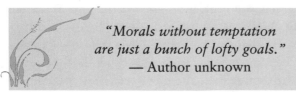

"Morals *without temptation*
are just a bunch of lofty goals."
— Author unknown

You may wonder what food has to do with morals. The answer is that how you deal with temptation to cheat on a diet shouldn't be any different from how you deal with temptation to cheat on a moral obligation or commitment.

You will be tempted to cheat on this diet—no question about it. It probably won't be because you're just dying for a bagel, but more because that bagel is now off limits. It doesn't take a psychologist to figure out that when you can't have something, you usually want it more, so now that you can't eat wheat or gluten, you'll probably want them more than ever.

The best way to deal with temptation is to just say no. Maybe that sounds simplistic or idealistic, but temptations surround us every day of our lives in many ways: the temptation to run a red light, to covet thy neighbor's spouse, to eat more Godiva chocolate than you should. Temptation isn't unique to this diet, and the way you deal with it should be the same as how you'd deal with any other temptation when you know the right thing to do.

If you cheat on your diet, how can you expect others to take it seriously? If your spouse sees that you cheat, you'd better not complain that he or she won't cook wheat- or gluten-free meals for you. It *obviously* isn't that important to you, or you wouldn't cheat. Why should your spouse care more about you sticking to your diet than you do? (Oh, and if you cheat, you'd better not whine about your bowel movements, either.)

The choice is yours, as are the consequences. In this case, the consequences of cheating could have an impact on your health. If it's a one-time indulgence, you're probably not going to do long-term harm (*no*, it's not okay "just this once") unless you suffer from a severe allergy and have an anaphylactic response. One of the best things about gluten intolerance is that many people have a severe gastrointestinal reaction when they ingest gluten, and the gas, bloating, and diarrhea act as a negative reinforcement, making them less likely to intentionally indulge when they shouldn't. Even without that type of reaction, if you have celiac disease or gluten intolerance, remember that prolonged exposure to gluten—even in small amounts—could be harmful and could put you at risk for many associated conditions.

What about Special Occasions?

Sometimes special occasions don't seem so special anymore when you realize that nearly all of these events involve food, usually of the wheat- or gluten-containing variety. The words "You're cordially invited to" can elicit feelings of panic or sadness if you're not comfortable with how to handle yourself in social situations because of your restricted diet. If you want to throw a party, you may be haunted with questions about whether you should serve all wheat-free or gluten-free foods, or if you should have goodies for your guests that you can't indulge in.

This is yet another situation where there are no right or wrong answers, but here are some basic guidelines that may help you feel more sociable during special occasions.

Fill up before you go: You've heard this basic rule before, but it's well worth repeating. It's always important to fill up before you leave the house, but when you're attending a special event where you will, undoubtedly, be surrounded by tempting wheat- or gluten-laden gourmet delicacies, it's especially important not to be hungry.

Call ahead to discuss the menu: Don't be shy; your host obviously wants you to attend, and would want you to be comfortable and content. People aren't usually offended when you ask what they plan to serve, especially if they realize you're asking because you have a restricted diet. For some reason, people always worry that this offends a host, but it doesn't. Ask yourself, "Would I be offended if someone asked me that question?" If you still hesitate to ask what they're serving, turn it into an offer to bring something. It's not the least bit rude say, "I'm so excited about your event. I have a restricted diet, and was wondering if we could discuss the food that will be served so I know if I should bring my own." Which brings me to the next rule . . .

Offer to bring food: Whether you offer to bring the dessert or to bring your own meal, always offer to bring something. Not only is it good etiquette, but it will usually prompt the host to tell you what's on the menu, so you have an idea of what to expect. Best of all, by bringing something, you know there will be at least one thing at the party that you can eat.

If you're the host, consider a wheat-free/gluten-free menu: You don't need to tell anyone the food they're eating is wheat- or gluten-free, nor would I recommend serving the types of foods that may not go over so well with people who aren't used to the diet, such as bread products. Lots of incredible hors d'oeuvres are inherently wheat-free/gluten-free, or can easily be made so with simple ingredient substitutions.

Potlucks aren't lucky: Potlucks can be tough, because they involve several cooks. Fill up before you go, and bring something you love, just in case that's all you get to eat. You can politely ask people what's in their dish, veiling your question in the form of a compliment: "Oh, this looks delicious! What's in it?" If you get a thorough answer, you can decide if it's okay or not. If the cook won't divulging his secret recipe and you really want to pursue it, you can say, "I have a restricted diet, and can't eat anything with wheat/gluten in it. Do you mind if I ask what's in the dish you brought? It looks delicious."

Can I Have Cake (and Eat it, Too)?

When you think of birthdays, what do you think of? Chances are, the first thing that popped into your mind was a vision of a cake—a big old glob of gluten—complete with candles. If it's a child on the gluten-free diet, it can be heartbreaking to think he or she won't be able to dive into the devil's food and feast on the frosting.

There's no need to miss out on special birthday fun. A few years ago, I wouldn't have recommended serving a gluten-free cake to party guests, especially kids, because chances that more than just a few of them would spit the cake across the room were good. Nothing dims the birthday candles faster than a group of guests spitting out cake, making faces, and rushing for their glasses of milk.

Today, though, things have changed. Thanks to mixes that are better than ever, it's easy to whip up a gluten-free cake topped with store-bought or homemade frosting that everyone will love. If you're less the mix type and more the Betty Crocker sort, new flours and terrific cookbooks offer hundreds of options for delicious birthday cakes. There's nothing wrong with serving two types of cakes (subtly, of course, so they don't draw attention to the gluten-free eater), but with the great-tasting, gluten-free alternatives, I no longer see the point.

You always have the option of serving something other than cake. Interestingly, a lot of kids don't like cake all that much; they lick off only the frosting or opt for ice cream instead. (When Tyler was little, I'd provide candy bars as a treat when other kids had birthday parties. Most of the kids complained about having to eat cake when Tyler "always got the good stuff.") If you want to avoid the issue altogether, consider serving ice cream sundaes, frozen yogurt, or chocolate-dipped fruit instead of cake.

How Do I Handle the Holidays?

Like most days ending in "y," seasonal and religious holidays usually center around—you guessed it—food. So, like all days ending in "y," it's important to follow some of the golden rules that have been laid down in this book, such as calling the host to discuss menu plans, offering to bring something, filling up before you leave the house, and bringing an emergency stash of food in case you need it. I know I've said this before, but please remember that, holiday or not, it's never anyone else's responsibility but yours to figure out what you're going to eat that day.

Some occasions, however, present unique food challenges. Christmas and Thanksgiving, for instance, generally feature a turkey (which is sometimes basted in a sauce that can include soy sauce), ham (often coated with soy sauce or seasonings), gravy (usually thickened with flour), stuffing (featuring loads of bread filling), rolls, and a pie (with crust, of course). Except for the cranberries (watch the seasonings) and the water served with dinner, there's not a whole lot for someone on a wheat-free/gluten-free diet to choose from.

If you're the entertaining type, you might want to consider hosting the holiday dinner. If you don't want to host the meal but are close enough to the hosting family member to suggest some substitutions, suggest a recipe like the one that follows.

Classic Turkey Dinner—Wheat-Free/Gluten-Free Style

Most meals aren't hard to revise so they're wheat-free/gluten-free. The classic turkey dinner is another matter. It may be a little more tricky, but with a few revisions and an extra touch of creativity, it's certainly not impossible to make the entire meal wheat-free/gluten-free. Remember, I'm not a measurer, nor am I a precision cook (no two meals ever turn out the same when I make them), so use the following recipe only as a guideline, adding your own personal touches as you like.

Turkey: Many turkeys are gluten-free. Watch, however, for turkeys that have been basted or injected with seasonings or soy sauce. Check the label carefully, then cook as you'd like.

Stuffing: Stuffing is a reflection of your personality (or whatever's left in your fridge from the week before). Start with the basics of traditional stuffing: sauteed celery, carrots, onion, garlic, and salt and pepper. Then it's time to get creative. You need flavor (hot Italian sausage works well) and, for lack of a better term, bulk. Rice is a great bulk ingredient, especially if you can find a gluten-free Rice-A-Roni substitute that has lots of flavor already built in. Add black olives, oysters, even gluten-free bread crumbs if you have them, a cup or two of chicken stock or broth, and cook as you traditionally would, either stuffed in the turkey or baked directly in the oven.

Gravy: Gravy is hard to make, even for the most seasoned chefs. Heat some turkey fat in a small saute pan. If you want a healthier, less fatty version, use less fat and more of something else, such as chicken broth. While it's heating, mix a few tablespoons of cornstarch with water (equal parts of water and cornstarch) until dissolved. Once the fat-broth mixture is heated, remove it from the heat and slowly stir in the cornstarch-water mixture. Keep stirring, wildly if you have to, lest lumps form when you least expect them. Heat again, add salt and pepper, and cross your fingers.

Pie: There are several options for pies, since in many cases the "innards" are gluten-free. It's often just the crust that presents the problem. Either make your pies crustless, or whip up a gluten-free crust using crushed cookies (or sweet cereal) mixed with butter and baked. A dollop of ice cream on top of a warm pie, and you're set for a happy holiday!

Passover

For those on a wheat-free/gluten-free diet, Passover is a blessed event, regardless of your religious affiliations or lack thereof, because it's the only holiday that's celebrated almost entirely gluten-free. Not only do clear labeling and strict laws about forbidden foods make it easy to determine what foods might be safe, but Passover foods are readily available at most grocery stores in a section dedicated to the holiday festivities.

Forbidden during the Passover season is *Chametz,* which includes wheat, rye, barley, oats, and spelt. Foods marked "Kosher for Passover" are gluten-free, *except* those with matzo, which is made with wheat and water. Matzo flour and matzo meal are ground forms of matzo, so they are not wheat- or gluten-free. Cake flour is also derived from wheat and is therefore off-limits, but is clearly indicated on the ingredients label as cake flour. As further evidence of the clearly marked labels we can enjoy on Kosher foods, the word *Parve* indicates that the product is milk-free.

Can I Take Holy Communion?

What should be a blessed sacrament is creating quite a stir in some religious communities. The traditional communion wafer offered for the Eucharist is made from wheat and, as such, is not allowed on a wheat-free/gluten-free diet. Options in the past have included adopting the "once a week won't hurt me" attitude (disputed by many medical professionals); foregoing the host and accepting only the wine; or substituting a low-gluten or gluten-free wafer for the Eucharist.

Gluten-free wafers are available, and in many denominations this is the preferred alternative. Church members can discuss the situation with their pastor or priest in advance of services, and arrangements can be made to provide a special host.

The Catholic Church, however, does not allow a gluten-free host for Eucharist, calling it "invalid matter for the celebration of the Eucharist," because they believe that the "confection of bread" is a fundamentally important characteristic of the host. Elders at an Episcopal conference in 1994 ordained that low-gluten hosts will be considered "valid matter" for celebration of the Eucharist, as long as they have enough gluten to obtain the "confection of bread," contain no foreign materials, and are prepared in a process that does not alter the substance of the bread.

While the low-gluten (as opposed to no-gluten) alternative is not acceptable for many, those who wish to take advantage of this substitution must submit a certificate of permission from their parish priest. Refer to the "Doctrine of the Faith: Norms concerning the use of low-gluten altar breads and mustum as a matter for the celebration of the Eucharist, 22 June 1995."[1]

Still praying for a gluten-free alternative, some are appealing to a higher source on the subject. Marisa Frederick, of Celiac Kids' Club in New York, has written a letter to the Pope, asking for dispensation for Catholic celiacs to receive a non-wheat-based host. She has also written a letter of petition, asking interested Catholics to sign and hoping that the Pope will understand the magnitude of celiac disease and provide a compassionate response and allow gluten-free wafers.

What If I'm Not Feeling Better on the Diet?

Most people who go gluten-free because they've been diagnosed with celiac disease or gluten intolerance feel better—not just a little better, but a *lot* better—within a week or two. If you aren't improving, there are four possible explanations. gluten is sneaking into your diet, you have additional food sensitivities, you need to be patient and hang in there, or you have what doctors call refractory sprue.

Gluten is sneaking into your diet: The first thing you should do if you're not improving or if you have continual setbacks is to take a close look at your diet. Reread labels over and over again, and call manufacturers to see if you still get the same responses. Have someone else who is knowledgeable about gluten-free foods go through your typical diet with you, and even have them tour your kitchen and pantry if they live close enough. Remember, ingredients change, and foods that were gluten-free yesterday aren't necessarily gluten-free today.

You have additional food sensitivities: If you're absolutely positive that your diet is completely gluten-free, but you're still not feeling better, you may have additional food sensitivities. Many people who have sensitivities to one food have them to others as well. You can develop sensitivities at any point in your life, so even foods that you used to be able to tolerate may cause you problems. Eliminate everything but the basics. Common sensitivities include milk, corn, meat, soy, and eggs, so be sure to avoid those. Slowly reintroduce foods back into your diet (except gluten, of course), until you've figured out which foods are causing the problem. Remember also that sometimes it can take several hours or days to feel the response, so look at all the foods you've eaten, even for several days preceding your reaction.

You need to be patient and hang in there: Some people take longer to improve than others. This can be especially frustrating when you hear claims of immediate improvement on the diet and fail to see your own results, but try to hang in there. Chances are you will feel better, even if it takes longer for you than it does for others. If you don't see improvement within six months or so, see your doctor again.

You may have refractory sprue: People who have refractory sprue either never respond positively to the gluten-free diet, or they respond well at first, and then experience a setback. This relapse is characterized the same as when celiacs eat gluten: high antigliadin antibody levels and abnormal cells on the lining of the small intestine. The only difference is, these people aren't eating gluten. Treatment options for refractory sprue are drastic, including parenteral nutrition (intravenous nutrition), steroids, and immunosuppressive therapies.

You're Ready for Your New Lifestyle

With this book, a desire to improve the way you feel, a touch of creativity, and a little extra effort, you have all the tools you need to live a happy, healthy, gluten-free lifestyle. As a summary and reminder, the following list offers quick-reference tips for success on starting and maintaining your new wheat-free/gluten-free diet.

Ten Tips for Success on a Wheat-Free/Gluten-Free Diet

1. Go "cold turkey." It's healthier and easier than sliding into the diet.
2. Educate yourself.
3. Educate others, especially those who prepare food for you or attend social functions with you.
4. Print the safe and forbidden lists in this book (or get them from **www.celiac.com**).
5. Order mixes, buy a breadmaker, and learn to order foods online.
6. Have realistic expectations of yourself as well as others.
7. Don't put yourself in inordinately difficult situations. (Stay out of doughnut shops!)
8. Be prepared; bring safe foods everywhere you go.
9. Eat before you leave the house.

10. Keep your chin up. This gets easier, I promise, and the healthy benefits far outweigh the initial difficulties you may face.

Before I send you out into the wonderful world of wheat-free/gluten-free living, I'd like to share a favorite parable about a chef and his daughter. It reminds me of how my family and I felt when we embarked upon the wheat-free/gluten-free lifestyle, and the little nudges I still need from time to time to keep me focused on what life really is about.

A young girl was being picked on by her friends at school, her grades were falling, and she was becoming depressed and feeling hopeless. She told her father that she wanted to give up; life was too hard, and she didn't know how to handle her problems.

Her father, a chef, took out three pots and filled them with water. He put each one on the stove and began heating the water. Once the water was boiling, he put carrots into the first pan, eggs into the second, and coffee beans into the third. After about 20 minutes, he fished the carrots out of the water and put them into a bowl. Then he took the eggs out of the water and put them into another bowl, and ladled the coffee out of the pan and poured it into a cup. He asked his daughter what she saw.

"I don't know," she said with some irritation at his silly demonstration. "Carrots, eggs, and coffee?"

He brought her closer and asked her to feel the carrots. She did and noted that they were soft. He then asked her to take an egg and break it. After pulling off the shell, she observed the hard-boiled egg. Finally, he asked her to sip the coffee. She smiled as she tasted its rich aroma.

She humbly asked, "What does it mean, Father?" He explained that each of the three items had faced the same adversity—boiling water—but each had reacted differently.

"The carrot went in strong, hard, and unrelenting,"
he said. "But after being subjected to the boiling water, it
softened and became weak. The egg had been fragile," he
continued. "Its thin outer shell had protected its liquid
interior. After sitting in the boiling water, its inside became
hardened."

Then he said, "But the ground coffee beans were
unique. After they were subjected to the boiling water,
they changed the water. They actually made it better."

Which are you most like? When adversity knocks on your door, how do you respond? Are you a carrot who seems hard, but when faced with pain and adversity, wilts and becomes soft, losing its strength? Are you an egg, starting off with a malleable heart, but after life's difficulties you become hardened and stiff? Your shell looks the same, but are you bitter and tough, with a stiff spirit and heart?

Or are you like the coffee bean? The bean *changed* the hot water—the "adversity" that it faced. When the water got the hottest, it just tasted better. If you are like the bean, when things are at their worst, you get better and make things better around you.

Beyond learning to deal with this lifestyle, I challenge every person reading this book to *change the water*. You can make a big difference in someone else's life by sharing your knowledge, your experience, and your enthusiasm. Become an activist in changing labeling laws to clarify when wheat or gluten are present; encourage your local store managers to carry wheat-free/gluten-free products you like; help someone new to the diet; or quietly offer something of yourself in any way that you feel is appropriate. The point is that you, like the little coffee bean, can change the water.

Tech Talk

Medical, Nutritional, and Scientific Details

If you're still hungry for more detailed answers to your technical, scientific, and medical questions, this is the section you've been waiting for! In this last part of the book, you'll find a section on nutrition written by Nancy Patin Falini, a registered dietitian who specializes in the wheat-free/gluten-free diet and celiac disease. She thoroughly describes the nutritional requirements and recommendations for those on a wheat-free/gluten-free diet.

If you want more detailed information about the specific tests for celiac disease, you'll find it here. If you're diabetic and you use the carbohydrate counting system, the carbohydrate exchange chart should prove helpful in controlling your blood-sugar levels. Finally, you'll discover the latest news about current research in the fields of wheat allergies, gluten sensitivities, and celiac disease.

Author's Note: This section, written by a dietitian who specializes in celiac disease and other food sensitivities, will help you make good nutritional choices given the restrictions you face.

Described here is a wide spectrum of information that ranges from the Dietary Guidelines for Americans to the nutritional adequacy of the wheat-free/gluten-free diet. After reading, digesting, and absorbing (pardon the puns) all that this chapter has to offer, you will be better equipped to play a proactive role in seeing that your health care needs are met. The goal here is to help you attain optimal health, given your particular food sensitivity, so that you can give all you can to life and get all you can out of it.

Nutritional Requirements and the Wheat-Free/Gluten-Free Diet

by Nancy Patin Falini, M.A., R.D.

The Dietary Guidelines for Americans: Know Your ABCs

The Dietary Guidelines are goals designed by the federal government for the general public ages two and older to make healthful food choices to reduce the risk of major chronic diseases. These diseases and medical conditions include obesity, diabetes, cancer, blindness, food-borne illness, cardiovascular disease, cavities, gum (periodontal) disease, and high blood pressure. You may even be able to compensate for years of ill health and chronic malabsorption of vital nutrients and phytochemicals by following these guidelines to the best of your ability.

Do keep in mind that these are only guidelines, because everyone's nutritional needs differ based on gender, age, culture, genetics, and whether or not they have an existing medical condition. The advice of the Dietary Guidelines is adjusted to better accommodate the specific issues pertaining to wheat allergy, gluten sensitivity, gluten intolerance, and celiac disease. However, if your food hypersensitivity has left you with chronic ill health, debilitating weakness, nutrient deficiencies, edema (fluid accumulation, particularly in the feet and ankles), dehydrating diarrhea, substantial weight loss, and/or you have related complications, you should either disregard or cautiously implement some of the guidelines. Before making any new dietary changes, especially if you have other diseases in addition to wheat allergy, gluten sensitivity, gluten intolerance or celiac disease, be sure to consult your physician.

In contrast, many individuals after diagnosis and continued treatment recover in a timely manner and become vibrant. They are basically "in remission," and are normal, healthy people. Don't be discouraged or overwhelmed by all the potential alterations these guidelines imply; begin by making only one or two changes at a time. It's like math. It all adds up to something greater—that is, optimal health and a feeling of well-being.

For clarity, the ten Dietary Guidelines are organized in an ABC format: Aim for Fitness, Build a Healthy Base, and Choose Sensibly. The goals, their benefits, and methods for implementation are described below.

A: Aim for Fitness

Dietary Guideline #1:
Aim for a Healthy Weight

Those within a healthy weight range should maintain it. Overweight individuals should control weight gain, then if genetically possible, should strive to lose initially 5 to 10 percent of their weight over a six-month period. A simple method for determining obesity (excess body fat) in adults is to determine your body mass index (BMI). This can be determined with the following equation:

1. Multiply your weight in pounds by 704.5.

2. Divide that result by your height in inches.

3. Divide that result by your height in inches a second time to determine your BMI.

A BMI of 30 or greater indicates obesity. When it is 25–29.9, the person is considered overweight. A BMI of 18.5–24.9 indicates healthy weight. Keep in mind the BMI is not without its flaws. It does not measure body composition. So a person may be heavy due to abundant muscle mass and not fat.

Where fat is stored in your body is important, too. A pear-shaped body, with fat on the buttocks and hips, as opposed to an apple shape characterized by excess fat stored in the abdomen, is healthier. Excess abdominal fat increases the risk for some diseases, such as heart disease and type 2 diabetes. Additionally, it produces high levels of insulin, which is linked with an increased risk of colon cancer,[1] a common malignancy in the United States. Adult females should have a waistline of 35 inches or less, and men should have waists no greater than 40 inches.

Once a person is overweight, he or she is more susceptible to becoming obese. Obesity can increase the risk in both children and adults for developing chronic diseases, such as heart disease; stroke; high blood pressure; diabetes; gallstones; and cancers of the breast (after menopause), endometrium, esophagus, gallbladder, kidney, and prostrate.

Conversely, being underweight can have its drawbacks, too. If you are confined primarily to a chair or bed, you are at greater risk for developing pressure sores. Also, you are more likely to suffer injury to vital organs, such as the kidneys, if you experience trauma, such as an auto accident.

There is no one standard to identify unhealthy weight in children. An undesirable weight should be determined by a medical professional, such as a registered dietitian (R.D.) or physician. In most circumstances, due to growth and development, overweight children are not advised to lose weight but are counseled in techniques to help them grow into their weight. Weight loss in children is encouraged only when assessed as safe and appropriate by a medical professional.

The ideal ways to manage your weight include increasing your daily physical activity, controlling your portion sizes, and replacing high-calorie foods with lower-calorie foods such as fruits and vegetables.

Dietary Guideline #2: Be Physically Active Each Day

Children should participate in a minimum of 60 minutes of physical activity daily, while adults should get at least 30 minutes most days, but every day is ideal. For those of us who love to be physical as in exercise, this goal is music to our ears. But for those who don't, the initial response may be "No way!" The good news is that physical activity does not necessarily mean calisthenics. Even routine physical activity can count as exercise.

Exercise not only helps to control weight, but also decreases the risk of developing cardiovascular disease and type 2 diabetes; increases the high-density lipoprotein (HDL) level (the good cholesterol); builds and maintains healthy bones, joints, and muscles, which consequently helps prevent or curtail osteoporosis (a common bone disease in celiac disease); helps control blood pressure; increases energy; improves sleep; and can strengthen your psyche by decreasing feelings of depression and anxiety while enhancing self-esteem. The latter four benefits are quite significant, particularly for the celiac population, as some experience one or more of these even after healing occurs.

There are two types of physical activity: aerobic, which strengthens cardiovascular fitness; and strength and flexibility, which helps build and maintain bones. In general, those with a chronic health problem, such as osteoporosis, cardiovascular disease, and/or diabetes, should consult with a health-care provider before becoming more physically active or changing their exercise routines. This is imperative for those who are physically impaired.

B: Build a Healthy Base
Dietary Guideline #3:
Let the Pyramid Guide Your Food Choices

Figure 2
Food Guide Pyramid

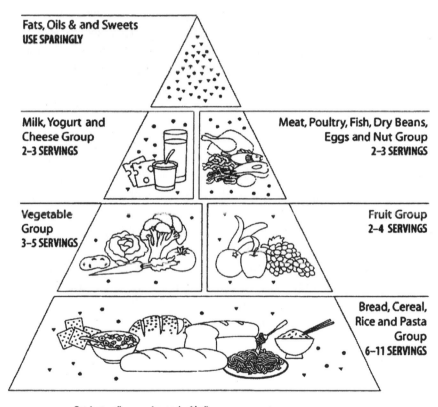

● Fat (naturally occurring and added)
▼ Sugars (added)

These symbols show fat and added sugars in foods.

Source: HealthNews 5 (5): 1–2 (April 15, 1999).

Since no one food supplies all the nutrients and substances needed for good health, adequate daily food variety is necessary. The Food Guide Pyramid, like the Dietary Guidelines, is designed for those aged 2 through 70. (See "Specific Nutritional Concerns of the Aging" later in this section for the Modified Food Pyramid for 70+ Adults.)

The Food Guide Pyramid is a graphic representation of the foods you should base your diet on and those you should consume in lesser amounts. Instead of climbing to the top to succeed, to eat your way to good health you are best off staying near the bottom. The lower part of the pyramid consists of plant products, which should be your predominant food choices. The steeper part consists of animal products, which you should moderate. The top contains oils, fats, and sweets, which you want to consume sparingly.

Water is the often-forgotten nutrient. The majority of our bodies are made up of water, though the concentration decreases as we age. Water is required for biochemical reactions to occur in the body. It is even required for mental work to the point where concentration can become impaired when a person is thirsty. It also regulates body temperature and promotes regular bowel movements.

Bread, Cereal, Rice and Pasta Group (Grain Products): Some people, until they become familiar with all the tasty, wonderful variety of wheat-free/gluten-free grain products, limit the numbers of servings chosen from this food group. All too often celiacs choose candy to replace calories (not to mention nutrition) that would otherwise come from making selections from this food group.

Complex carbohydrates, B vitamins such as thiamin and pyridoxine (vitamin B6), and minerals such as iron and zinc may be obtained from this group. Furthermore, whole grains provide significant amounts of fiber, magnesium, manganese, copper, chromium, and potassium. Grain products also are rich in phytochemicals, natural substances in plant foods that possess various yet not well understood roles in hindering the development of some chronic diseases.

Fruit Group: Fresh fruits or 100 percent fruit juices contain valuable nutrients such as vitamin A, vitamin C, folate, and potassium.

Vegetable Group: These food groups are rich in nutrients such as folate, potassium, carotene (the plant form of vitamin A), and vitamin C. The latter two vitamins are antioxidants, providing protection against chronic disease, such as cancer and cardiovascular disease.

Meat, Poultry, Fish, Dry Beans, Eggs, and Nuts Group (Meat Group): Various B vitamins such as niacin, iron, protein, and variable levels of fat, are found in foods in this group. Animal products specifically supply vitamin B12, selenium, zinc, chromium, and cholesterol. Nuts and seeds contain folate, vitamin E, magnesium, copper, essential fatty acids, fiber, and phytochemicals. Dried beans, peas, and lentils supply folate, calcium, iron, magnesium, copper, fiber, and phytochemicals. Soybeans possess a unique function to serve as a probiotic by stimulating the growth of healthy intestinal bacteria. This wonderful attribute can help prevent bacterial overgrowth in the intestine, which can result from gluten sensitivity, gluten intolerance, or celiac disease.

Milk, Yogurt, and Cheese Group (Dairy Group): The dairy group supplies calcium, and some products are fortified with vitamin D. Phosphorus, potassium, and small amounts of vitamin K are among some of the other nutrients, as are B vitamins such as riboflavin.

Dietary Guideline #4:
Choose a Variety of Grains Daily, Especially Whole Grains

At least six servings of grains (bread, cereal, rice, and pasta group) should be eaten daily, and a minimum of three should be whole grains. Grains are naturally fat-free or low in fat unless fat is added during the processing or preparation processes.

Pyridoxine (vitamin B6) is among the important nutrients in grains. It, along with folate/folic acid and vitamin B12, helps prevent elevated homocysteine (a product of protein metabolism) levels. Elevated homocysteine levels increase your risk of cardiovascular disease.

Whole grains have not had their fiber stripped away and thus are better foods to eat for more fiber. Refined grains are low-fiber foods because most of their fiber is removed along with major nutrients during the milling process. Some nutrients may be replaced by an enrichment process, or a particular grain product may be fortified with other nutrients. Unfortunately, in the case of most gluten-free grain products made especially for gluten-free consumers, neither the enrichment nor fortification processes are mandated.

When choosing these foods, try to choose (unrefined) whole grains and enriched grains such as ground flaxseed, brown rice and its flour, brown rice flakes, rice bran, wild rice, enriched white rice, enriched cream of rice and baby rice cereal, stone-ground whole kernel corn tortillas, enriched cornmeal, and corn flour. Feast on flours made from beans such as fava and chickpea (garbanzo); and nut flours, such as almond flour. (The full-fat versions are more nutritious than partially defatted nut flours.)

The Flack on Flax

Based on clinical studies, adults are advised to eat one to two tablespoons of ground flaxseed and/or one teaspoon of flaxseed oil each day. Because of a lack of research in certain life stages, certain groups of people should limit their intake of flaxseed/ground flaxseed because they are rich in lignans, which are phytoestrogens. Children under ten, women trying to become pregnant, pregnant women, and breastfeeding women should avoid eating flaxseed on a regular basis, as should women with breast cancer.[2] Flaxseed oil without added lignans is safe for anyone except children, whose fatty acid requirements have not yet been determined.

Dietary Guideline #5:
Choose a Variety of Fruits and Vegetables Daily

Everyone should eat a minimum of five fruits and vegetables each day. The majority of Americans eat only two or three servings a day. The most nutritious types of produce are red, yellow, or orange fruits, and dark green, yellow, or orange vegetables.

Studies show these foods, when eaten in quantities beyond the minimum recommendations, specifically nine to ten servings daily, provide even more protection against chronic diseases such as cancer and hypertension. They also supply non-nutritive substances. For example, sulforaphane contained within cruciferous vegetables (cauliflower, broccoli, kale, Brussels sprouts, and cabbage) is an indirect antioxidant that protects entire cells against the cancer process.[3]

Dietary Guideline #6:
Keep Food Safe to Eat

Keeping foods free of harmful organisms such as bacteria, parasites, and fungal growth is essential to good health. This prevents foodborne illness that can incidentally mimic wheat allergy, gluten sensitivity, gluten intolerance, or celiac disease with its symptoms of nausea, vomiting, abdominal pain, and/or diarrhea. Additionally, when grains are stored for long periods of time in a relatively warm and moist place, mycotoxins can form and cause a risk for liver cancer.

Some tips for keeping your food safe from harmful living organisms include appropriate washing, separating, cooking, chilling, serving, and storing methods. For more information on food safety call the FDA's Food Information Line at 888-SAFE FOOD or the USDA's Meat and Poultry Hotline at 800-535-4555.

C: *Choose Sensibly*

Dietary Guideline #7:
Choose a Diet That Is Low in Saturated Fat
and Cholesterol and Moderate in Total Fat

Generally speaking, Americans have decreased their total fat consumption but their saturated fats remain high. In contrast, many have increased their daily calories. Saturated fat is found in varying levels in a variety of foods, including meat, poultry, seafood, eggs, dairy products, and palm and coconut oils. An excess of this type of fat increases the risk of cardiovascular disease and certain types of cancer, such as colon, rectum, breast, and prostate. Additionally, saturated fat is used by the liver to make cholesterol. This, in addition to excess dietary cholesterol (cholesterol is found only in animal products), contributes to atherosclerosis, or hardening of the arteries.

Trans-fatty acids are unsaturated fats whose structure is synthetically changed and consequently whose effects on the body are adversely altered. Stick margarine, shortening, and partially hydrogenated vegetable oil provide trans-fatty acids. High amounts of trans-fatty acids promote atherosclerosis. Also, due to their structural change, trans-fatty acids likely alter cell walls, thus increasing susceptibility to free-radical damage. (Free radicals are unstable biochemical structures that must find another structure to stabilize.) This could be the reason for their suspected role in the onset of some chronic diseases. Additionally, moderating total fat is an effective method for preventing excess calorie consumption.

Europeans who consume what is called a Mediterranean diet have affirmed the benefits of modifying the types of fats we eat. Their primary sources of dietary fat are those obtained from fish, nuts, and olive and flaxseed oils. Their consumption of red meat, eggs, whole milk cheese, and butter (foods high in saturated fat and cholesterol) is less than that of Americans. The Mediterranean diet, also based on grains, fruits, vegetables, and dried beans (the base of the Food Guide Pyramid), is correlated with less cardiovascular disease.

By decreasing saturated fat, cholesterol, and trans-fatty acids, you can focus on incorporating more of a balance of unsaturated fats. Unsaturated fats predominantly supply essential fatty acids found in vegetable oils, nuts, seeds, and seafood. Olive oil, predominantly a monounsaturated fat, is an exception. Although it offers benefits like reducing cardiovascular disease, it is not a significant source of essential fatty acids.

Essential fatty acids (linoleic and linolenic) are not produced by the body, but are critical for the normal function of all tissues, particularly in the development and maintenance of cells and hormones. Eating excess trans-fatty acids can interfere with the conversion of essential fatty acids into their final and usable forms. Good sources of essential fatty acids are oils and their soft, pourable spreads from any of these sources: flaxseed, canola, safflower, soybean, corn, peanut, cottonseed, sesame, sunflower, or walnut. Whole nuts and seeds supply essential fatty acids. Whole soy foods containing low or high fat content, including soy milk, soy flour, and tofu, as well as some seafood, also contain essential fatty acids.

Omega 3 fatty acids are polyunsaturated fats, primarily found in flaxseed, canola oil, walnuts, soy products containing fat, and seafood (coldwater fish are rich in these fatty acids). Omega 3 fatty acids are believed to inhibit inflammation and prevent cardiovascular disease and cancer.

Some people in the gluten-sensitive, gluten-intolerant, and celiac world are concerned that the gluten-free diet is inherently high in fat, because of the need for relatively more fat to compensate for the absence of gluten in baking. Whether or not this is true is still questioned. There is, however, some evidence that the gluten-free diet is high in fat in those individuals who select more animal products over grains once they are diagnosed. A physician with expertise in celiac disease claims there is less cardiovascular disease in the celiac population, probably because of years of having experienced chronic malabsorption.

Dietary Guideline #8:
Choose Beverages and Foods to
Moderate Your Intake of Sugars

This refers to sugars (like table sugar or sucrose) and syrups (like high-fructose corn syrup) that are added to foods in processing and/or preparation. This does not include sugars like those found naturally in milk (lactose) or in fruit (fructose). Sugar by itself and when added to foods provides empty calories (no nutritional value other than calories/energy), and can lead to tooth decay, gum disease, weight gain, and suppression of appetite for nutritious foods.

Dietary Guideline #9:
Choose and Prepare Foods with Less Salt

In general, most people consume excess sodium in the form of table salt. We need 2,400 milligrams of sodium daily, which is one teaspoon of salt. Moderating sodium can help control blood pressure and prevent strokes. Excess sodium leads to excess calcium loss in the urine, which can increase the risk for osteopenia and osteoporosis. There is a greater risk for stomach cancer with excess sodium in your diet.

Dietary Guideline #10:
If You Drink Alcoholic Beverages, Do So in Moderation

Children and adolescents should not drink alcoholic beverages. If you as an adult do not drink alcohol, don't start. If you do drink, do it in moderation. If, however, you have newly diagnosed wheat allergy with gastrointestinal symptoms, gluten sensitivity, gluten intolerance, or celiac disease, or your intestine is still healing, it is wise to eliminate alcoholic drinks. Alcohol is a solvent and can promote inflammation, whether or not you have an intestinal condition. Consequently, you may experience intestinal distress from the effects of alcohol, further worsening your symptoms.

Nutrients Prone to Be Affected by
Gluten Sensitivity/Intolerance and Celiac Disease

The damage from gluten sensitivity, gluten intolerance, and celiac disease initially affects the upper part of the small intestine (duodenum) where the gluten enters the intestinal tract from the stomach. Damage can vary from mild to severe and potentially can work into the middle part of the small intestine (jejunum), then to the lower part of the small intestine (ileum) if allowed to progress. Malabsorption of one or potentially all nutrients can occur in active celiac disease. As a rule of thumb, the longer you go without a diagnosis, the greater the extent of malabsorption.

Within 3 to 12 months, the small intestine theoretically can heal, although one expert physician in celiac disease feels it may take up to five years to heal, particularly if there are related complications such as secondary pancreatitis.

A wheat allergy stimulates the release of histamine and other chemicals that impact blood supply, muscle contractions, secretion of mucus, and inflammation. When these changes occur in the gastrointestinal tract they can cause such symptoms as nausea, vomiting, abdominal pain, and diarrhea. Because these symptoms obviously suppress appetite and can cause loss of nutrients such as magnesium, zinc, potassium, sodium, and chloride, they can contribute to nutrient imbalances and deficiencies. Also, adequate nutrients may be missed in the process of eliminating wheat.

Carbohydrates

Carbohydrates provide energy. Carbohydrate (glucose) is the fuel that makes your brain function. It helps promote growth when eaten in sufficient amounts, thereby sparing dietary protein to be used for its primary purpose, growth and maintenance of all body tissues.

Carbohydrate malabsorption can run the gamut from inflicting lactose intolerance (one form of disaccharidase deficiency) to starch malabsorption.

Do You Have a Disaccharide (Lactose, Sucrose, Maltose) Intolerance?

A disaccharide intolerance is a manifestation of carbohydrate malabsorption. Disaccharides are sugars that include lactose (milk sugar), sucrose (well known as table sugar and syrups), and maltose (a near-fully digested sugar from starch, such as bread). The corresponding enzymes lactase, sucrase, and maltase are required for digesting each of these disaccharides/sugars. When these enzymes are absent or lacking, you develop varying degrees of disaccharide intolerance.

The part of the villi in which these enzymes are located influences tolerance of the different disaccharides. Lactase is stored in the tips of the villi, while sucrase is located in the center, and maltase is at the base. The more extensive your villous atrophy, the more likely you are to experience disaccharide intolerance involving all of the sugars. In most cases, newly diagnosed gluten-sensitive, gluten-intolerant, and celiac individuals have some degree of lactose intolerance that, for many, is transient and will improve or resolve after the intestine heals.

If you experience any one of these intolerances, the disaccharide passes through the small and large intestines undigested. It absorbs water and undergoes fermentation, ultimately resulting in diarrhea, nausea, gas/flatulence, bloating/abdominal distention, and/or abdominal pain. These intolerances mimic or otherwise can worsen gastrointestinal symptoms caused by wheat allergy, gluten sensitivity, gluten intolerance, and celiac disease.

Lactose intolerance can be determined by standardized tests (the stool acidity test for infants and young children, the lactose tolerance test, and the hydrogen breath test). As for sucrose and maltose intolerance, the hydrogen breath test may be used. Some physicians will analyze sucrase and maltase, as well as lactase levels in the intestinal mucosa, at the same time the intestinal biopsy is conducted. If you suspect you are disaccharide intolerant, be sure to ask your physician and request formal testing.

Protein

Protein is essential for the growth and maintenance of cells and tissues, and is required for wound healing. It helps regulate fluid balance in the form of albumin (in the blood), thus preventing fluid accumulation (edema), which characteristically begins in the feet and ankles.

A lack of hormones and enzymes needed to digest protein to its component parts, amino acids, can occur. Also, the intestinal damage inflicted by gluten sensitivity, gluten intolerance, and celiac disease can cause protein loss from destroyed cells.

Fat

Fat provides a concentrated form of energy. In moderation, it contributes to normal weight and allows for growth, thereby enabling protein to be spared for growth and maintenance of all body tissues. Fat is required for the absorption of fat-soluble vitamins as described below, and for providing essential fatty acids.

Fat malabsorption is most likely to occur when there is damage to the jejunum. Secondary pancreatic insufficiency caused by the intestinal damage can result in fat malabsorption.

Fat-Soluble Vitamins (Vitamins A, D, E, K)

Vitamin A/carotene (plant source of vitamin A) is required for night vision, and is associated with preventing the development of macular degeneration, a blinding disease. Used in the development and maintenance of epithelial cells, such as those that line the gastrointestinal and respiratory tracts and prevent infection, it also functions as an antioxidant, preventing free-radical damage to cells.

Vitamin D is required for the absorption of calcium. It promotes bone and teeth formation and maintenance and prevents osteomalacia (softening of the bones) and rickets (a childhood version of osteomalacia that is rare in the United States due to vitamin D fortification in milk). Vitamin D also prevents osteopenia and osteoporosis.

Vitamin E acts as an antioxidant, protecting cells from free-radical damage. It is needed for normal reflex function, and may help ward off dementia.

Vitamin K is required for normal blood clotting. It appears to play a role in bone and teeth formation and maintenance.

Damage to the duodenum can cause fat-soluble vitamin malabsorption. In the presence of fat malabsorption, the absorption of these vitamins gets worse. If you have substantial fat malabsorption, until it improves, you should use vitamin supplements that contain these nutrients in a water-miscible form to allow for optimal absorption.

Calcium

Calcium is essential for bone and teeth formation (see Table 7). It prevents retarded growth, osteopenia, and osteoporosis. It is required for muscle contractions and nerve impulses, thereby preventing muscle pain and twitching, as well as heart palpitations.

Regardless of age, calcium is one of the most commonly, if not the most commonly, malabsorbed nutrients. Additionally, research reveals that some people with celiac disease have a problem metabolizing calcium.

Table 7
Calcium Recommendations

Life-Stage Group	Adequate Intake—mg/day
0– 6 months	210
6–12 months	270
1–3 years	500
4–8 years	800
9–13 years	1,300
14–18 years	1,300
19–30 years	1,000
31–50 years	1,000
51–70 years	1,200
more than 70 years	1,200
Pregnancy	
less than 18 years	1,300
19–50 years	1,000
Lactation	
less than or equal to	
18 years	1,300
19–50 years	1,000

Source: Reprinted with permission from Dairy Council Digest, November/December 1997. Confirmed with author that information is current as of February 2002.

Magnesium

Necessary for bone and teeth formation and maintenance, magnesium helps prevent osteopenia and osteoporosis. It plays a role in over 300 enzyme reactions in the body, enhances glucose metabolism, and aids in insulin secretion. Magnesium helps facilitate nerve impulses and muscle contractions, helps prevent insomnia and depression, and regulates body temperature. It is required for energy production.

This is another frequently malabsorbed nutrient that is also commonly underconsumed.

Zinc

Zinc plays a role in numerous enzyme reactions, and is essential for growth, especially in children. It promotes wound healing and maintains the sense of taste and normal appetite. It prevents alopecia (hair loss) caused by a deficiency state.

This mineral is more likely to be affected when diarrhea is a problem.

Iron

Iron is required for producing hemoglobin and myoglobin, which carry oxygen throughout the body. It prevents iron-deficiency anemia (diminished number of red blood cells) and microcytic anemia (unusually small red blood cells), thus positively influencing your energy level and strength. It enhances vibrant, healthy skin tone, and contributes to growth. Since iron deficiency may impede or slow your ability to function mentally, it is important to get adequate iron to prevent this potential problem.[4]

Like calcium, iron is a commonly malabsorbed mineral. However, its loss is also attributed to blood seeping from the damaged intestine.

Folate/Folic Acid

This vitamin is required for red blood cell division. Consequently, it, along with vitamin B12, prevents macrocytic anemia (abnormally large red blood cells). Like pyridoxine (vitamin B6), it lowers the risk for cardiovascular disease by preventing elevated homocysteine levels and may play a role in preventing Alzheimer's disease.

Folate is the plant version of this B vitamin, while folic acid is the synthetic form of folate and is actually better absorbed. Folic acid is the form used in vitamin supplements and in the fortification of foods.

Vitamin B12 (Cobalamin)

Like folate/folic acid, this vitamin is required for red blood cell division. It prevents megaloblastic anemia (larger than normal and irregularly shaped red blood cells), maintains normal nerve functions, and prevents pernicious anemia, which results in neurological damage and is characterized by loss of balance, tingling, and numbness in the toes and fingers. Like pyridoxine (vitamin B6) and folate/folic acid, vitamin B12 lowers the risk for cardiovascular disease by preventing elevated homocysteine levels and may play a role in preventing Alzheimer's disease.

This vitamin is malabsorbed when intestinal damage extends into the ileum. A deficiency is rare in children, but is more probable beyond childhood. Additionally, bacterial overgrowth can complicate malabsorption of vitamin B12.

Potassium, Sodium, Chloride (Electrolytes)

Electrolytes regulate fluid and mineral balance, maintain normal blood pressure, and facilitate nerve impulses and muscle contractions.

They can become imbalanced or depleted when there is damage to the jejunum, chronic vomiting, and/or diarrhea. Furthermore, damage to the duodenum adds to chloride malabsorption.

Does the Gluten-Free Diet Supply Adequate Nutrition?

This question doesn't have an easy answer. According to Tricia Thompson, R.D., new evidence indicates the possibility of nutritional inadequacies in the gluten-free diet. Her research has focused on B vitamins, specifically thiamin (vitamin B1), riboflavin (vitamin B2), niacin (vitamin B3), folate/folic acid, as well as iron and fiber. Analysis of these nutrients in gluten-free grain products and comparisons made to gluten-containing grain products reveals that one or more of these are lacking in most gluten-free products.

We shouldn't conclude that the wheat-free or gluten-free diet is inadequate nutritionally, but we should take care to be more aware of making good food choices.

When and Why Nutrient Supplementation Is Needed

Generally speaking, supplements providing B vitamins and folate/folic acid (especially for women) may be important for those with wheat and gluten intolerances or sensitivities. Because excess iron in the body functions as a free radical, contributing to atherosclerosis and cancer, iron should not be supplemented unless necessary (that is, if you're anemic due to iron deficiency).

Selenium is a mineral typically present in soil, so grains and lean meat, organ meats, poultry, and seafood supply selenium. Unfortunately, much of our soil is selenium-depleted. For this reason and because selenium is a potent antioxidant, it should be included in your multivitamin and mineral supplement.

Various conditions in celiac disease create a greater need for calcium, vitamin D, and magnesium, the bone- and tooth-building nutrients. Many celiacs have some degree of lactose intolerance upon diagnosis, which can hinder adequate calcium and vitamin D consumption if appropriate milk alternatives are not chosen. Second, because of malabsorption, gluten sensitivity/intolerance or celiac disease places you at higher risk for bone diseases such as osteopenia and osteoporosis. In fact, many newly diagnosed patients have one of these diseases. For these reasons, adequate calcium, vitamin D, and/or magnesium may be obtained only with the addition of supplements.

Magnesium may be an important supplement. Ross Pelton, R.Ph., reports that approximately 75 percent of adults in the general population do not meet the recommended dietary allowance (RDA) for magnesium. Magnesium is often malabsorbed in active celiac disease. Also, magnesium deficiency is commonly associated with osteoporosis. Estrogen-containing medications can also deplete magnesium levels. Since calcium and magnesium work in balance, calcium supplementation without magnesium worsens the blood level imbalance and consequently induces leaching of magnesium from the bones.[5]

When using nutrient supplements, beware that adverse interactions can occur if you take too much. Since calcium interferes with iron absorption, take the two supplements at separate times. Take no more than 500 to 600 milligrams of calcium at a time. Iron supplements should preferably be taken with juice. Folic acid greater than 1 milligram daily can mask the signs of blood work, indicating vitamin B12 deficiency. Vitamin E acts as a mild blood thinner and if taken in large doses can cause excess bleeding, especially if taken with routine aspirin or prescription blood-thinning medications. Vitamin E also interferes with vitamin K (especially pertinent if you are taking vitamin K injections) by counteracting its ability to clot blood. Vitamin A in excess is harmful to the liver. Zinc in extreme amounts can decrease copper levels and impair immunity.

Specific Nutritional Concerns of the Adolescent

Adolescents are at particular risk of nutrient deficiencies for a variety of reasons. They grow rapidly, which increases their calorie and nutrient requirements. As they become more independent and spend less time at home, their nutritional intake is inconsistent. Often they skip breakfast and lunch, snack frequently, and eat only dinner. Skipping breakfast alone puts them at nutritional risk. Furthermore, fast foods are most appealing to the adolescent population, but those are usually packed with fat and calories and lack nutrient density. The requirements of a wheat-free/gluten-free diet potentially further limit nutrient selection.

The average adolescent is low or deficient in calcium, iron, zinc, folic acid, vitamins A and E, and pyridoxine (B6). Lower milk consumption is exchanged for increased meat consumption, contributing to inadequate calcium and vitamin A. Yet adolescents tend not to eat enough lean meats and poultry, which are better sources of iron, zinc, and pyridoxine. A lack of whole grains, which is even more of a challenge for those with wheat or gluten intolerance or celiac disease, likely contributes to inadequate pyridoxine. This, along with increased requirements for iron, particularly in menstruating females, contributes to iron deficiency. Minimal consumption of vegetable oils and fruits/vegetables contribute respectively to inadequate vitamin E and folate/folic acid.

Special attention should be paid to vitamin D as well, especially in the celiac teen. The primary food source is vitamin D-fortified milk. Since vitamin D is required for calcium absorption, it is critical that sufficient quantities of this mineral are consumed daily. We only have until age 30 to accumulate as much bone calcium as possible; this is when bone mass peaks.

Due to wheat allergy, gluten sensitivity, gluten intolerance, or celiac disease where food variety can be potentially limited and malabsorption a problem, nutrient supplementation to help contribute sufficient amounts of these nutrients may be necessary. If you are concerned about the adequacy of your adolescent's diet, consult with a registered dietitian experienced with these medical conditions and pediatrics.

Specific Nutritional Concerns During Pregnancy

Pregnancy imposes increased nutritional requirements. In healthy women, this includes an additional 300 calories and an average of 60 grams of protein daily. Since the average American consumes 80 to 100 grams of protein daily, getting adequate protein is not usually a concern. Most vitamin and mineral requirements are increased (not vitamin D). The need for vitamin A is ever so slightly higher. Active celiac disease can further increase these needs, depending on the mother's nutritional status and disease severity. Generally, a pregnant woman should be careful not to exceed her need for vitamins A and D. If consumed in excess, these can cause birth defects.

Although in general calcium requirements aren't increased in pregnancy, it is critical that the pregnant woman consume adequate amounts daily. This will prevent her calcium stores from being used to develop the unborn baby's bones. Pregnancy typically promotes increased calcium absorption, but this capacity is hindered in the case of villous atrophy caused by active gluten sensitivity, gluten intolerance, and celiac disease.

Iron requirements are greater during pregnancy to allow for production of the mother's increased blood supply, to prevent iron-deficiency anemia, and to enable iron accumulation to occur in the unborn baby during the last trimester. Folate/folic acid needs are greater during pregnancy, but prior to conception this nutrient is just as vital. A deficiency has been correlated with neural tube birth defects such as spina bifida. Sadly, many women are unaware of their pregnancy during the first trimester, when neural tube development occurs.

In addition to supplementing iron and folic acid, it seems prudent for the pregnant gluten-sensitive, gluten-intolerant, and celiac woman to take a prenatal multivitamin and mineral daily. The need for a multivitamin and mineral should also be considered for the wheat-allergic woman. Nutrient supplementation should be advised and monitored by a physician and may or may not include vitamin A, depending on the mother's individual medical status. If vitamin A supplementation is recommended, it is more likely to be in the form of carotene, which, incidentally, does not inflict birth defects.

Remember that essential fatty acids are critical during pregnancy because of the sudden and rapid fetal growth taking place (pregnant women should avoid flax/flaxseed oil).

Finally, the pregnant woman should be certain she completely eliminates wheat/gluten if she is sensitive or intolerant. Not only will this help produce a healthy baby, but it will also free her from the challenges of differentiating between the causes of her discomforts, which can mimic or result from wheat allergy, gluten sensitivity, intolerance, or celiac disease.

Specific Nutritional Concerns of the Aging

A variety of factors can increase the risk of malnutrition among senior citizens, especially those with medical conditions such as wheat allergies or celiac disease. These include difficulty chewing or swallowing, decreased physical activity, and alteration in normal bodily functions (such as decreased lactase secretion). Also, since many seniors eat alone, they are less likely to eat regularly.

Since activity level usually decreases as we age (although this does not necessarily have to occur), we generally require fewer calories. This means it's even more important that the elderly do not fill up on junk food or foods of little nutritional value, such as chips. Because they have a smaller calorie requirement, their food choices should be rich in nutrients as represented by Figure 3, the Modified Food Pyramid for 70+ Adults.

Figure 3
Modified Food Pyramid for 70+ Adults

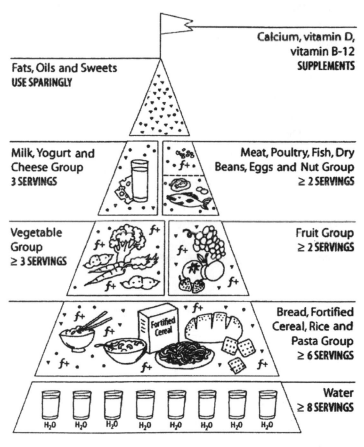

Calcium, vitamin D, vitamin B-12 **SUPPLEMENTS**

Fats, Oils and Sweets **USE SPARINGLY**

Milk, Yogurt and Cheese Group **3 SERVINGS**

Meat, Poultry, Fish, Dry Beans, Eggs and Nut Group **≥ 2 SERVINGS**

Vegetable Group **≥ 3 SERVINGS**

Fruit Group **≥ 2 SERVINGS**

Bread, Fortified Cereal, Rice and Pasta Group **≥ 6 SERVINGS**

Water **≥ 8 SERVINGS**

H₂O H₂O H₂O H₂O H₂O H₂O H₂O H₂O

- • Fat (naturally occurring and added)
- ▼ **Sugars (added)**
- *f*+ **Fiber (should be present)**

These symbols show fat, added sugars and fiber in foods.

Source: HealthNews 5 (5): 1–2 (April 15, 1999).

Sufficient protein is vital, especially in the aging population. We have an increased tendency to lose lean body mass, which is primarily muscle, as aging occurs, usually after age 65. If too little protein is eaten, muscle loss continues, decreasing physical strength and compromising immune function, ultimately increasing susceptibility to infection and illness. If a senior citizen loses weight, as in the case of wheat allergy, gluten sensitivity, gluten intolerance, or celiac disease, the lost muscle will be more difficult to regain. It is possible that aging actually imposes a greater need for protein after age 65.

Seniors have difficulty getting adequate amounts of some key vitamins and minerals. Calcium (especially for the lactose intolerant) and Vitamin D are especially important; a supplement may be necessary.

Suppressed stomach acid and enzyme production accounts for vitamin B12 malabsorption in the aging. This process seems to begin at age 51 and affects approximately 10 to 30 percent of the aging population. Gluten sensitivity, gluten intolerance, or celiac disease–induced vitamin B12 malabsorption will only compound these conditions. Because synthetic vitamin B12 is easier to absorb, most of the RDA (2.4 micrograms daily) should be satisfied in the form of a supplement and/or foods fortified with (synthetic) vitamin B12. Getting more than the RDA is advantageous. Folate, as mentioned earlier, is challenging for all age groups to get, and the elderly are not exempt from this because they often do not eat enough folate-rich foods, which primarily include fruits, vegetables, and legumes.

To Be or Not to Be Vegetarian, along with Wheat- or Gluten-Free

For reasons including culture, religion, health, and concern for animals and our precious Earth, we see a trend toward vegetarianism. Vegetarianism is also associated with various health benefits, including potentially stronger bones, a lowered strain on the kidneys by consuming moderate amounts of protein, and a reduced risk of cardiovascular disease and certain types of cancer. Interestingly, you can achieve these benefits by following the Dietary Guidelines.

Vegetarianism is a diet based on plant foods, with some or total exclusion of animal products. Although there are personal variations to vegetarianism, the standard vegetarian diets range from lacto-ovovegetarianism, which includes the dairy group and eggs, to a strict vegetarian/vegan diet where all animal products, possibly to the extreme of honey, are totally excluded. While this type of diet may be healthful depending on food choices, when part of a food group or an entire food group is eliminated, there is always the risk of nutrient deficiencies.

The scientific literature indicates that even in the case of the vegan diet, all nutrient requirements may potentially be achieved through the diet itself without nutrient supplementation. This, however, is under the best of circumstances, limited primarily to those people not necessarily required to incorporate a therapeutic dietary regimen such as the wheat-free/gluten-free diet into their vegetarianism.

Vegetarianism will imply further limitations on your food selection while it will require a deeper working understanding of food and nutrition and greater vigilance in label reading (depending on how extensively you omit animal products). If you are newly diagnosed and have experienced any of the following conditions, you should highly consider postponing vegetarianism until you have recovered: nutritional deficiencies, malnutrition, substantial weight loss, or other debilitating symptoms such as chronic diarrhea.

In any case, if you are considering vegetarianism or were a vegetarian prior to your wheat allergy, gluten sensitivity, gluten intolerance, or celiac disease, it's vital that you seek medical nutrition therapy from a registered dietitian experienced with vegetarianism and your particular adverse food reaction.

Adequate calorie consumption is important, but especially so for strict vegetarians and children on a vegetarian diet. All people need enough calorie-dense foods to enable the use of their protein for growth and maintenance of all body tissue. However, it is imperative that children get enough calories to facilitate their rapid growth and normal development. With vegetarianism comes the wonderful benefit of increased fiber in the diet. But eating excessive fiber is sometimes a problem in childhood and is more likely to be an issue in the vegan diet. Too much fiber can interfere with the absorption of minerals, including iron, zinc, magnesium, copper, and calcium.

In terms of protein, we all need amino acids, the building blocks of protein. Our bodies make nonessential amino acids, but we need to get those that we can't produce (essential amino acids) from the foods we eat. These essential amino acids are found in all animal products, including the dairy and meat groups. The only plant products that contain essential amino acids are soybeans and buckwheat (higher in amino acids than soybeans). Foods with lower quality protein, referring to their incomplete amino acid content, include legumes (dried beans, peas, and peanuts), nuts, seeds, and grain products. Each of these supplies differing levels of the various essential amino acids.

Lacto-ovovegetarians who consume non-meat-group animal products don't need to concern themselves with getting enough essential amino acids. In contrast, vegans do. In the past, nutritionists recommended complementing (combining two different sources) or eating plant proteins in the same meal to get a balance of amino acids. The current advice is just to be sure you eat these plant foods over the course of the day. For example, beans and corn may be eaten over two separate meals or snacks. However, investigation on children has revealed that there may be an advantage to complementing in the same meal or within six hours of each other.[6] Since children usually eat more often than every six hours, this may not be a practical concern.

Approximately 85 percent of the protein in plant foods is digestible, as compared to 97 percent of that from animal products. This reduction in digestion increases a vegan's protein needs minimally. Additionally, since the elderly after age 65 may need more total protein than what the current RDA designates is important for a vegetarian, senior citizens need to focus a bit more on protein-rich foods.

Since soy is a commonly used protein source for vegetarians, it is especially important for certain groups of vegetarian women to be aware of precautions that they must take. Like flaxseed, soy has phytoestrogens, so women who are at high risk for breast cancer, or who currently have or have had estrogen-dependent breast cancer or who are presently taking tamoxifen, should limit eating soy products. If any of these conditions describe you or you're unaware of your risk for breast cancer, check with your physician about soy safety and your particular medical history. Soy supplements and soy powders are best avoided.

Various nutrients that I call "nutrients of concern" require extra attention to ensure that enough are consumed to maintain optimal stores and thus prevent deficiencies. These nutrients include vitamin D, omega 3 fatty acids (a common source is seafood), calcium, iron, zinc, and vitamins B12 and B2 (riboflavin). Vegans are vulnerable to lacking any of these; lacto-ovovegetarians are most prone to lack iron and zinc, because heme iron and substantial sources of zinc are missing from their diet. There are, however, some interesting considerations. Iron's status is generally no different in vegetarians than in meat eaters. This may be explained by the premise that vegetarians eat relatively more vitamin C, which improves absorption of non-heme iron. Vitamin B12-fortified meat analogs are also advantageous.

While there are specific nutritional concerns for people on a wheat-free/gluten-free diet, overall it is extremely healthy. If disease or malnourishment existed prior to beginning the diet, once the gut heals, nutritional needs are similar to those of any other healthy person.

Diabetic and Wheat-Free/ Gluten-Free: Carbohydrate Exchange Information

Courtesy of Cynthia Kupper, R.D., C.D.,
Executive Director of the Gluten Intolerance Group

One of the newer techniques for managing the diabetic diet is carbohydrate counting, which involves keeping track of the carbohydrates eaten at each meal, and planning meals throughout the day accordingly. Rather than limiting all meals to low-sugar foods, carbohydrate counting allows more flexibility and special treats from time to time.

Diabetics on the wheat-free/gluten-free diet will find the following table (Table 8) to be an excellent resource for determining the carbohydrate content of gluten-free foods. Remember, every product is different, and reading labels is essential. Consult a dietitian/nutritionist for carbohydrate information on other gluten-free products, or for specific information on managing the diabetic diet.

Table 8
Carbohydrate Information on
Selected Gluten-Free Foods and Ingredients

Food	Measurement/Serving	Carbohydrates (grams)
Wheat-Free/Gluten-Free Ingredients		
Rice flour, white	1 cup	70
Rice flour, brown[1]	1 cup	110
Rice bran[1]	1 ounce	141
Potato flour	1 cup	80
Potato starch	1 cup	128
Tapioca flour	1 cup	99
Corn flour (masa)	1 cup	123
Cornmeal[1]	1 cup	181
Cornstarch	1 tablespoon	8
Amaranth[2]	1 cup	129

324

Sorghum	½ cup	70
Soy flour[2]	1 cup	28–33
Arrowroot flour	1 cup	113
Sweet rice flour	1 cup	91
Quinoa[2]	½ cup	59
Garfava flour (combination bean flour)[2]	¼ cup	23
Four Flour Blend (Authentic Foods)	¼ cup	32
Egg Replacer (Ener-G Foods)	1½ teaspoon	94
Xanthan gum	2 tablespoons	85

Yeast Breads

Pizza crust	2 slices of 12" pizza	30
Sandwich bread	1 slice	16
Breadsticks	1 each 6" stick	18
Hamburger buns	1 bun	29
Bagels	1 (3" diameter)	52
English muffins	1	54
Raisin bread	1 slice	35
French bread	1 slice	13

Quick Breads

Yeast-free hamburger buns	1 bun	40
Yeast-free sandwich bread	1 slice	20
Irish soda bread	1 slice of 7-inch round	40
Corn breadone	1½"–1" piece	25
Drop biscuits/spoon bread	1 slice of 9-inch round	18
Zucchini bread	1 slice	53
Pizza crust (yeast free)	2 slices of 12" pie	30
Basic muffin	1 standard muffin cup	36
Pancakes (with or without eggs)	2 (4" diameter)	24
Waffles (with or without eggs)		148
Baked donuts with frosting		164
Baked donuts without frosting		147
Banana bread (with or without eggs)	1 slice	52
Biscuits		118
Basic quick bread	1 slice	35
Basic scone	1 slice of 8" pie	44
Flavored scones (meat or cheese)	1 slice of 8" pie	38
Pretzels	25 each	70

Misc. Starches

Crackers, handmade	one 1½" cracker	6
Crackers, manufactured	6 each	60
Spaghetti/rice	½ cup	37.2
Macaroni/rice	½ cup	38

Cereals

Cold cereals

— Unsweetened	1 cup (30 grams)	27
— Sweetened	1 cup (30 grams)	23–26
— Puffed, unsweetened	1 cup (16 grams)	13
Hot cereals	¼ cup (40 grams)	31–38

Cookies

Basic cookie	1 small cookie	22
Chocolate chip cookies	1 small cookie	20
Brownie	1" square	33
Graham crackers	1	11
Gingersnap/vanilla wafers	1 small cookie	20

Source: Chart excerpted from *Diabetes, Celiac Disease, and Me* and used with permission of chart author Cynthia Kupper, R.D., C.D., Executive Director of the Gluten Intolerance Group, Seattle, WA.

---

[1]Extra fiber may slow absorption and aid glucose control.

[2]Higher protein may slow absorption and aid glucose control.

Blood Tests for Celiac Disease

Earlier in the book you learned that the accepted method of diagnosing celiac disease is a blood screen, followed, if the screen is positive, by a biopsy of the small intestine. For those interested in knowing more about blood testing, this section describes the specific tests that are done and why each is important.

The purpose of the blood test is to look for antibodies in the bloodstream. Specifically, the tests look for:

- Antigliadin antibodies (AGA)—both IgA and IgG

- Antiendomysial antibodies (EMA) (sometimes referred to as AEA)—IgA and sometimes IgG

- Anti-tissue transglutaminase (tTG)—IgA (the tTG test is done with either human or guinea pig testing materials; the type done with human materials is a superior test, but costs more)

- Total serum IgA (this test isn't always done, but it should be if AGA IgG is positive but AGA IgA is normal)

- Sometimes the test will look for anti-reticulin antibodies (ARA), which correlate to the degree of intestinal damage. This test is less sensitive than other blood tests, so it is considered less valuable in making a diagnosis and is used less often.

EMA and tTG Antibodies

The EMA and tTG antibodies, evaluated in combination, are the most important in screening for celiac disease. The immune systems of people with celiac disease make EMA antibodies in reaction to the ingestion of gluten. EMA is important in testing for celiac disease because it is very specific to celiac disease, meaning if someone *doesn't* have celiac disease, they most likely will have a negative EMA test result. EMA has a very high positive predictive value, meaning that patients with a positive EMA very likely have celiac disease (nearly 100 percent).

Tissue transglutaminase (tTG) (IgA and IgG) is the antigen responsible for making the EMA response positive. The tTG enzyme is present in the gut and in other areas of the body. In celiac patients, wheat is made *more reactive* (technically, gliadin is made more antigenic) by tTG. For testing purposes, it is important to know that the tTG test is highly specific and extremely sensitive (the human tTG test is superior to the guinea pig tTG test). It is not adversely affected by interfering antibodies and smooth muscle antibodies, and is therefore considered to be more reliable than other antibody tests.

It's a good idea to have an antibody test every year or so after you've gone on the gluten-free diet, just to ensure that your diet is, in fact, 100 percent gluten-free. This is especially important for people who are asymptomatic, or feel only mild symptoms after eating gluten. If you're inadvertently eating gluten (or worse yet, cheating), your antibody levels will be elevated, and you'll need to take a closer look at your diet.

The following tables show normal antibody levels (Table 9) and the probability of celiac disease based on a combination of the presence of three antibodies (Table 10).

Table 9
Normal Antibody Levels

Antigliadin IgA	Less than 18
Antigliadin IgG	Less than 24
EMA	Reads positive or negative
tTG IgA	Less than 13
tTG IgG	Less than 30

Source: Celiac Disease: Going Against the Grains, by Michelle M. Pietzak, M.D.

Table 10
Probability of Celiac Disease Based on
Three Antibodies in Combination

EMA IgA	AGA IgA	AGA IgG	Interpretation
+	+	+	CD 99 % probable
+	-	+	CD probable
+	+	-	CD probable
+	-	-	CD probable
-	+	+	CD less likely[1]
-	-	+	CD less likely[1]
-	+	-	CD less likely
-	-	-	CD very unlikely[2]

Source: Celiac Disease: Going Against the Grains, by Michelle M. Pietzak, M.D.

---

[1]If patient is IgA sufficient; AGA IgG>100 warrants work-up for enteropathy
[2]If patient is on a gluten-containing diet

Summary of Serological (Blood) Tests

There are several blood tests for celiac disease because some are more "specific," while others are more "sensitive." The following definitions are used for celiac blood tests:

Sensitivity: The probability of a positive test result in a patient with disease

Specificity: The probability of negative test result in a patient without disease

Positive predictive value: The probability of disease in a patient with positive test result

Negative predictive value: The probability of no disease in a patient with negative test result

Table 11
Sensitivity, Specificity, Positive Predictive Value (PPV),
and Negative Predictive Value (NPV) of the
Serologic Markers for Celiac Disease

Test	% Sensitivity	% Specificity	% PPV	% NPV
AGA IgG	57–100	42–98	20–95	41–88
AGA IgA	53–100	65–100	28–100	65–100
AEA IgA[1]	75–98	96–100	98–100	80–95
guinea pig tTG[2]	90.2	95		
human tTG	98.5	98		

Source: Celiac Disease: Going Against the Grains by Michelle M.
Pietzak, M.D.

---

[1]Patients older than 2 years of age
[2]IgG + IgA antibodies

IgA Deficiency

Some people are IgA deficient, meaning that they produce less IgA
than normal. While IgA deficiency occurs in only 1 out of 200 people or so, a significant percentage (about 5 percent) of those with IgA
deficiency have been found to have celiac disease.

When the antigliadin IgA and IgG tests are performed on someone who has celiac disease but has an IgA deficiency, only the
antigliadin IgG level will be elevated. An analysis of the total serum
IgA will determine if a person is IgA-deficient.

Can You Trust Your Test Results?

Unfortunately, the tests for celiac disease aren't perfect. Sometimes
the results are negative when they should be positive (called a false

negative), and sometimes they're positive when they should be negative (false positive).

There are several reasons for false negatives in celiac testing, both with the blood test and the biopsy, including the following:

- *Not eating gluten (or enough gluten) prior to testing.*

- *A mistake on the part of the person doing the analysis.*

- *Patient not old enough (blood test).* Sometimes very young children have not been making antibodies long enough to show up in the blood. Children under two years old who have a negative antibody screening should be reevaluated, especially if symptoms persist or a biopsy is positive.

- *Patient is IgA deficient (blood test).* If a celiac person is IgA deficient, the IgA antibody screen will appear normal and the test will be interpreted as negative. Total serum IgA should be measured, especially if immunoglobulin G (IgG) levels are high.

- *Area clipped for biopsy was not affected.* Sometimes the affected areas of the small intestine are spotty, meaning that in one area the villi will be blunted, and in other areas they will appear normal or near normal. Even with several samples, there is a chance that samples will be taken from unaffected areas.

- *Villi are partially blunted, but not totally.* Many pathologists have been taught that unless there is total villous blunting, the condition is not celiac disease—a conclusion no longer considered current. Pathologists who are up on the latest research will consider the extended spectrum of celiac disease, and will do further analysis before reaching a conclusion.

Just as there is the possibility of a false negative, there is the possibility of a false positive in celiac testing, for the following reasons:

- *High antigliadin IgG levels could indicate other conditions (blood test).* Assuming someone's IgA levels are normal and they are not IgA deficient, high IgG levels could indicate other conditions such Crohn's disease, parasitic infections, allergic gastroenteropathy, colitis, lymphoma, or other disorders involving greater permeability of the gut.

- *High tTG can occur with other conditions (blood test).* The tTG test may be elevated in other organ-specific immune responses such as liver disease and thyroid disease.

- *Elevated IgA levels (blood test).* A significant portion of the general population has high IgA levels, so elevated IgA in and of itself does not indicate celiac disease. Elevated IgA levels can also be an indication of other disorders of the gut.

New Finger-Prick ("Dot-Blot") Blood Test on the Horizon

The University of Maryland's Center for Celiac Research (CFCR) has developed a "dot-blot" test that uses human antibodies and requires just one drop of blood. The test can be done quickly in any doctor's office, making testing much more reliable and less cumbersome (it's sent to a lab for interpretation, so test results aren't immediate).

Preliminary results indicate that the assay is as reliable as the current comparable test. If the sensitivity and specificity of the new dot-blot tests can be confirmed on a large scale, it may be possible in the not-too-distant future to use this as a replacement for the intestinal biopsy procedure as the "gold standard" for diagnosing celiac disease. This would result in early identification and treatment for patients with celiac disease at a significant cost savings, and in a much less invasive manner.

Research Update:
Wheat and Gluten May
Be in Your Future

(Contributions by Michelle Maria Pietzak, M.D.
and Alessio Fasano, M.D.)

*"Every oak tree started out as a couple of nuts
who decided to stand their ground."*
— Anonymous

In the last several years, researchers around the world have focused on potential treatments for wheat sensitivities, gluten intolerance, and celiac disease. Specific research on celiac disease has attempted to understand the mechanisms by which gluten causes the presentation of this disease. In the past few years, some exciting new discoveries have been made in this area that may have equally important impacts on other conditions as well, such as diabetes and multiple sclerosis. Recently, scientists at the University of Maryland who were looking for the key to unlock some of the most baffling mysteries about celiac disease shouted a very loud, "Eureka!" followed by an equally loud, "Open sesame!"

Zealots for Zonulin

"Zonulin" may sound like a character from a science fiction movie, but it's actually a protein made by the human body, and may represent an important piece of the puzzle in the development of autoimmune diseases, including celiac disease.

The small intestine contains billions of cells that are packed so tightly together that they act as a barrier against toxins, viruses, bacteria, and other foreign invaders, protecting the body's tissues. Between these cells are the "tight junctions" (also referred to as the zonula occludens).

Researchers wondered how gluten, a relatively large molecule, was getting through the tightly packed cellular barrier and into the immune system where it caused an autoimmune response. The answer, they discovered recently, is that exposing the small intestine of the celiac patient to gluten causes an increase in the production of the protein zonulin. Zonulin decreases the resistance of the small intestinal barrier by opening the tight junctions, which can then open the spaces between cells, allowing some substances to pass through. In other words, zonulin acts as the gatekeeper for the body's tissues. People with celiac disease and some other disorders have higher levels of zonulin, which, in essence, means the gates are "stuck open," allowing gluten and other harmful substances to pass through.

An Unexpected Discovery

The story of the discovery of zonulin is an interesting and unique example of how scientists can learn from microorganisms (for example, bacteria). Researchers at the Center for Vaccine Development at the University of Maryland were trying to develop a vaccine for the cholera bacterium (cholera is one of the leading causes of death in children worldwide, and it causes a profuse, watery diarrhea). The researchers discovered that cholera causes diarrhea by secreting a toxin called Zot (zonula occludens toxin), which can open the tight junctions (zonula occludens), thereby contributing to the severe, life-threatening diarrhea. Being keen scientists, they realized that these smart bacteria were likely mimicking a natural process in the human body. Using the latest techniques in molecular biology, they identified zonulin, a human protein that binds to the same receptor as Zot and performs similar actions.

The researchers found that zonulin was elevated in the tissues of subjects with many different diseases, such as celiac disease, type 1 diabetes (insulin-dependent or childhood diabetes, also an autoimmune disorder), and multiple sclerosis. They hypothesized that zonulin opens the tight junctions in these individuals, and allows molecules to pass across the intestinal barrier that normally would not pass through.

In a person with celiac disease, production of zonulin increases in response to eating gluten. This leads to more open tight junctions between the intestinal epithelial cells, allowing the passage of toxic portions of gluten (which are normally too large to pass through). These toxic portions then interact with our friend tTG (tissue transglutaminase; see section on antibody testing for celiac disease), which changes the gluten fraction to a form that can interact with the immune system's lymphocytes (specialized white blood cells).

These interactions lead to the production of cytokines, chemicals that attract more lymphocytes to the affected area. The lymphocytes then attack the small intestinal epithelium, leading to blunted or flat villi. Some lymphocytes will also be stimulated to produce specialized antibodies, the antigliadin, antiendomysial, and anti-tissue transglutaminase antibodies. These antibodies do not damage the intestine, but can be used as markers for celiac disease when they are found in the blood in elevated concentrations.

Zonulin and the Blood-Brain Barrier

Researchers at the University of Maryland were on a roll. Having discovered the importance of zonulin in opening the spaces between the cells that serves as a barrier in the small intestine, they turned their attention to the blood-brain barrier. The blood-brain barrier, like the barrier created by tightly packed cells in the small intestine, is a collection of tightly packed endothelial cells that line the blood vessels of the brain and prevent some substances in the blood from entering, while allowing others to pass through. Until now, scientists knew very little about why some molecules were allowed to pass through and others were not. The researchers hypothesized that zonulin could play a similar role in the blood-brain barrier to the one it plays in the intestinal epithelial barrier, by opening the tight junctions or gates between the cells in the blood vessels of the brain.

Their theories have been substantiated; they have now verified that the receptor that binds both zonulin and Zot exists in the brain. This discovery may lead to novel treatments of diseases in which there is blood-brain barrier dysfunction, such as multiple sclerosis, brain tumors, and HIV infection.

The fact that zonulin receptors exist in the brain, and that zonulin is increased in the tissues of patients with celiac disease, may provide an explanation for some of the neurological symptoms of the disease. Also, the possibility that doctors may be able to deliver new types of medications (linked to Zot or zonulin) across the blood-brain barrier could open the door to a whole new world of treatment options for many neurological diseases.

Dreams of Wheat and Gluten in the Future

It may be hard to believe, but the future for people with wheat or gluten intolerance may not be a gluten-free diet. Before you start cheering and reaching for a Domino's pizza and beer, I'd like to take a moment to pay my personal respects to the gluten-free diet. It's very healthy, and thanks to new products that are becoming more readily available, even treats we could once only dream about are now a reality—and they're *great* tasting!

Furthermore, as a treatment to a lifelong condition, the gluten-free diet is benign *and* effective. Would you rather have chemotherapy? Surgery? Radiation? Worse yet, no treatment at all? I think it's great that researchers are taking the time and devoting the resources to finding a cure and treatment alternatives so that someday the gluten-free diet will not be a medical necessity for celiacs. But let's not forget how fortunate we are that for now it's what we have.

Okay, off my soap box and back to business. So what's in store for the future? Researchers have explored a number of alternatives, some more feasible than others.

Gluten-Free Wheat

Genetic engineering has definitely taken on a new and more dominant role in our modern society, but not without a lot of controversy. The idea of modifying wheat and other grains so that they don't contain gluten has been discussed, and actually, some wheat is currently modified to contain more gluten than normal. But what about taking the gluten out of wheat? Considering the fact that there are more than 50 toxic fractions of gluten, it's likely not a viable scientific alternative.

Digestive Enzymes: A Pill to Take Before
You Eat Gluten to Prevent Its Effects

Several products usually referred to as digestive enzymes are being marketed as having the ability to break down gluten. Many of these products are intentionally marketed to the celiac and autism communities, claiming that they will "inactivate gluten," and may therefore help people who are supposed to follow a strict gluten-free diet, but who accidentally or intentionally ingest gluten.

One such enzyme is called SerenAid, which contains protease and peptidase enzymes that the manufacturer claims are designed to "completely break down the proteins in grains (gluten) and dairy products (casein)." Its peptidase enzyme is said to work on caseomorphins and gluteomorphins, which are specific peptides within the gluten and casein molecules. The manufacturer concludes that these enzymes result in a more "complete breakdown of casein and gluten molecules, minimizing the absorption of peptides and protein fragments through the intestinal lining into the bloodstream."

Dr. Pietzak advises against relying on this type of product: "The claim that these enzymes 'completely' break down gluten isn't substantiated by scientific research. If someone with celiac disease relies on this product to eliminate the harmful effects of gluten, especially on an ongoing basis, they could be putting themselves at great risk."

The idea of popping a pill that would allow you to eat gluten is enticing, and researchers are working on just such an antidote. But for now, there isn't enough evidence supporting the claims that these enzymes do, in fact, completely break down the gluten molecules, and conducting human experimentation to test for yourself just isn't wise.

A Pill to Block Zonulin

One potential way to treat celiac disease and other autoimmune disorders in which zonulin has been shown to be produced excessively would be to prevent zonulin from "opening the gates," or in other words, from binding to its receptor, keeping the "gut barrier" intact and preventing gluten from getting across. How would this be accomplished? One way would be to take a pill that interacts with the zonulin receptor, and blocks zonulin from binding. This pill could be taken prior to eating gluten, so that even celiacs and those who have an extreme sensitivity to gluten will be able to eat it without symptoms, without intestinal damage, and without an immune response. This would be a way to manage celiac disease similar to the way lactose-intolerant people take a lactase pill prior to ingesting milk products.

tTG Enzyme Blockers

Since tTG is the enzyme responsible for altering the toxic portions of gluten to a form that can interact with our immune system, would it be possible to block the effects of this enzyme with a medication? Unfortunately (or perhaps fortunately), tTG is necessary for many different reactions in the body, and altering it would likely have many unwanted side effects. Therefore, for the moment, this does not seem to be a future potential treatment for celiac disease.

Oral Vaccine to Create "Immune Tolerance"

As stated above, after gluten is altered by the tTG enzyme, it can interact with different white blood cells, or lymphocytes, in the immune system. One of these cells is called the "antigen presenting cell" or APC. APCs are a variety of cell types that carry an antigen (in this case the portion of the gluten protein altered by tTG) in a form that can stimulate lymphocytes. It may seem counterintuitive, but one way to decrease the response of the immune system is by giving small amounts of antigen (a molecule that induces the formation of antibodies, in this case gluten) all the time. This actually works to desensitize the immune system to the offending agent, similar to when people receive allergy shots.

People with autoimmune disorders where zonulin has been shown to be produced excessively, such as celiac disease, type I diabetes, and multiple sclerosis, may benefit from this type of treatment. Celiacs, for instance, would receive an oral vaccine containing small amounts of the toxic portions of gluten. These would bind to the APCs continuously, and help induce tolerance. Perhaps the vaccine could also be used in people who are at higher risk to develop the disease, to prevent the disease from ever developing. Think of it as a "celiac immunization."

Cytokine Blockers

One way in which celiac disease self-perpetuates is by the release of cytokines, chemicals released by the lymphocytes to attract more lymphocytes to the small bowel lining and cause damage. Could we block the release of these chemicals or inactivate them to stop the disease from progressing?

This would be a case of "the cure is worse than the disease."

Although there are medications available to treat other diseases, such as cancer and Crohn's disease, blocking the release of cytokines by white blood cells, or suppressing white blood cells in general, produces many severe side effects. Many of these medications, such as steroids and chemotherapies, suppress the immune system so much that the person taking them is at much higher risk for severe infections. And a common side effect of many chemotherapies that suppress white blood cells is diarrhea. These would be far less preferable than a gluten-free diet.

However, researchers are studying the different cytokines that play a role in celiac disease. Although this currently does not look like a potential treatment, it certainly holds some hope for the future.

The Foreseeable Future

Of the options mentioned above, two are the most probable for the near future are the pill to block zonulin from creating holes in the intestinal wall's protective barrier, and the vaccine against celiac disease, which would create an immune tolerance to gluten.

In the meantime, scientists continue to work on more reliable and less invasive tests to diagnose celiac disease. And since the human tTG antibody test can now be run on just one drop of blood, even general practitioners will be able to run this test in their offices in the near future.

The Camera Pill: Replacement for the Biopsy?

In 2001, the Food and Drug Administration approved the use of a small video camera the size of a large pill. This miraculous little device offers doctors a close-up view of the small intestine. The patient swallows the camera, which winds its way painlessly through the digestive tract, and, using wireless technology, beams back color pictures of the gut. While the camera pill offers a look at areas of the small bowel not easily seen through an endoscope, it doesn't replace endoscopy.

The damage done to the small intestine in celiac disease is microscopic, and therefore not easily seen through this camera. These changes can only be seen in a biopsy specimen that has been stained correctly and examined under a microscope.

So what will this camera pill be good for? Its main utility will be to look for large cancers of the gastrointestinal tract that are too deep to be seen by conventional endoscopy. It may benefit the celiac population by providing easier screening for intestinal lymphomas, which occur much more commonly in patients with untreated celiac disease.

The exciting and promising therapies on the horizon for celiacs will most likely eliminate the requirement for a strict gluten-free diet. The convenience and ability to eat a wider variety of foods will surely be welcome, but as you know from reading this book, the gluten-free diet isn't as restrictive as it first appears. With the tools you now possess, waiting for a cure should be a lot easier.

Endnotes

Chapter 2

1. Walsh, S. J.; and Rau, L. M. "Autoimmune Diseases: A Leading Cause of Death among Young and Middle-aged Women in the United States." *American Journal of Public Health* 90: 1463–1465 (2000).

2. *Scandinavian Journal of Gastroenterology* 28 (7): 595–598 (1993).

Chapter 3

1. Corrao, G.; Corazza, R.; Bagnardi, V.; et al. "Mortality in Patients with Coeliac Disease and Their Relatives: A Cohort Study." *Lancet* 358 (9279): 356.

2. The Health Insurance Portability and Accountability Act (HIPAA) of 1996.

3. Cooper, B. T.; Holmes, G. K.; Ferguson, R.; et al. "Gluten-Sensitive Diarrhea Without Evidence of Celiac Disease." *Gastroenterology* 79: 801 (1980).

Chapter 4

1. Ventura, A.; Magazzu, G.; Greco, L; for the SIGEP study group for autoimmune disorders in celiac disease. "Duration of Exposure to Gluten and Risk for Autoimmune Disorders in Patients with Celiac Disease." *Gastroenterology* 117: 297–303 (August 1999).

2. Hadjivassiliou, M.; Grunewald, R. A.; Lawden, G. A. B.; et al. "Headache and CNS White Matter Abnormalities Associated with Gluten Sensitivity." *Neurology* 56: 385–388 (2001).

3. Ludvigsson, J. F.; and Ludvigsson, J. "Coeliac Disease in the Father Affects the Newborn." *Gut* 49: 169–175 (2001).

4. Telephone conversation, February 2002.

5. Sanders, D. S.; Carter, M. J.; Hurlstone, D. P.; et al. "Association of Adult Coeliac Disease with Irritable Bowel Syndrome: A Case-Control Study in Patients Fulfilling ROME II Criteria Referred to Secondary Care." *Lancet* 358 (9292): 1504–1508 (November 2001).

Chapter 5

1. Hunter, B. T., *Gluten Intolerance: The Widespread Genetic Defect That Can Cause Arthritis, Enteritis, Schizophrenia, and Other Health Problems.* Keats Publishing, Los Angeles, 1987, p. 13.

2. Hunter, B. T., *Gluten Intolerance: The Widespread Genetic Defect That Can Cause Arthritis, Enteritis, Schizophrenia, and Other Health Problems.* Keats Publishing, Los Angeles, 1987, p. 12.

3. Lafee, Scott. "With Rates Rising, Researchers Race to Find the Cause of Autism and Better Treatment." *San Diego Union-Tribune,* edition 1, 2, 6, 7: F1 (January 9, 2002).

4. www.mercola.com

5. Scahill, L.; Schwab-Stone, M.; Merikangas, J.; et al. "Psychosocial and Clinical Correlates of ADHD in a Community Sample of School-Age Children." *Journal of the American Academy of Child and Adolescent Psychiatry,* 11 (August 1, 1999).

6. *Archives of General Psychiatry* 56: 1088–1096 (1999).

Chapter 8

1. Current Good Manufacturing Practice in Manufacturing, Packing, or Holding Human Food, 21 CFR Part 110, Subpart C, 110.40a.

2. Whelan, A. Personal correspondence, February 2002.

Chapter 9

1. Quinoa Corporation promotional pamphlet: www.quinoa.net

2. Janatuinen, E. K.; Kemppainen, T. A.; Pikkarainen, P. H.; et al. "Lack of Cellular and Humoral Immunological Responses to Oats in Adults with Coeliac Disease." *Gut* 46: 327–331 (2000).

3. Hoffenberg, E.; Haas, J.; Drescher, A.; et al. "A Trial of Oats in Children with Newly Diagnosed Celiac Disease." *Journal of Pediatrics* 137: 356–366 (2000).

Chapter 18

1. www.celiac.com

TECH TALK: Nutritional Requirements

1. "Obesity: The Overlooked Cancer Risk." *American Institute for Cancer Research Newsletter* 74 (Winter, 2002).

2. "The Facts about Flaxseed." *American Institute for Cancer Research Science News* 22 (December 2001).

3. "Fighting Cancer, Naturally." *American Institute for Cancer Research Newsletter* 74 (Winter 2002).

4. Brown, D. "Link Between Iron and Youth Cognitive Skills?" *Journal of the American Dietetic Association* 101:1308–1309 (2001).

5. Pelton, R. "Don't Forget Magnesium." *American Druggist* (December 1999).

6. Messina, V.; Mangels, A. "Considerations in Planning Vegan Diets: Children." *Journal of the American Dietetic Association* 101:661–669 (2001).

Advisors

Alessio Fasano, M.D.

Dr. Fasano is Professor of Pediatrics, Medicine, and Physiology at the University of Maryland School of Medicine. He is an internationally recognized expert in the area of gastrointestinal pathophysiology, particularly in the field of diarrheal diseases. In January 1993, Dr. Fasano was appointed Head of the Division of Gastroenterology and Nutrition in the Pediatrics Department and Section Chief of Gastrointestinal Pathophysiology for the Center for Vaccine Development (CVD) at the University of Maryland School of Medicine.

Dr. Fasano is regarded as one of the foremost authorities worldwide on celiac disease, and his pilot epidemiology studies in the United States have changed the long-held concept that celiac disease is a rare disorder in this country. In 1995, he organized the first international meeting on celiac disease in the United States. That same year, he was appointed a member of the Board of Directors of the Digestive Disease National Coalition, as the representative of the American Celiac Society. In 1997, together with Dr. Karoly Horvath, Dr. Fasano established the Center for Celiac Research at the University of Maryland, the first national center in which clinical care, diagnostic support, education, and basic and clinical science research on celiac disease are offered by a single institution. Because of his expertise, commitment, and achievement in celiac research, Dr. Fasano successfully organized the 9th International Symposium on Celiac Disease, held for the first time in the United States in August 2000. He served as Co-chair for the Section on Celiac Disease at the 13th International Histocompatibility Workshop in Seattle in 2002.

Michelle Pietzak, M.D.

Michelle Maria Pietzak, M.D., is an Assistant Professor of Clinical Pediatrics at the University of Southern California. She is board-certified in both pediatrics and gastroenterology, and practices as a pediatric gastroenterologist at Childrens Hospital Los Angeles. In her practice, she not only cares for children with celiac disease, but those with other autoimmune inflammatory bowel diseases (such as Crohn's disease and ulcerative colitis), short bowel syndrome, and those who have special nutritional needs requiring either intravenous nutrition or special formulas.

As described in the section, "Why Your Doctor Won't Test You for Celiac Disease," Dr. Pietzak was first exposed to gluten and celiac disease in 1995. Since that time, she has been intimately involved with the Center for Celiac Research based at the University of Maryland, and has co-authored numerous papers and abstracts describing the occurrence of the disease in the United States and California. In an effort to raise awareness about celiac disease, she lectures around the country to both laypeople and those in the scientific community. She is also a medical advisor to both the Celiac Disease Foundation in Studio City, California, and the Celiac Sprue Association in Orange County, California.

Dr. Pietzak lives in Glendale with her husband, Derek; daughter, Olivia; mother, Lillian; and two boxers named Beavis and Barkley.

Cynthia S. Rudert, M.D., F.A.C.P.

Cynthia Rudert, M.D., is a board-certified gastroenterologist practicing in Atlanta, Georgia. Her practice is largely devoted to screening and following patients with celiac disease, and she has one of the largest practices in the United States devoted to managing and following both adults and teenagers with celiac sprue. Dr. Rudert lectures nationally on celiac disease and has been committed to educating both the public and patients about this commonly missed disorder.

Dr. Rudert is the Medical Advisor for the Celiac Disease Foundation and the Gluten Intolerance Group of North America. She is the Medical Director for the Gluten Sensitive Support Group of Atlanta and is one of the founding members of the Celiac Standardization Group. She answers questions on celiac disease throughout the United States on Clan Thompson's Website, **www.clanthompson.com**. Her e-book *Ask the Doctor* is available from Clan Thompson. This online publication answers frequently asked questions on the diagnosis, treatment, management, and complications of celiac disease.

Dr. Rudert is also the founder and president of the Atlanta Women's Medical Alliance, the largest alliance of female physicians in the United States.

Peter H. R. Green, M.D.

Peter H. R. Green, M.D. is a Clinical Professor of Medicine at Columbia University College of Physicians and Surgeons in New York. He is also an attending physician at the New York-Presbyterian Hospital. He graduated from the Faculty of Medicine of the University of Sydney, Australia, and completed his internship, residency, and gastroenterology fellowship in Sydney. A research fellowship at Harvard Medical School and the Beth Israel Hospital in Boston was followed by a move to Columbia Presbyterian Medical Center in New York, where he currently practices as a gastroenterologist.

With more than 450 celiac patients under his care, Dr. Green started the Celiac Disease Center at Columbia University. The aims of the center are threefold: first, to provide comprehensive care and counseling to patients with celiac disease; second, to coordinate collaborative research into clinical and pathophysiological aspects of celiac disease and its complications; and third, to provide patient and physician education about celiac disease.

Dr. Green lectures at many celiac support groups and medical centers around the country as well as at national and international gastroenterology meetings. In addition, he serves on the Medical Advisory Board of the Celiac Disease Foundation and the Westchester Celiac Support Group, and is on the Editorial Advisory Board of the publication *Gluten-Free Living*.

Nancy Patin Falini, M.A., R.D.

Nancy Patin Falini, M.A., R.D., holds a master's in nutrition education from California State University, Chico. Her specialty in celiac disease began in 1988 when she completed her graduate thesis on pediatric celiac disease. Since 1995, she has counseled individuals and families as a registered dietitian in private practice, specializing in celiac disease. She has been the Nutrition Advisor for the Greater Philadelphia Celiac-Sprue Support Group since 1989. She is a past Contributing Editor to *Gluten-Free Living* and currently serves on the Dietitian Advisory Board for this publication. She is a member of the American Dietetic Association and the American Dietetic Association's Complementary/Integrated Care Practice Group.

In addition to serving as an advisor for this book, Nancy wrote "Nutrition Basics," a chapter in *Kids with Celiac Disease: A Family Guide to Raising Happy, Healthy, Gluten-Free Children.* She co-authored the Greater Philadelphia Celiac-Sprue Support Group's Pharmacy Card and other literature published as a result of that card, and she has published numerous articles and literature on celiac disease. She lectures nationally on the topic to medical professionals and support groups. Also, she has served as a reviewer of peer-related literature. *Marquis Who's Who in America* has published her achievement biography in their *26th Edition of Marquis Who's Who in the East,* and her achievement was also published in their *Millennium Edition of Who's Who of American Women.*

Nancy's love for different cultures and countries has taken her around the world, where she has partaken in numerous missionary experiences, including one with the late Mother Teresa of Calcutta. Her background as a dietitian and her work with nutrition and hunger in developing countries have broadened her ability to implement nutritional sciences and nutrition counseling.

Nancy, a native of California, lives in West Chester, Pennsylvania, with her husband and four internationally adopted children whom she home-schools.

Elaine Monarch, Executive Director, Celiac Disease Foundation

After living for years with "mysterious symptoms," Elaine Monarch was, in 1981, only the second patient to be diagnosed with celiac disease by a prominent gastroenterologist in Los Angeles. Once diagnosed, Elaine discovered that no support groups existed for individuals and their families living with the disease on the West Coast, and little medical information was available.

In 1990, driven by her own need to find answers to questions about celiac disease and her desire to help others, Elaine founded the Celiac Disease Foundation (CDF). As Founder and Executive Director, Elaine has worked with an international medical advisory board to create a universally recognized nonprofit organization dedicated to raising awareness of this vastly underdiagnosed disease. For the past 11 years, CDF has provided services to the growing celiac community with programs of education, patient support, and advocacy.

Under Elaine's leadership, CDF has become a vital link between the medical community and people living with celiac disease. CDF was instrumental in establishing the Celiac Disease Standardization Group, and has coordinated lectures by experts on celiac disease to the medical community. Elaine represents celiac disease annually at Digestive Disease Week and the American College of Gastroenterologists, and is a member of the Digestive Disease National Coalition, where she strives to encourage funding from the National Institutes of Health (NIH) for additional research.

Elaine has received much recognition for her dedication to helping people with celiac disease from groups including the National Society of Fundraising Executives; *The Los Angeles Times*; the city of Los Angeles; and the Marilyn Magaram Center for Nutrition, California State University, Northridge.

Resource Directory

This section contains important resources that are helpful for people with allergies, sensitivities, intolerances, and celiac disease. Reference information is current at the time of printing, but changes frequently.

The author and publisher of this book do not endorse suppliers, manufacturers, distributors, and stores mentioned in this directory. These listings are provided for your benefit; you need to pursue those that meet your needs.

National Organizations and Support Groups

Many of these organizations have local chapters; contact the national support group to obtain contact information.

Allergies/General Nutrition

Allergy and Asthma Network/
Mothers of Asthmatics
3554 Chain Bridge Road, Suite 200
Fairfax, VA 22030
800-822-2762
www.aanma.org

American Academy of Allergy,
Asthma, and Immunology
611 E. Wells Street
Milwaukee, WI 53202-3889
414-272-6071
www.aaaai.org

American College of Allergy,
Asthma, and Immunology
85 West Algonquin Road
Arlington Heights, IL 60005
http://allergy.mcg.edu

American Dietetic Association
216 W. Jackson Blvd.
Chicago, IL 60606-6995
312-899-0040; 800-366-1655;
312-899-4899 (fax)
hotline@eatright.org
www.eatright.org

Asthma and Allergy
Foundation of America
1233 20th Street, N.W., Suite 402
Washington, DC 20036
202-466-7643; 202-466-8940 (fax)
800-7ASTHMA
www.aafa.org

Food Allergy and Anaphylaxis
Network (FAAN)
10400 Eaton Place, Suite 107
Fairfax, VA 22030
800-929-4040; 703-691-2713 (fax)
www.foodallergy.org
www.fankids.org (for kids)

International Food
Information Council Foundation
1100 Connecticut Ave. N.W., #430
Washington, DC 20036
foodinfo@ificinfo.health.org
http://www.ific.org

Autism

Autism Network for
Dietary Intervention (ANDI)
P.O. Box 17711
Rochester, NY 14617-0711
609-737-8453 (fax)
www.autismndi.com

Autism Society of America
7910 Woodmont Avenue, Suite 300
Bethesda, MD 20814-3015
800-3AUTISM; 301-657-0869 (fax)
www.autism-society.org

Center for the Study of Autism
P.O. Box 4538
Salem, OR 97302
www.autism.org

Cure Autism Now
5225 Wilshire Boulevard, Suite 226
Los Angeles, CA 90036
323-549-0500; 888-8AUTISM
info@cureautismnow.org
www.canfoundation.org

Attention Deficit Disorder (ADD)/Attention Deficit Hyperactivity Disorder (ADHD)

Feingold Association of the U.S.
P.O. Box 6550
Alexandria, VA 22306
800-321-3287
www.feingold.org

Attention Deficit
Disorder Association
1788 Second Street, Suite 200
Highland Park, IL 60035
847-432-2332
www.add.org

Autoimmune Diseases

American Autoimmune
Related Diseases Association, Inc.
22100 Gratiot Ave.
Eastpointe MI 48021-2227
800-598-4668; 586-776-3900;
586-776-3903 (fax)
www.aarda.org

Immune Deficiency Foundation
P.O. Box 67324
Scotts Valley, CA 95067-7324
408-353-1861; 408-353-1861 (fax)
idbon@gte.net

Celiac Disease (Celiac Sprue)

American Celiac Society
59 Crystal Ave.
West Orange, NJ 07052-3570
973-325-8837

Celiac Disease Foundation (CDF)
13251 Ventura Blvd., Suite 1
Studio City, CA 91604-1838
818-990-2354; 818-990-2379 (fax)
cdf@celiac.org
www.celiac.org

Celiac Sprue Association (CSA/USA)
P.O. Box 31700
Omaha, NE 68131-0700
402-558-0600; 402-558-1347 (fax)
cekliacs@csaceliacs.org
www.csaceliacs.org

Gluten Intolerance
Group of North America (GIG)
15110 10th Avenue S.W., Suite A
Seattle, WA 98166-1820
206-246-6652; 206-246-6531 (fax)
info@gluten.net
www.gluten.net

R.O.C.K. (Raising Our Celiac Kids)
National Support Group for Families
with Gluten-Free Children
3527 Fortuna Ranch Road
Encinitas, CA 92024
858-395-5421
info@celiackids.com
www.celiackids.com

Government Agencies

Office of the Americans
with Disabilities Act
Public Access Section
Civil Rights Division
U.S. Department of Justice
P.O. Box 66738

Washington, DC 20035-6738
800-514-0301; 800-514-0383 (TDD)
www.usdoj.gov/crt/ada/adahom1.htm

Office of Special Education
Programs (OSEP)
Mary E. Switzer Building,
Room 3006
330 C Street, S.W.
Washington, DC 20202
202-205 5465
www.ed.gov/offices/OSERS/OSEP
/index.html

U.S. Department of Agriculture
Food and Nutrition Service
3101 Park Center Drive, Room 819
Alexandria, VA 22302
703-305-2286
webmaster@fns.usda.gov
http://www.fns.usda.gov/fns

U.S. Department of Education
Office for Civil Rights
Customer Service Team
Mary E. Switzer Building,
Room 5000
330 C Street S.W.
Washington, DC 20202
202-205-5413; 800-421-3481;
877-521-2172 (TTY);
202-205-9862 (fax)
OCR@ED.Gov
www.ed.gov/offices/OCR

International Organizations

Canadian Celiac Association (CCA)
190 Britannia Road East, Unit #11
Mississauga, Ontario, Canada
L4Z 1W6
905-507-6208; 800-363-7296;
905-507-4673 (fax)
www.celiac.ca;
www.celiac.edmonton.ab.ca;
www.penny.ca/Hamilton.htm

Coeliac Society of Australia
11 Barlyn Road,
Mount Waverley, 3149
P.O. Box 89, Holmesglen, 3148
03-9808-5566; 03-9808-9922 (fax)
www.coeliac.org.au

Coeliac Society of New Zealand
27 Tuna Terrace
Titahi Bay, New Zealand
09-820-5157; 09-820-5187 (fax)

Coeliac Society of the
United Kingdom
P.O. Box 220
High Wycome, Bucks
HP 11 2HY, England, UK
44-494-437278; 44-494-474349 (fax)
www.coeliac.co.uk

Deutsche Zoeliakie-Gesellschaft
(German Celiac Society)
Filderhauptstrasse 61
D-70599 Stuttgart 70, Germany
+49-0-711-45-45-14;
+49-0-711-4-56-78-17 (fax)
http://home.t-online.de/home/
DZG.E.V./homepage.htm

Gluten Enteropathy/
Coeliac Support Group
73 Old Mill Way
Durban North, South Africa 4051
031-563-3109
lucoll@mweb.co.za

Other Support Organizations

Autism and Diet Website
www.advimoss.no/GFCF_results.htm

Celiac Disease On-Line Support
Group (Chat Room)
Operator and Chat Moderator:
Abigail Neuman
www.delphi.com/celiac

Celiac Disease Resources
for Medical Professionals
Contact: David A. Nelsen, Jr., M.D., M.S.
http://www.uams.edu/celiac/

Celiac Kids' Club (Westchester
Celiac Sprue Support Group)
Contact: Marisa Frederick
264 Scotchtown Road
Goshen, NY 10924
845 615-1227
CeliacsWestchNY@aol.com

Celiac Support Group for Children
Contact: Tanis Collard
11 Level Acres Road
Attleboro, MA 02703
508-399-6229; 508-399-6685 (fax)
csgc@ix.netcom.com
www.members.home.net/kellyleech/
celiac.csgc.html

Celiac Support Page
postmaster@celiac.com
www.celiac.com

Celiac Kids' Support Page
info@celiackids.com
www.celiackids.com

Gluten Free Casein Free (GFCF)
Diet Support Group
P.O. Box 1692
Palm Harbor, FL 34682
www.gfcfdiet.com

Tri-County Celiac Sprue Support
Group (TCCSSG)
34638 Beechwood
Farmington Hills, MI 48335
248-926-1228
tccssg@yahoo.com

Westchester Celiac
Sprue Support Group
Contact: Sue Goldstein
9 Salem Place
White Plains, NY 10605
914-428-1389
CeliacsWestchNY@aol.com

Research Organizations and Centers

An Experimental
Intervention for Autism
Understanding and Implementing
a Gluten and Casein Free Diet
Lisa S. Lewis, Ph.D.
156 E. Delaware Avenue
Pennington, NJ 08534
lisas156@aol.com
www.princeton.edu/~serge/ll/
gfpak.html

Childrens Hospital Los Angeles
Michelle Pietzak, M.D.
4650 Sunset Blvd.
MS #78-Division of Gastroenterology
Los Angeles, CA 90027
323-669-2181; 323-664-0718 (fax)
http://chla.org/gastroenterology.cfm

The Celiac Disease Center at
Columbia University
The Columbia Genome Center
Columbia University College of
Physicians and Surgeons
Peter H. R. Green, M.D.
161 Fort Washington Avenue,
Room 645
New York, NY 10032
212-305-5590; 212-305-3738
www.columbia.edu

Mayo Clinic
Joseph Murray, M.D.
200 First Street S.W.
Rochester, MN 55905

507-284-2511; 800-291-1128;
507-284-0161 (fax)
www.mayohealth.org;
www.mayoclinic.com

University of California,
San Diego (UCSD)
Martin Kagnoff, M.D.
9500 Gilman Drive
La Jolla, CA 92093
858-534-4622
immunology@ucsd.edu
www.medicine.ucsd.edu

The University of Chicago
Celiac Disease Program
at The University of Chicago
Children's Hospital
Stefano Guandalini, M.D.
Contact: Michelle Melin-Rogovin
5839 S. Maryland Avenue, MC 4065
Chicago, IL 60637
773-702-7593; 773-702-0666 (fax)
www.celiacdisease.net

University of Maryland
Center for Celiac Research (CFCR)
Alessio Fasano, M.D., and Karoly
Horvath, M.D.
700 West Lombard Street
Baltimore, MD 21201
410-706-3734
afasano@umaryland.edu;
khorvath@umaryland.edu
www.celiaccenter.org

University of Utah
391 Chipeta Way, Suite D
Salt Lake City, UT 84108
801-581-5075; 800-444-8638
x15075
erin@episun5.med.utah.edu

Fundraising Organizations

Friends of Celiac Disease
Research, Inc.
8832 North Port
Washington Road, # 204
Milwaukee, WI 53217
414-540-6679; 414-540-0587 (fax)
www.friendsofceliac.com

Raising Our Celiac Kids (R.O.C.K.)
3527 Fortuna Ranch Road
Encinitas, CA 92024
858-395-5421; 858-756-0431 (fax)
support@celiackids.com
www.celiackids.com

Testing Laboratories

EnteroLab
10851 Ferguson Rd., Ste. B
Dallas, TX 75228
email@enterolab.com
www.enterolab.com

IMMCO Diagnostics, Inc.
60 Pine View Drive
Amherst, NY 14228
800-537-TEST; 716-691-0466
www.immcodiagnostics.com

Prometheus Laboratories Inc.
5739 Pacific Center Blvd.
San Diego, CA 92121
858-824-0895; 888-423-5227;
858-824-0896 (fax)
www.prometheus-labs.com

Specialty Laboratories
2211 Michigan Avenue
Santa Monica, CA 90404-3900
310-828-6543; 800-421-7110;
310-828-6634 (fax)
www.specialtylabs.com

Medical and Nutritional Reference Information

American Journal of
Clinical Nutrition
9650 Rockville Pike, L-2310
Bethesda, MD 20814-3998
301-530-7038; 301-571-5728 (fax)
www.ajcn.org

Better Health USA
1620 W. Oakland Park Blvd.,
Suite 401
Ft. Lauderdale, FL 33311
800-684-2231; 954-739-2780 (fax)
www.betterhealthusa.com

Finer Health and Nutrition
Kenneth Fine, M.D.
www.finerhealth.com

Healthfinder
A Service of the U.S. Department
of Health and Human Services
200 Independence Avenue S.W.
Washington, DC 20201
202-619-0257; 877-696-6775
healthfinder@health.org
www.healthfinder.gov

Healthgate
800-434-GATE
support@healthgate.com
www.healthgate.com

Medscape, Inc.
20500 N.W. Evergreen Parkway
Hillsboro, OR 97124
503-531-7000; 503-531-7001 (fax)
member_services@mail.medscape.com
www.medscape.com

The Merck Manual
Merck & Co., Inc.
One Merck Drive
P.O. Box 100
Whitehouse Station, NJ 08889-0100

800-819-9546; 732-594-1187 (fax)
Merck_index@merck.com
www.merck.com

National Digestive Diseases
Clearing House (NDDIC)
A Service of National Institute of
Diabetes & Digestive & Kidney
Diseases (NIDDK-NIH)
2 Information Way
Bethesda, MD 20892-3570
301-654-3810
nddic@info.niddk.nih.gov

National Health
Information Center (NHIC)
P.O. Box 1133
Washington, DC 20013-1133
800-336-4797; 301-565-4167;
301-984-4256 (fax)
nhicinfo@health.org
www.nhic.org

National Organization for Rare
Disorders, Inc. (NORD)
P.O. Box 8923
New Fairfield, CT 06812-8923
203-746-6518; 800-999-6673
203-746-6481 (fax)
orphan@rarediseases.org
www.rarediseases.org

Nutribase Directory of Food and
Supplement Manufacturers
Info@nutribase.com
www.nutribase.com/dfm.htm

Sprue-nik Press Medical/Research
Articles Index
34638 Beechwood
Farmington, MI 48335
248-926-1228
www.enabling.org/ia/celiac/
sn/spinmed.html

United States National Library
of Medicine (NLM)
8600 Rockville Pike
Bethesda, MD 20894
888-FIND-NLM
custserv@nlm.nih.gov;
pubmednew@ncbi.nlm.nih.gov
www.nlm.nih.gov;
www.ncbi.nlm.nih.gov/PubMed/

Subscription Publications

Many national support groups also
have subscription publications.

Bob & Ruth's Gluten-Free
Dining and Travel Club
22 Breton Hill Road
Baltimore, MD 21208
410-486-0292
bobolevy@erols.com

The Gluten-Free Baker Newsletter
361 Cherrywood Drive
Fairborn, OH 45324-4012
937-878-3221
thebaker@concentric.net

Gluten-Free Living
Contact: Ann Whelan
P.O. Box 105
Hastings-on-Hudson, NY 10706
914-969-2018
www.glutenfreeliving.com

The Gut Reaction
(Gluten-Free Pantry)
800-291-8386
pantry@glutenfree.com
www.glutenfree.com

Sully's Living Without
P.O. Box 132
Clarendon Hills, IL 60514-0132
630-415-3378
pwagener@livingwithout.com
www.livingwithout.com

Activities and Camps Specifically Designed for Children with Celiac Disease

Camp Celiac for Kids (Northeast)
Celiac Support Group for Children
11 Level Acres Road
Attleboro, MA 02703
508-399-6229; 508-399-6685 (fax)
csgc@ix.netcom.com
www.members.home.net/kellyleech /celiac/csgc.html

GIG Kid's Camp (West)
Gluten Intolerance Group
15110 10th Ave S.W., Suite A
Seattle WA 98166-1820
206-246-6652; 206-246-6531
info@gluten.net
www.gluten.net

Ben's Friends Camp (Midwest)
Friends of Celiac Disease Research
8832 North Port Washington Road, #204
Milwaukee, WI 53217
414-540-6679; 414-540-0587 (fax)
friends@aero.net
www.friendsofceliac.com

Internet Resources

Listservs: A Listserv is a "mailing list" in which participants can post questions, answers, and comments on a list that is distributed by e-mail to all participants.

Autistic Kids on a
Gluten-free Diet Listserv
To subscribe: Visit **www.onelist.com** and subscribe to the list called "gfcfkids."

Celiac Listserv
To subscribe: Send e-mail to **List-serve@maelstrom.stjohns.edu** with "subscribe celiac" in subject heading (be sure to send this e-mail from the address you want your Listserv e-mails sent to).

Celiac Listserv—Cel-Kids
News Group
To subscribe: Send e-mail to **List-serve@maelstrom.stjohns.edu** with "subscribe cel-kids" in subject heading (be sure to send this e-mail from the address you want your Listserv e-mails sent to).

Website Collections/Links

Celiac Information
Listowners: Bill Elkus (**Maxwell@lamg.com**); Michael Jones (**mjones@digital.net**); Jim Lyles (**lyles@tir.com**)
www.enabling.org/ia/celiac

Database of Gluten-Free Manufacturers
Operator: Linda Blanchard
Linda@ccgs.com
www.nowheat.com

Gluten-Free Links
Operator: Don Wiss
Donwiss@panix.com
www.gflinks.com

The Kitchen Link: Wheat-Free and Gluten-Free Recipes and Resources
help@kitchenlink.com
www.kitchenlink.com/wheatfree.html

Grandma Whimsy (Carol Roberts)
www.grandmawhimsy.com

Gluten-Free Shopping Guides

The Celiac Database
Operator: Chuck Brandt
P.O. Box 5605
Wilmington, DE 19808-0605
302-999-1144; 302-999-9794 (fax)
info@celiacdatabase.org
http://www.celiacdatabase.org

Erewhon Natural Foods Market
Celiac Shopping Guide
shop@erewhonmarket.com
www.erewhonmarket.com/celiac-
shoppingguide.html

Gluten Free Food List
Operator: Abigail Neuman
www.geocities.com/HotSprings/Spa/
4003/gf-index.html

Gluten-Free Food Vendor Directory
Operator: Don Wiss
donwiss@panix.com
www.gfmall.com

Gluten-Free InfoWeb
2422 Fox Hollow Drive
Pittsburgh, PA 15237
CeliacInfo@aol.com
www.glutenfreeinfo.com

Gluten-Free Pocket Guides
and Databases for Food/Drugs
Operator: Clan Thompson
951 Main Street
Stoneham, ME 04231
207-928-3303
celiac@clanthompson.com
www.clanthompson.com

Commercial Products Listing
CSA/USA, Inc.
(see contact information under
Celiac Disease)

The Tri-County Shopping Guide
TCCSSG Shopping Guide
(see contact information under
Other Support Organizations)

Pharmaceutical Companies and Drug Information

Abbott Laboratories
200 Abbott Park Road
Abbott Park, IL 60064
847-937-6100; 800-441-4987;
847-937-9826 (fax)
www.abbott.com

AstraZeneca LP
725 Chesterbrook Blvd.
Wayne, PA 19087
610-695-1000; 800-237-8898
www.astrazeneca.com

Barr Labs
2 Quaker Road
Pomona, NY 10970
800-222-4043; 914-353-4530 (fax)
www.barrlabs.com/home.html

Drug Company Phone Numbers
www.needymeds.com/companies.html

Gluten-Free Drug and
Food Database
Operator: Clan Thompson
951 Main Street
Stoneham, ME 04231
207-928-3303
info@clanthompson.com
www.clanthompson.com

Johnson & Johnson Merck
750 Camp Hill Road
Fort Washington, PA 19034
800-469-5268; 215-273-4070 (fax)
www.jnj.com

Ortho-McNeil Pharmaceutical
1000 U.S. Route 202
P.O. Box 300
Raritan, NJ 08869
800-682-6532
www.ortho-mcneil.com;
www.jnj.com

Parke Davis/Warner Lambert (Pfizer)
Patient Assistance Program
P.O. Box 1058
Somerville, NJ 08876
908-725-1247; 800-223-0432;
908-707-9544 (fax)
www.warner-lambert.com;
www.pfizer.com

Pfizer, Inc.
Pfizer Prescription Assistance
P.O. Box 25457
Alexandria, VA
800-646-4455; 800-438-1985
www.pfizer.com

Pharmacia & Upjohn
RxMAP
P.O. Box 29043
Phoenix, AZ 85038
888-691-6813; 602-314-7163 (fax)
ptinfo@pnu.com
www.pnu.com

Procter & Gamble Pharmaceuticals
Patient Assistance Program
17 Eaton Avenue
Morwich, NY 13815
800-448-4878; 800-836-0658;
800-283-8915
atyourservice.im@pg.com
www.pg.com/main.jhtml

Stokes Pharmacy
"Celiac Sprue, A Guide Through
the Medicine Cabinet"
639 Stokes Road
Medford, NJ 08055

800-754-5222; 800-440-5899 (fax)
pharmacist@stokesrx.com
www.stokesrx.com

Wyeth Consumer
5 Giralda Farms
Madison, NJ 07940
973-660-5500; 973-660-7111 (fax)
www.wyeth.com

Restaurants and Fast-Food Chains

Applebee's International Restaurant
4551 W. 107th Street, Suite 100
Overland Park, KS 66207
913-967-4000;
800-354-7363, x 4087;
913-967-8984
www.applebees.com

Baskin-Robbins
600 North Brand Blvd., 6th Floor
Glendale, CA 91203
818-956-0031; 800-859-5339
www.baskinrobbins.com

Burger King
Corporation Consumer Relations
17777 Old Cutler Road
Miami, FL 33157
305-378-3535; 305-378-7011
www.burgerking.com

Chevy's
2000 Powell Street, Suite 200
Emeryville, CA 94608
800-4-Chevys; 510-768-1330 (fax)
www.chevys.com

Dairy Queen/Orange Julius
7505 Metro Blvd.
P.O. Box 39286
Edina, MN 55439
952-830-0200; 952-830-0480 (fax)
www.dairyqueen.com

Denny's
203 East Main Street
Box 3-6-9
Spartanburg, SC 29319
800-733-6697
tell_us@advantica-dine.com
www.dennys.com

El Pollo Loco
3333 Michelson Drive, Suite 550
Irvine, CA 92612
949-399-2000
www.elpolloloco.com

In N Out Burgers
4199 Campus Drive, 9th Floor
Irvine, CA 92612
800-786-1000
www.in-n-out.com

Jack-in-the-Box, Inc.
9330 Balboa Avenue
San Diego, CA 92123-1516
858-571-2121; 800-955-5225
www.jackinthebox.com

McDonald's
999 Waterside Drive, Suite 2300
Norfolk, VA 23510
757-626-1900; 757-640-3615 (fax)
www.mcdonalds.com

Outback Steakhouse
2202 N.W. Shore Blvd.
Tampa, FL 33607
813-282-1225; 813-282-1209 (fax)
irenewenzel@outback.com
www.outbacksteakhouse.com

Rubio's Baja Grill (Fish Tacos)
Rubio's Restaurants, Inc.
1902 Wright Place, Suite 300
Carlsbad, CA 92008
760-929-TACO; 800-354-4199;
760-929-8203 (fax)
www.rubios.com

Taco Bell
Consumer Affairs
17901 Von Karman
Irvine, CA 92614-6221
800-822-6235
www.tacobell.com

TCBY Yogurt
2855 Cottonwood Parkway,
Suite 400
Salt Lake City, UT 84121-7050
800-323-1156; 800-688-8229
consumer@tcby.com;
tcbycs@mrsfields.com
www.tcby.com

Tony Roma's
9304 Forest Lane, Suite 2000
Dallas, TX 75243
800-286-7662; 214-343-2680 (fax)
www.tonyromas.com

Wendy's International, Inc.
Wendy's Customer Service
4288 W. Dublin-Granville Road
Dublin, OH 43017
614-764-3100; 800-82-WENDY
www.wendys.com

Cookbooks, Online Recipes, and General Information Books

Against the Grain: The Slightly Eccentric Guide to Living Well Without Gluten or Wheat
Jax Peters Lowell
Henry Holt

Allergies and Your Family
Doris Rapp
Practical Allergy Research
Foundation

Best Gluten-Free Recipes
Operator: Allan Gardyne
Lot 12 Esplanade
Tuan, Queensland, Australia 4650
coeliac@ozemail.com.au
www.ozemail.com.au/~coeliac/
index.html

Best of Lifeline
Montez Fowlkes and Kathy Hayes
(Obtain through CSA/USA)

Best Recipes from Celiacs
Yvonne Goulart
(Obtain through CSA/USA)

Beyond the Staff of Life
Kief Adler
Naturegraph Publishers

*Brain Allergies: The Psychonutrient
and Magnetic Connections*
William Philpott and Dwight Kalita
NTC/Contemporary Publishing
Company

*Cajun and Southern
Gluten-Free Delights*
Aileen Bennett
A&G Publishing

*The Complete Food Allergy
Cookbook: The Foods You've
Always Loved Without the
Ingredients You Can't Have!*
Marilyn Gioannini
Prima Publishing

Coping with the Gluten-Free Diet
Marion N. Wood
Charles C Thomas Publisher, Limited

Creative Rice Baking
P.O. Box 6281
Rock Island, IL 61204
creativericebaking@home.com
http://members.home.net/
creativericebaking

*Easy Breadmaking for
Special Diets: Wheat-Free,
Milk- and Lactose-Free, Egg-Free,
Gluten-Free, Yeast-Free, Sugar-Free,
Low-fat, High-to-Low Fiber*
Nicolette Dumke
Allergy Adapt Inc.

Easy, Successful, Gluten-Free Recipes
Carolyn Randall
(Obtain through CSA/USA)

*Feeding Your Allergic Child: Happy
Food for Happy Kids: 75 Proven
Recipes Free of Wheat, Dairy, Corn,
and Eggs for the Millions of
Miserable Children*
Elisa Meyer
St. Martin's Press, Inc.

*The Food Allergy Field Guide:
A Lifestyle Manual for Families*
Theresa Willingham
Savory Palate, Inc.
Food and Gut Reaction
Elaine Gottschall
Kirkton Press

For Newly `Diagnosed Celiacs
Yvonne Goulart
(Obtain through CSA/USA)

Full of Beans
Violet Currie and Kay Spicer

*Gluten-Free Diet:
A Comprehensive Resource Guide*
Shelley Case, B.Sc., R.D.
www.glutenfreediet.ca

Gluten Free/Casein Free Recipes
gfcfrecipes@hotmail.com
http://gfcfrecipes.tripod.com

The Gluten-Free Cookbook:
Over 50 Delicious and Nutritious
Recipes to Suit Every Occasion
(The Healthy Eating Library)
Anne Sheasby
Anness Publishing, Ltd.

Gluten-Free Cooking
Rita Greer
Athene Publishing Company, Ltd.

The Gluten-Free Gourmet
Bakes Bread: More than 200
Wheat-Free Recipes

The Gluten-Free Gourmet Cooks
Fast and Healthy: Wheat-Free
Recipes with Less Fuss and Less Fat

The Gluten-Free Gourmet:
Living Well Without Wheat

The Gluten-Free Gourmet: Living
Well Without Wheat, 2nd Edition

More From the Gluten-Free Gourmet:
Delicious Dining Without Wheat
The Gluten-Free Gourmet
Makes Dessert

All the above by Bette Hagman
Henry Holt & Company, Inc.
Gluten-Free International Recipes
Sandra Leonard
(Obtain through CSA/USA)

The Gluten-Free Pantry Companion
Beth Hillson
Published by Gluten-Free Pantry
http://www2.mailordercentral.com/
glutenfree/

Gluten-Free Pantry Companion:
Great Recipes for a Wheat-
Free/Gluten-Free Kitchen
Beth Hillson
Published by Gluten-Free Pantry
www.glutenfreepantry.biz/store

Gluten-Free Recipes and Cooking Tips
http://celiac.automated-shops.com

GlutenFreeda Online
Cooking Magazine
http://www.glutenfreeda.com

The Gluten, Wheat, and Dairy Free
Cookbook
Anjtoinette Saville
Published by Thorsons 2000

Good Food, Gluten Free
Hilda C. Hills
Keats Publishing

Gourmet Food on a Wheat-Free Diet
Marion N. Wood
Charles C Thomas Publisher, Limited

Holiday Menus
Sandra Leonard and Carolyn Randall
(Obtain through CSA/USA)

The Impossible Child in School—
At Home: A Guide for Caring
Teachers and Parents
Doris Rapp
Practical Allergy Research Foundation

Living Healthy with Celiac Disease
Wendy Wark
AnAffect Marketing
115 Andover Drive
Exton, PA 19341

Microwave Recipes
Esther Wyant
(Obtain through CSA/USA)

Prescription for Nutritional Healing:
A Practical A-Z Reference to Drug-
Free Remedies Using Vitamins, Min-
erals, Herbs, and Food Supplements
James Balch and Phyllis Balch
Avery Publishing Group

RecipeSource
SOAR: The Searchable Online
Archive of Recipes
Gluten Free Recipes
www.recipesource.com

Special Diet Celebrations:
No Wheat, Gluten, Dairy, or Eggs
Carol Fenster, Ph.D.
Savory Palate, Inc.
www.savorypalate.com

Special Diet Solutions: Healthy
Cooking Without Wheat, Gluten,
Dairy, Eggs, Yeast, or Refined Sugar
Carole Fenster, Ph.D.
Savory Palate, Inc.

Special Diets for Special Kids
(books 1 and 2)
Lisa Lewis, Ph.D.
Future Horizons
800-489-0727
www.futureHorizons-autism.com

A Quick Look at Celiac Disease for
Those Who Work with Children
Gluten-Free Living
P.O. Box 105
Hastings-on-the-Hudson, NY 10706
gfliving@aol.com

Wheat-Free Gluten-Free
Children's Cookbook

Wheat-Free Gluten-Free
Reduced Calorie Cookbook

Wheat-Free Gluten-Free
Dessert Cookbook

All the above by Connie Sarros
3270 Camden Rue
Cuyahoga Falls, OH 44223
330-929-1651
gfcookbook@hotmail.com
www.wfgf.homestead.com/gf.html

The Wheat-Free Kitchen:
A Celebration of Good Food
Jacqueline Mallorca
The Farthing Press
1700 Broadway, Suite 601
San Francisco, CA 94109
415-441-4142

Wheat-Free Recipes and Menus:
Delicious Dining Without
Wheat or Gluten
Carol Fenster, Ph.D.
Savory Palate, Inc.

Specialty Foods

Cecilia's Gluten-Free Grocery
PMB 171
3702 S. Virginia Street G12
Reno, NV 89502-7510
775-827-0672; 800-491-2760;
775-827-5850 (fax)
info@glutenfreegrocery.com
www.glutenfreegrocery.com

DeRoMa (Glutino Brand)
1118 Rue Berlier
Laval, Quebec, Canada H7L 3R9
450-629-7689; 800-363-DIET
info@glutino.com
www.glutino.com

Dietary Specialties
1248 Sussex Turnpike, Unit C2
Randolph, NJ 07869
888-640-2800; 973-895-3742 (fax)
info@dietspec.com
www.dietspec.com

El Peto Products
41 Shoemaker St.
Kitchener, Ont.
N2E 3G9 CANADA
800-387-4064; 519-748-5211;
 519-748-5279 (fax)
elpeto@golden.net
www.elpeto.com

Ener-G Foods
P.O. Box 84487
Seattle, WA 98124-5787
800-331-5222; 206-764-3398
heidi@ener-g.com
www.ener-g.com

Frankferd Farms Foods
717 Saxonburg Blvd.
Saxonburg, PA 16056
724-352-9500; 724-352-9510 (fax)
carel@frankferd.com
www.frankferd.com

Gluten-Free Cookie Jar
P.O. Box 52
Trevose, PA 19053
215-355-9403; 888-GLUTEN-0;
215-355-7991 (fax)
glutenfreecookiejar@yahoo.com
www.glutenfreecookiejar.com

Gluten Free Delights
P.O. Box 284
Cedar Falls, IA 50613
319-266-7167; 888-403-1806;
319-268-7355 (fax)
ZEJG11A@prodigy.com
www.glutenfreedelights.com

Gluten-Free Mall
info@glutenfreemall.com
www.glutenfreemall.com

Gluten Free Pantry
P.O. Box 840
Glastonbury, CT 06033
860-633-3826; 800-291-8386;
860-633-6853 (fax)
pantry@glutenfree.com
www.glutenfree.com

The Gluten-Free Trading Company
604A W. Lincoln Avenue
Milwaukee, WI 53215
414-385-9950; 888-993-9933;
414-385-9915 (fax)

gftc@GLUTEN_FREE.TC
info@gluten-free.net
www.gluten-free.net

Gluten Solutions, Inc.
3810 Riviera Drive, #1
San Diego, CA 92109
1-888-845-8836
info@glutensolutions.com
www.glutensolutions.com

Glutino
See DeRoMa

Kinnikinick Foods
10306-112 Street
Edmonton, Alberta, Canada
T5K 1N1
780-424-2900; 877-503-4466;
780-421-0456 (fax)
info@kinnikinnick.com
www.kinnikinnick.com

Miss Roben's
P.O. Box 1149
Frederick, MD 21702
301-665-9580; 800-891-0083;
301-665-9584 (fax)
info@missroben.com; orders@
missroben.com
www.missroben.com

Really Great Food Co.
P.O. Box 2239
St. James, NY 11780
800-593-5377; 631-361-6920 (fax)
chris@reallygreatfood.com
www.reallygreatfood.com

Schär
Dr. Schär GmbH
Winkelau 5
I-39014 Postal (BZ)
+39-0473-293300
info@schaer.com
www.schaer.com/p5100uk.html

The Square Meal
www.thesquaremeal.com

Sylvan Border Farm
Gluten-Free Products
Mendocino Gluten-Free Products, Inc.
P.O. Box 277
Willits, CA 95490
800-297-5399; 707-459-1834 (fax)
sylvanfarm@pacific.net
www.sylvanborderfarm.com

Twin Valley Mills
Rt. 1, Box 45
Ruskin, NE 68974
402-279-3965
www.twinvalleymills.com

General (Products, Manufacturers, Stores, Services)

Albertson's (Supermarkets)
250 Parkcenter Blvd.
Boise, ID 83706
888-746-7252; 208-395-3302 (fax)
customerservice@albertsons.com
www.albertsons.com

Alpineaire Foods
DG Management
P.O. Box 1799
Rocklin, CA 95677
800-322-6325; 916-824-6050 (fax)
info@aa-foods.com
www.aa-foods.com

Amy's Kitchen, Inc.
P.O. Box 7868
Santa Rosa, CA 95407
707-578-7188; 707-570-0306
susanshimm@amyskitchen.net

Annie's Naturals
792 Foster Hill Road
North Calais, VT 05650

802-456-8866; 800-434-1234;
802-456-8865 (fax)
info@anniesnaturals.com
www.anniesnaturals.com

Arrowhead Mills
P.O. Box 2059
Hereford, TX 79045
800-749-0730; 806-364-8242 (fax)

Aurora Foods Inc.
1000 St. Louis Union Station
St. Louis, MO 63103
314-241-0303; 888-349-1998;
314-613-5567 (fax)
www.aurorafoods.com

Authentic Foods
1850 West 169th Street, Suite B
Gardena, CA 90247
800-806-4737; 310-366-7612;
310-366-6938 (fax)
sales@authenticfoods.com;
authenti@pacbell.net
www.authenticfoods.com

Balance Bars
1015 Mark Avenue
Carpinteria, CA 93013
800-678-4246; 805-566-0235 (fax)
healthy@balance.com
www.balance.com

Beatrice Group, Inc.
770 N. Springdale Road
Waukesha, WI 53186
262-782-2750; 800-227-6202;
800-988-7808

Ben & Jerry's Homemade
Holdings, Inc.
30 Community Drive
South Burlington, VT 05403-6828
802-846-1500; 800-726-6748
www.benandjerrys.com

Best Foods
International Plaza
700 Sylvan Avenue
Englewood Cliffs, NJ 07632-9976
201-894-4000; 800-338-8831
www.bestfoods.com

Betty Crocker (Signature
Brands/General Mills)
P.O. Box 279
Ocala, FL 34478-0279
800-328-8360; 800-456-9573;
800-328-1144; 352-402-9451 (fax)
www.bettycrocker.com

Blue Diamond Growers
1802 C Street
Sacramento, CA 95814
916-442-0771; 800-987-2329
customerservice@bluediamond
growers.com
www.bluediamondnuts.com

Bob's Red Mill
5209 S.E. International Way
Milwaukie, OR 97222
800-553-2258; 503-654-3215;
503-653-1339
www.bobsredmill.com

Cabot Creamery Cooperative
Main Street
Cabot, VT 05647
188-TRY-CABOT
info@cabotcheese.com
www.cabotcheese.com

Cadbury/Schweppes
25 Berkeley Square
London, England
W1X6HT
www.cadbury.co.uk

Campbell's Soup Company
Campbell Place
Camden, NJ 08103-1701
800-257-8443; 800-410-7687
www.campbellssoup.com

'Cause You're Special Co.
P.O. Box 316
Phillips, WI 54555
715-339-6959; 603-754-0245 (fax)
info@causeyourespecial.com
www.causeyourespecial.com

Cecilia's Gluten-Free Grocery
PMB 171
3702 S Virginia Street G12
Reno, NV 89502-7510
775-827-0672; 800-491-2760;
775-827-5850 (fax)
info@glutenfreegrocery.com
www.glutenfreegrocery.com

Celestial Seasonings Tea
4600 Sleepy Time Drive
Boulder, CO 80301
800-351-8175; 303-581-1294 (fax)
www.celestialseasonings.com

Charms
See Tootsie Roll Industries, Inc.

Chebe Bread (Prima Provisions)
P.O. Box 27085
West Des Moines, IA 50266
(515-223-5007; 800-217-9510
info@chebe.com
www.chebe.com

Chicken of the Sea International
Consumer Affairs
P.O. Box 85568
San Diego, CA 92138-5568
www.chickenofthesea.com

Classico International
Gourmet Specialties Company
180 E. Broad Street
Columbus, OH 43215-3799
800-727-8260
www.classico.com

Coca Cola
Industry and Consumer Affairs
P.O. Drawer 1734
Atlanta, GA 30301
800-GET-COKE
www.cocacola.com

Coldstone Creamery
16101 N. 82nd Street, #A4
Scottsdale, AZ 85260
480-348-1704; 480-348-1718 (fax)
bconley@coldstonecreamery.com
www.coldstonecreamery.com

Colgate-Palmolive
800-338-8388; 800-468-6502
www.colgate.com

Costco (Price Club)
P.O. Box 34331
Issaquah, WA 98027
800-774-2678
www.costco.com

Culinary Imports
100 Schillhammer Road
Jericho, VT 05465
800-958-7678; 802-899-4678 (fax)
www.vermontspecialtyfoods.org/
members/culinary.html

Dannon
Consumer Response Center
P.O. Box 90296
Allentown, PA 18109-0296
800-321-2174; 877-DANNONUS
www.dannon.com

Delimex
See Heinz

DeRoMa (Glutino Brand)
1118 Rue Berlier
Laval, Quebec, Canada H7L 3R9
450-629-7689; 800-363-DIET
info@glutino.com
www.glutino.com

Dietary Specialties
1248 Sussex Turnpike, Unit C2
Randolph, NJ 07869
888-640-2800; (973-895-3742 (fax)
info@dietspec.com
www.dietspec.com

Dixie USA, Inc.
P.O. Box 1969
15555 FM 2920
Tomball, TX 77377
800-233-3668
info@dixieusa.com
www.dixiediner.dom

Dowd & Rogers
3504 J Street
Suite 16
Sacramento, CA 95816
916-451-6480; 916-736-2349 (fax)
www.dowdandrogers.com

Dreyer's
5929 College Avenue
Oakland, CA 94618
877-437-3937
www.dreyers.com

Duncan Hines
1000 St. Louis Station, Suite 300
St. Louis, MO 63103
800-845-7286
www.duncanhines.com

Edy's Ice Cream
5929 College Avenue
Oakland, CA 94618
800-777-3397
www.edys.com

ELISA Technologies
(gluten detection kits)
4581-L NW 6th Street
Gainesville, FL 32609
352-337-3929; 352-337-3928 (fax)
elisa@fdt.net
www.elisa-tek.com

Ener-G Foods
P.O. Box 84487
Seattle, WA 98124-5787
800-331-5222; 206-764-3398
heidi@ener-g.com
www.ener-g.com

Epicurean International, Inc.
(Thai Kitchen)
P.O. Box 13242
Berkeley, CA 94701
510-268-0209; 800-967-8424;
510-834-3102 (fax)
info@thaikitchen.com
www.thaikitchen.com

Fantastic Foods
1250 N. McDowell Blvd.
Petaluma, CA 94954
707-778-7607; 800-888-7801;
707-778-7607 (fax)
AskUs@fantasticfoods.com
www.fantasticfoods.com

Farley's (Nabisco)
2945 W. 31st Street
Chicago, IL 60623
312-254-0900; 800-541-1222;
312-254-0795 (fax)
www.nabisco.com

Farmer John
Clougherty Packing Company
3049 E. Vernon Avenue
Los Angeles, CA 90058
323-583-4621; 800-432-7637;
323-584-1699 (fax)
farmerjohn@farmerjohn.com
www.farmerjohn.com

Favorite Brands International
(Nabisco)
Nabisco Consumer Affairs
100 DeForest Avenue
P.O. Box 1911
East Hanover, NJ 07936-1911
800-244-4596
www.nabisco.com

Fisher Nuts
John B. Sanfilippo & Son, Inc.
2299 Busse Road
Elk Grove Village, IL 60007-6057
847-593-2300; 847-593-3085 (fax)
www.fishernuts.com

Fleischmann's
See Beatrice Group, Inc.

Foods by George
3 King Street
Mahwah, NJ 07430
201-612-9700; 201-634-0334 (fax)

Food For Life Baking Co., Inc.
2991 E. Doherty Street
Corona, CA 91719
800-797-5090; 888-458-8360;
909-279-1784 (fax)
info@food-for-life.com
www.food-for-life.com

Frankferd Farms Foods
carel@frankferd.com
www.frankferd.com

FREEDA Vitamins
36 East 41 Street
New York, NY 10017
800-777-3737; 212-685-4980;
212-685-7297 (fax)
FreedaVits@aolcom

Friendly Ice Cream Corporation
1855 Boston Road
Wilbraham, MA 01095
800-966-9970
www.friendly.com

Frito Lay
P.O. Box 660634
Dallas, TX 75266-0634
800-352-4477
www.fritolay.com

Frookie
2070 Maple Street
Des Plaines, IL 60018
888-FROOKIE; 847-699-3201 (fax)
www.frookie.com

G! Foods
3536 17th Street
San Francisco, CA 94110
415-255-2139, 415-863-3359 (fax)
gfoods@SHELL12.BA.BEST.COM
www.g-foods.com

Genisoy Products Company
2351 N. Watney Way, Suite C
Fairfield, CA 94533
707-399-2510; 888-GENISOY;
707-399-2518 (fax)
sales@mloproducts.com
www.genisoy.com

Gifts of Nature
P.O. Box 309
Corvallis, MT 59828
406-961-1529; 406-961-3491 (fax)
giftsofnature@netzero.com
www.giftsofnature.net

Gillian's Foods, Inc.
462 Proctor Avenue
Revere, MA 02151-5730
781-286-4095; 781-286-1933 (fax)
R357BOBO@aol.com
www.gilliansfoods.com

Glutano
Unit 270 Centennial Park,
Centennial Avenue
Elstree, Borehamwood Herts
WD6 3SS
020-8953-4444;
020-8953-8285 (fax)
info@glutenfree-foods.co.uk
www.glutenfree-foods.co.uk

Gluten-Free Cookie Jar
P.O. Box 52
Trevose, PA 19053
215-355-9403; 888-GLUTEN-0;
215-355-7991 (fax)
questions@glutenfreecookiejar.com
www.glutenfreecookiejar.com

Gluten Free Delights
P.O. Box 284
Cedar Falls, IA 50613
319-266-7167; 888-403-1806;
319-268-7355 (fax)
ZEJG11A@prodigy.com
www.glutenfreedelights.com

The Gluten Free Exchange
P.O. Box 5046
Clover, SC 29710
803-631-1519
ginger@gfexchange.com
www.gfexchange.com

Gluten-Free Mall
info@glutenfreemall.com
www.glutenfreemall.com

Gluten-Free Pantry
P.O. Box 840
Glastonbury, CT 06033
860-633-3826; 800-291-8386;
860-633-6853 (fax)
pantry@glutenfree.com
www.glutenfree.com

The Gluten-Free Trading Company
604A W. Lincoln Avenue
Milwaukee, WI 53215
414-385-9950; 888-993-9933;
414-385-9915 (fax)
gftc@GLUTEN-FREE.TC;
info@gluten-free.net
www.gluten-free.net

Gluten Solutions, Inc.
737 Manhattan Blvd., Suite B
Manhattan Beach, CA 90266
310-939-7559; 888-8-GLUTEN
info@glutensolutions.com
www.glutensolutions.com

Glutino
See DeRoMa

Haagen-Dazs
Glen Pointe Center East
Teaneck, NJ 07666
800-767-0120
www.haagendazs.com

Health Valley
16100 Foothill Blvd.
Irwindale, CA 91706-7811
800-423-4846
www.healthvalley.com

Heinz U.S.A.
P.O. Box 57
Pittsburgh, PA 15230
800-255-5750; 800-568-8602 (fax)
www.heinz.com
www.naturesgoodness.com

Herb-Ox
See Hormel

Hershey's
P.O. Box 815
Hershey, PA 17033-0815
800-468-1714
www.hersheys.com

Hidden Valley
Oakland, CA 94612
800-53-SAUCE
www.hiddenvalley.com

Hillshire Farm & Kahn's
P.O. Box 25111
Cincinnati, OH 45225
800-328-2426
www.hillshirefarm.com

Hormel
P.O. Box 800
Austin, MN 55912
800-523-4635
www.hormel.com

Hunt-Wesson Inc.
P.O. Box 4800
Fullerton, CA 92634-4800
800-633-0112; 800-457-6649
www.hunt-wesson.com

Imagine Foods, Inc.
350 Cambridge Avenue, #350
Palo Alto, CA 94306
415-327-1444; 800-333-6339;
415-327-1459 (fax)
www.imaginefoods.com

International Home Foods
1633 Littleton Road
Parsippany, NJ 07054
800-544-5680

Jet-Puffed Marshmallows (Nabisco)
100 DeForest Avenue
P.O. Box 1911
East Hanover, NJ 07936-1911
800-244-4596
www.jetpuffed.com

Jimmy Dean Foods
8000 Centerview Parkway, Suite 400
Cordova, TN 38018
800-925-DEAN
www.jimmydean.com

Just Born
1300 Stefko Blvd.
Bethlehem, PA 18016
800-445-5787; 800-543-4981 (fax)
www.justborn.com

Kelloggs
Consumer Affairs
1 Kellogg Square
Battle Creek, MI 49016-1986
800-962-1413
www.kelloggs.com

Kelloggs (UK)
www.kelloggs.co.uk

Kingsmill Foods Co. LTD
416-755-1124; 800-737-7976
peggy@kingsmillfoods.com
www.kingsmillfoods.com

Kinnikinnick Foods
10306-112 Street
Edmonton, Alberta, Canada
T5K 1N1
780-424-2900; 877-503-4466;
780-421-0456 (fax)
info@kinnikinnick.com
www.kinnikinnick.com

Kitchen Basics, Inc.
P.O. Box 41022
Brecksville, OH 44141
440-838-1344; 480-998-8622
info@kitchenbasics.net
www.kitchenbasics.net

Kozy Shack, Inc.
83 Ludy St.
Hicksville, NY 11802-9011
714-538-1718; 714-538-1755 (fax)
www.kozyshack.com

Kraft General Foods, Inc.
Consumer Response and Information
Kraft Court
Glenview, IL 60025
800-323-0768; 800-543-5335
www.kraftfoods.com

Land-O-Lakes
P.O. Box 64050
St. Paul, MN 55164-0050
800-328-4155; 651-481-2959 (fax)
www.landolakes.com/new

Lawry's Foods, Inc.
700 Palisade Avenue
Englewood Cliffs, NJ 07632
800-745-9232; 800-9LAWRYS
www.lawrys.com

Lay's Products
See Frito Lay

Lea & Perrins
800-987-4674; 800-338-8831
lpinfo@leaperinnsus.danone.com
www.lea-and-perrins.com

Legumes Plus
N. 204 Fairweather Street
Fairfield, WA 99012
800-845-1349; 509-283-2314 (fax)
www.legumesplus.com

Lifesavers (Nabiscso)
P.O. Box 41
Salem, OR 27102
800-541-1222
www.nabisco.com

Lipton
700 Palisade Avenue
Englewood Cliffs, NJ 07632
800-697-7887; 800-697-7897
www.lipton.com

Lipton (Canada)
800-565-7273

Log Cabin
See Aurora Foods, Inc.

Louis Rich
P.O. Box 7188
Madison, WI 53707
800-722-1421
www.louisrich.com

M&M Mars
High Street
Hackettstown, NJ 07840
908-852-1000; 800-222-0293;
800-627-7852
www.mmmars.com

McCormick & Co., Inc.
211 Schilling Circle
Hunt Valley, MD 21031
800-632-5847; 410-527-6267 (fax)
www.mccormick.com

MacBar Distributors
(Quejos cheesebuns)
P.O. Box 434
Santa Monica, CA 90406
310-829-6802

Mahatma
c/o Riviana Foods Inc.
P.O. Box 2636
Houston, TX 77252
800-226-9522; 713-942-1826 (fax)
info@riviana.com
www.mahatmarice.com

Malt-O-Meal
701 W. 5th Street
Northfield, MN 55057-0180
800-753-3029
ca@malt-o-meal.com
www.malt-o-meal.com

Manischewitz Food Products Corp.
One Manischewitz Plaza
Jersey City, NY 07302
201-333-3700 – ask for
Deborah Ross
info@manischewitz.com
www.manischewitz.com

Miss Roben's
P.O. Box 1149
Frederick, MD 21702
301-665-9580; 800-891-0083;
301-665-9584 (fax)
info@missroben.com;
orders@missroben.com
www.missroben.com

Motts USA
Stanford, CT 06905-0800
800-426-4891
www.motts.com

Mr. Spice
Lang Naturals
850 Aquidneck Avenue
Newport, RI 02842
401-848-7700; 800-SAUCE-IT;
401-848-7701 (fax)
customerservice@MrSpice.com
www.mrspice.com

Mrs. Butterworth's
See Aurora Foods, Inc.

Mrs. Leeper's Pasta
12455 Kerran Street, Suite 200
Poway, CA 92064-6855
858-486-1101; 858-486-1770 (fax)
www.mrsleeperspasta.net

Nabisco Brands, Inc.
P.O. Box 1911
E. Hanover, NJ 07936
800-622-4726
www.nabisco.com

Nature's Hilights, Inc.
P.O. Box 3526
Chico, CA 95928
916-342-6154; 800-313-6454;
916-342-3130 (fax)
nhi@maxinet.com

Nature's Life
7180 Lampson Avenue
Garden Grove, CA 92841
800-854-6837; 714-379-6501 (fax)
info@natlife.com
www.natlife.com

Nelson David of Canada
Celimix Brand Gluten-Free Foods
101-193 Dumoulin Street
Winnipeg, Manitoba R2H 0E4
Canada
204-237-9161; 204-231-2883 (fax)
www.glutenfreemall.com/cgi-
bin/2/webc.cgi/~sadams/st_main.ht
ml?catid=38

Nestlé
P.O. Box 39487
Salem, OR 44139-0487
800-441-2525; 800-258-6728;
800-851-0512
www.nestle.com

Nestlé (Willy Wonka Division)
800-299-6652

Newman's Own Organics
P.O. Box 2098
Aptos, CA 95001
408-685-2866; 800-444-8705
www.newmansownorganics.com

Nutribase Directory of Food and
Supplement Manufacturers
info@nutribase.com
www.nutribase.com/dfm.htm;
www.nutribase.com/tollfree

Ore-Ida Foods, Inc.(Heinz)
P.O. Box 10
Boise, ID 83707
800-892-2401
www.oreida.com

Oscar Mayer Foods Corporation
P.O. Box 7188
Madison, WI 53707
800-672-2710; 800-222-2323
www.oscarmayer.com

Pacific Grain Products, Inc.
P.O. Box 2060
Woodland, CA 95776
916-662-5056; 800-49-BEANS;
916-662-6074 (fax)
www.pacgrain.com

Pamela's Products
335 Allerton Avenue
South San Francisco, CA 94080
650-952-4546; 650-742-6643 (fax)
info@pamelasproducts.com
www.pamelasproducts.com

Pastariso (Rice Innovations Inc.)
1773 Bayly Street
Pickering, Ontario, Canada
L1W2Y7
905-451-7423

Pepsi-Co Food Services
6606 LBJ Freeway, #150A
Dallas, TX 75240
800-433-2652
www.pepsi.com

Planter's (Nabisco)
Nabisco Consumer Affairs
100 DeForest Avenue
P.O. Box 1911
East Hanover, NJ 07936-1911
800-8NABNET
www.planters.com

The Quaker Oats Company
P.O. Box 049003
Chicago, IL 60604-9003
312-222-7707; 800-234-6281;
800-856-5781
www.quakeroats.com

Quinoa Corp
P.O. Box 1039
Torrance, CA 90505
310-530-8666; 310-530-8764 (fax)
quinoacorp@aol.com
www.quinoa.net

Really Great Food Co.
P.O. Box 2239
St. James, NY 11780
800-593-5377; 631-361-6920 (fax)
chris@reallygreatfood.com
www.reallygreatfood.com

Red Star Yeast
800-4-CELIAC; 800-423-5422
carol.stevens@ufoods.com
www.redstaryeast.com

Rice Innovations Inc.
See Pastariso

Road's End Organics
120 Pleasant Street, Suite E-1
Morrisville, VT 05661
877-CHREESE; 802-888-2646 (fax)
roadsend@together.net
www.chreese.com

Safeway (Vons) Stores
P.O. Box 523
Clackamas, OR 92015
503-657-6279; 503-557-4008 (fax)
www.safeway.com

San-J International, Inc.
2880 Sprouse Drive
Richmond, VA 23231
804-226-8333; 800-446-5500;
804-226-8383 (fax)
sales@san-j.com
www.san-j.com

Sargento Products
800-CHEESES; 800-558-5802
www.sargento.com

Scenario International Co.
(Organic Gourmet)
4092 Deervale Drive
Sherman Oaks, CA 91403-4609
818-986-3777
www.organic-gourmet.com

Schär
Dr. Schär GmbH
Winkelau 5
I-39014 Postal (BZ)
+39-0473-293300
info@schaer.com
www.schaer.com/p5100uk.html

Schillings Spices
See McCormick

Signature Brands
See Betty Crocker
Silly-Yak Shirt Company
181 Lorraine Gate
East Meadow, NY 11554
www.silly-yak.com

Spangler Candy Company
400 N. Portland Street
P.O. Box 71
Bryan, OH 43506-0071
419-636-4221; 800-653-8638;
419-636-3695
Spangler@bright.net
www.spanglercandy.com

Special Foods
9207 Shotgun Court
Springfield, VA 22153
703-644-0991; 703-644-1006 (fax)
kslimak@IX.NETCOM.COM
www.specialfoods.com

Stagg
P.O. Box 800
Austin, MN
800-611-9778
staggchili@usmpagency.com
www.staggchili.com

Starkist Seafood Co.
One Riverfront Place
Newport, KY 41071
800-252-1587
www.starkist.com

Sylvan Border Farm
Gluten-Free Products
Mendocino Gluten-Free Products, Inc.
P.O. Box 277
Willits, CA 95490
800-297-5399; 707-459-1834 (fax)
sylvanfarm@pacific.net
www.sylvanborderfarm.com

Tamarind Tree, Ltd.
(Annie's Homegrown)
P.O. Box 128
Hampton, CT 06247
781-224-9639; 800-HFC-TREE;
781-224-9728 (fax)
www.tamtree.com

Tinkyada
120 Melford Drive, Unit 8
Scarborough, Ontario
M1B 2X5
416-609-0016; 416-609-1316 (fax)
www.tinkyada.com

Tom's of Maine
P.O. Box 710
Kennebunk, ME 04043
207-985-2944; 800-775-2388;
207-985-2196 (fax)
www.tomsofmaine.com

Tootsie Roll Industries, Inc.
7401 South Cicero
Chicago, IL 60629
773-838-3400; 800-877-7655
www.tootsie.com

Trader Joe's
P.O. Box 3270
South Pasadena, CA 91031
626-441-2024; 626-441-9573 (fax)
www.traderjoes.com

Twin Valley Mills
Rt. 1, Box 45
Ruskin, NE 68974
402-279-3965
www.twinvalleymills.com

Tyson Foods, Inc.
P.O. Box 2020
Springdale, AR 72765-2020
501-290-4000; 800-643-3410;
800-233-6332
www.tyson.com

U.S. Mills, Inc.
200 Reservoir Street
Needham, MA 02494
781-444-0440

Van's International Foods
20318 Gramercy Place
Torrance, CA 90501
310-320-8611
www.vansintl.com

Vons (Safeway) Stores
800-955-8667
www.vons.com

Whole Foods Market, Inc.
Research and Support Team
601 N. Lamar, Suite 300
Austin, Texas 78703
512-477-4455
www.wholefoodsmarket.com

Williams Foods, Inc.
13301 West 99th Street
Lenexa, KS 66215
800-255-6736
www.williamsfoods.com

Wishbone (Lipton)
Consumer Service Department
800 Sylvan Avenue
Englewood Cliffs, NJ 07632
800-697-7897
comments.wish-boneusa@unilever.com
www.wish-bone.com

Index

(Page numbers in **boldface** type refer to figures or tables.
Those in *italics* refer to footnotes or sidebars. Recipes are gathered under that heading.)

About the Author

Danna Korn is the author of *Kids with Celiac Disease: A Family Guide to Raising Happy, Healthy, Gluten-Free Children.* As an official spokesperson for celiac disease awareness, she appears frequently on national and local TV and radio, and is featured in newspaper and magazine articles. She has written dozens of articles on gluten-free living that have been published in national magazines and newspapers, and she speaks frequently around the country to health-care professionals, celiacs, parents of celiacs, parents of autistic kids involved in a gluten-free/casein-free dietary intervention program, and others on a wheat-free, gluten-free diet.

Danna has been researching celiac disease since her son, Tyler, was diagnosed with the condition in 1991. That same year, she founded R.O.C.K. (Raising Our Celiac Kids), a support group for families of children on a gluten-free diet. Today, Danna leads more than 85 chapters of R.O.C.K. throughout the country, inspiring others to help parents of newly diagnosed celiac, allergic, or autistic kids. R.O.C.K. recently became a nonprofit corporation and funds research, free celiac testing, gluten-free food donations, and awareness programs.

Danna and her husband, Paul, own and operate a high-tech recruiting firm called SearchNet Technical Recruiting, specializing in software engineering and computer professionals. They live in Encinitas, California, with their children, Tyler and Kelsie.

You can contact Danna at: **danna@celiackids.com.**

✿ ✿ ✿

We hope you enjoyed this Hay House book.
If you would like to receive a free catalog featuring additional
Hay House books and products, or if you would like
information about the Hay Foundation, please contact:

Hay House, Inc.
P.O. Box 5100
Carlsbad, CA 92018-5100

(760) 431-7695 or (800) 654-5126
(760) 431-6948 (fax) or (800) 650-5115 (fax)
www.hayhouse.com

✿ ✿ ✿

Hay House Australia Pty Ltd
P.O. Box 515
Brighton-Le-Sands, NSW 2216
phone: 1800 023 516
e-mail: info@hayhouse.com.au

✿ ✿ ✿